Salisbury Cathedral 800 Years of People & Place

Sarum Studies 7
2020

Edited by:
Emily Naish
John Elliott

Sarum Chronicle
recent historical research
on Salisbury & district

ISBN 978-1-9161359-2-5   ISSN: 1475-1844
Published 2020

How to contact us:
    To order a copy phone John Elliott on 01722 711665 or email
jpelliott@btinternet.com
    To submit material for consideration in future editions of *Sarum Chronicle* email
John Elliott at jpelliott@btinternet.com with the words Sarum Chronicle in the
subject line.

Editorial Team: Roy Bexon, Ruth Butler, Alan Castle, John Chandler, John Cox,
Stephen Dunn, John Elliott, Jane Howells, John Loades, Andrew Minting, Emily
Naish, Ruth Newman, and Margaret Smith

www.sarumchronicle.wordpress.com

Designed and typeset by John Elliott.

Contents

Salisbury Cathedral from the western end (Roy Bexon)

Foreword

Salisbury Cathedral lives. It is still doing what its builders intended 800 years ago. It offers the daily rhythms of a common life that not even the Covid-19 lockdown of 2020 has been able to silence. It lives – and it lives the values which brought Bishop Poore's generation from the hilltop to the valley. They came in pursuit of liberty to worship and liberty to grow: in its custodianship of Magna Carta and its vocation to pray for Prisoners of Conscience it champions liberty still. They unleashed the explosion of creativity which raised the Cathedral in under four decades and saw a city grow up around it: in its cultivation of historic crafts and its commitment to fine music-making it nurtures creativity still. And through their labour and their ministry here they bore lasting witness to the God of eternity: in its unceasing prayer it points to eternity still.

So to visit Salisbury Cathedral is to visit a place that lives. A visit here is never a dreary tour of a place where things once used to happen: a visit here may be punctuated by the offering of an act of worship, or enriched by a display of contemporary art, or enhanced by a glorious array of flowers, or enlivened by an exhibition of rare archival material. And a visit will almost certainly be animated by members of the Cathedral community of today: the staff on the donations desk or in the shop; the volunteer guides and stewards; the duty chaplains.

It is to this complex, rich life that *Sarum Studies* 7 bears witness. It takes the reader back to those who lived, worked, and worshipped on the hilltop of Old Sarum; it sets out Salisbury's unique status as the Cathedral that moved; it brings the reader right up to date with Cathedral life in the 21st century.

This packed and varied volume, like Salisbury Cathedral, testifies to the abundant living that Jesus Christ says he has come to bring. May Salisbury Cathedral flourish, and – through its stones and these pages – may many, many more come to know it, and be changed by it.

The Very Reverend Nicholas Papadopulos,
Dean of Salisbury,
May, 2020.

Acknowledgements

This book would not have been possible without the contribution of many people and organizations.

First, the authors of the various chapters who engaged with the project with such enthusiasm and then accepted many rounds of copy editing. Second, Roy Bexon and Ash Mills who produced most of the images which accompany the text; Jane Howells who did numerous rounds of copy editing and compiled the index; Alan Castle who systematically copy edited every word, spotted errors and also made helpful suggestions on how the chapters could be improved, Catriona Blaker who read the completed work and Ruth Newman who was a constant pillar of support and also copy edited the whole book several times. Third, the whole editorial board of Sarum Chronicle who read and commented upon all the chapters and supported the project throughout.

We owe a special thanks to the Dean for his support and for the Foreword.

We are especially grateful to all those institutions that have allowed us to use images from their collections and especially the staff of the Wiltshire and Swindon Archive who have been fully supportive of the project as have the staff of the Salisbury Museum.

It has been wonderful to be part of a project where so much positive enthusiasm has been generated and where the answer to any request was invariably yes without any hesitation. We are eternally grateful to all those who have contributed in any way.

Finally we are grateful to all those of you who have bought a copy of the book. Thank you for your interest in the history of Salisbury, in the cathedral, its history, and everything that it does to spread Christ's word amongst the people of Salisbury and the wider world.

John Elliott
Emily Naish

Introduction

It was fitting that much celebration should have been planned for 2020, especially on 28 April, which was exactly 800 years since the foundation stones were laid and the erection of a magnificent new medieval cathedral was begun in Salisbury. Then the coronavirus pandemic intervened.

This volume contains a series of chapters that were written during 2019 and early 2020 exploring both past and present aspects of the cathedral's life and its people. The authors have written from their own interests and experiences to create a rich picture of a very special community. Just as the sight of the cathedral dominates the skyline for miles around, so all the activity described here has made the cathedral central to the religious and cultural life of Salisbury over the centuries, no matter what one's personal beliefs may be.

A Papal Bull which authorized the move of the cathedral from Old to New Sarum was issued on 29 March 1218. A wooden chapel was built at New Sarum, and the first service held there on Trinity Sunday 1219. The foundation stones for the new cathedral were laid on 28 April 1220, and from 28 September 1225 services were being held at the eastern end of the building. Work progressed rapidly and the original cathedral, minus its tower and spire, was mostly completed by 1258.

Salisbury Cathedral is architecturally special, being built largely in a single Gothic style - the Early English - which was much lighter in structure than the Romanesque which preceded it, and used pointed arches and lancet windows. The tower and spire followed a little later, in the early 1300s, and contain much ballflower decoration which signalled the start of the next Gothic development; the decorated style.

This is not another history of the cathedral, but an exploration of some of the exciting variety of experiences to be found within its walls and beyond. At one end of the time spectrum there is a re-examination of the people and land at Old Sarum, and at the other, chapters on the floral displays that mark the liturgical calendar, and on the numerous art exhibitions. The 2020 art exhibition did take place despite the Covid-19 epidemic. but as an interactive digital experience.

The tower and spire have always been iconic expressions of Salisbury and there is much here on the various restorations that have been a constant feature of cathedral life and of the efforts to raise the money to pay for it.

The cathedral is the venue for big events, major services and many large concerts. It is crammed to capacity for the various services that precede Christmas and Easter, with long queues of people who are anxious to join in the celebrations. It is also supported by about 600 volunteers who act as guides, take people up the tower, steward services and concerts, arrange the flowers, act as chaplains and dust the furniture.

We hope that this book adds to the celebration of this significant anniversary, providing an insight for both local people and visitors into aspects of the cathedral that may not be widely known.

John Elliott
28 April 2020

The People and Places of 13th Century Old Sarum

June Effemey

In July 2019, ten medieval deeds relating to the abandoned medieval hill-top city of Old Sarum, (Fig 1) and the adjacent settlement of Stratford sub Castle, near Salisbury in Wiltshire, were re-discovered in the *Registrum Rubrum*, a medieval Register of the Bishops of Salisbury.[1] (Fig 2) The Register, a collection of hand-written copies of deeds, charters and Papal bulls, in medieval Latin, is held in the Wiltshire and Swindon History Centre in Chippenham. The deeds, dating to between 1284 and 1358, are highly significant because they provide information hitherto lacking for the population, landscape, and economy of Old

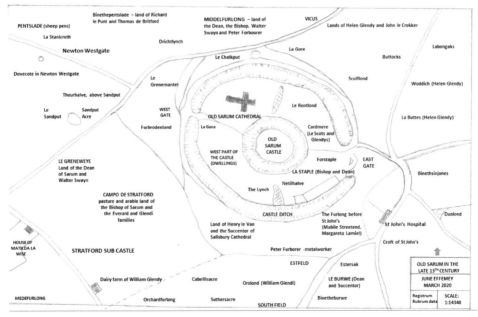

Fig 1: Working map by the author showing the position of individual plots

Sarum and the neighbouring Stratford sub Castle in the late 13th and early 14th centuries.

The first two deeds recount how a portfolio of plots of land and properties in and around Old Sarum, owned by the Bishops of Sarum, descended from one land-holder to another between the late 12th century and 1354. From Bishop Herbert Poore, the properties went to Peter de Mylford, to his son Richard de Mylford, then to Richard's son, also called Richard, who granted them to Hugo Glendy of Stratford sub Castle around 1240. William Glendy, Hugo's son, inherited the lands, and gave them to his son Bartholomew Glendy in 1284; deeds 3 and 4 record this transaction. (Fig 3) Bartholomew gave the lands to William Everard, son of Everard de Stratford, in 1292 (the subject of deeds 5 and 6). William Everard's son John and his wife Beatrice's acquisition of the properties from Bishop Robert Wyville is described in deeds 8 and 9, dated 1354 and 1356. Deed 10, an inspection by King Edward III of earlier charters, dated 17 January 1358, notes that this portfolio of lands, held of the Bishop of Sarum, reverted into the King's hands if the see was vacant.

The longest deeds, 3, 4 and 6, list, and give locations for, 12 plots of meadowland and over 100 plots of arable land, distributed across the landscape of Stratford sub Castle, as well as describing several urban plots within Old Sarum itself. (See Figs 4 & 5) The deeds provide names for many features, such as mills, fields and trackways, and mention over 130 neighbouring properties and their land-holders. In total, more than 80 local people, and over 370 different plots, topographical features and places are named. Several local inhabitants named do not appear in any other sources, for example Mabil Streetend, and many of the places listed, such as 'Orslond', 'Cardmere', and 'Le Rontland,' occur only in these *Registrum* deeds. A typical entry is 'one acre of land at *Le Borwe* next to the lands of the Succentor in a field called Eastfield.' Properties tend to be listed in

Fig 2: The *Registrum Rubrum* (*Emily Naish*)

Fig 3: Glendy family seal attached to a 1350 document. The seal is possibly the only depiction of a medieval woman for the Old Sarum area. (*Roy Bexon*)

sequence, in the manner of a medieval perambulation through the landscape around Old Sarum. Many of the toponyms given in the deeds for the furlongs, fields, lands and features in Old Sarum's rural hinterland, such as *Shulflond*, meaning a shovel-shaped piece of land, have an Anglo-Saxon etymology, perhaps indicating how local pre-Conquest inhabitants described and understood their physical environment.[2] Similarly, the toponym 'Le Stert,' an Anglo-Saxon word meaning a piece of land which juts out, perhaps alludes to the lie of the small meadow in Stratford which bore that name.[3] Although the deeds describe only a proportion of all the places and people of the area, they nevertheless represent a unique record of the medieval population and landscape of the locality.

THE TOPOGRAPHY OF THE AREA
The City

Old Sarum was laid out with a castle at its centre, a cathedral precinct, with

Above and opposite: Figs 4 & 5 Two pages from *Registrum Rubrum* reproduced by permission of Wiltshire and Swindon Archives.

cathedral, bishop's palace and cemeteries, in the north-west sector of the castle bailey, surrounded with massive earthwork defences. These structures were extensively examined in the Hope and Hawley excavations of 1909-15.[4] Located outside Old Sarum's main east gate were civilian dwellings, St John's Hospital (the medieval poor house), with its chapel and cemetery, as well as a house for lepers, near which Sarum bishops held some lands.[5] Several major medieval and Roman roads converged outside this east gate.[6] While much has been discovered about Old Sarum's royal and ecclesiastical buildings, and their inhabitants, less has been uncovered about the city's medieval civilian settlement, population and economy. Recently, however, geophysical surveys and archaeological investigations have significantly increased understanding of the city's layout. Inside Old Sarum's walls, a dense urban settlement was identified, particularly in the south-west sector, and an open courtyard area, bounded by massive structures flanking the city walls, was found in the south-east sector. The surveys also located suburban settlement immediately outside the walled city, to the west, east and south.[7]

Registrum deeds dated 1284 and 1292 mention a place called '*La Staple*' located at Old Sarum. The Staple was a specific term used to describe the markets set up in English towns in the 1280s by Edward I, primarily for the sale and taxation of

raw wool, prior to its export, chiefly to Bruges and Florence.[8] Given this wool trade context, it is highly likely that the courtyard with massive structures found by geophysical surveys represent this Staple market area, for in English towns which had Staple markets, the part of the town where the staple was held came to be known as the 'staple.' The Staple took place in a defined area, which was often bounded by the town walls, and within which were specialised buildings for dealing with the staple merchandise, such as warehouses, and the weigh-house with beam for weighing wool, which was taxed by weight.[9] At Old Sarum, the Staple was sited in the city's south-east sector, close to the main gate, enabling easy ingress and egress of cartloads of merchandise.

According to the *Registrum* deeds, the Staple at Old Sarum consisted of the forecourt area, the '*Le Forstaple*', and the main area, '*La Staple*'. There was also a half-acre plot within the Staple called '*Netilhalve*', or '*Netilacre in la Staple*'. This area could have been where plant materials such as flax and hemp, which could be turned into textiles, or nettles, which were used for cloth dyeing, were sold. Those holding property in the Staple between 1284 and 1292 included the Bishop, Dean, and Succentor, as well as laymen like William Payn, William Glendy, Bartholomew Glendy, William Everard, and Richard Pound, who held a plot in the Forestaple. These people were probably involved in the commerce in wool and other commodities, and the one-acre plot the Glendy family held in the Staple in 1284 must have represented a substantial part of the total market area. Wool was England's main export commodity in the 13th and early 14th centuries, and trade was dominated by companies of Italian merchant-bankers, who purchased wool across the country.[10] Locally, Italian merchants dominated the shipping of wool out of the south coast's major port, Southampton.[11] A letter from Pope Clement V dated 1305, contained in the *Registrum Rubrum*, notes the appointment of John Frescobaldi, son of Florentine nobleman Berti Frescobaldi, to Salisbury Cathedral's prebend of Highworth.[12] Berti Frescobaldi founded the most important Florentine merchant banking company operating in England between 1290 and 1311, the Frescobaldi Company. Frescobaldis acted as bankers to the Pope, financed the wool trade, exported wool from England to Europe, opened a branch in London, and lent money to Edward I. Salisbury Cathedral's Dean, Peter of Savoy (*Sabaudia*), of Rome, who was appointed in 1297, and who held land in Old Sarum's Staple, must have conducted business with the Frescobaldi Company, since he is recorded in 1318 as owing them 50 marks.[13]

Recent geophysical surveys indicated the highest density of urban dwellings in the south-west sector of Sarum Castle's outer bailey, to the west of the Staple. The *Registrum Rubrum* deeds concur with the notion expressed in Bishop Osmund's foundation charter of the Cathedral at Old Sarum, with descriptions of the city by 12th-century historian Henry of Malmesbury, and with descriptions by 13th century poet William of Avranches, that the cathedral and city of Old Sarum stood 'within the castle'.[14] Hence, urban plots are noted in the deeds as being located in 'the castle' rather than 'the city,' typically in the western side. In deed 6, a half-acre plot is said to lie in the castle of Sarum on its western side. A place called '*La Gore*' is also described as being inside the castle, on its western side, situated next to the 'lynch.' (This 'lynch' may be the medieval earthen cross-bank which divided this western residential area from the market to its east). The half-acre plot held by the Glendy family in 1284, and by William Everard in 1292, described as lying 'against the wall of the castle', was also probably a plot next to the city wall in this residential area. The understanding that the city lay within the castle may also explain why *Registrum* deeds describe Old Sarum city plots in terms of land size, usually half an acre, rather than employing the standard medieval terminology for urban plots, namely 'tenements' or 'messuages.'

The Suburbs

The *Registrum* deeds do not refer to any urban settlement on the north side of Old Sarum, but do mention mineral extraction activity, a chalkpit, north of the city. A chalkpit is indicated on 19th-century Ordnance Survey maps in this location. Suburban settlement to the south of Old Sarum, however, is indicated by the rows of plots mentioned in the deeds as laying against the ditch '*fosse*' of the castle. In 1284, the Glendys held two half-acre plots by the castle ditch, one sited between land of the Cathedral's Succentor and land of Henry le Van, and the other between the land of Michael le Scot and another plot of William Glendy. Given Old Sarum's topography, any plot located against the castle ditch probably stood within extra-mural urban areas. The south side is a promising location, since recent archaeological surveys indicated dense urban settlement to the south of the castle's outer ditch. A 1339 deed of John Everard also seems to refer to plots in this extra-mural southern settlement: 'in the south part of the castle between the road which extends from the castle towards New Sarum on one side and the land lately of John Pachet on the other'.[15]

The *Registrum* deeds indicate that the eastern part of the city was considered as standing within the city's precincts, stating that a piece of land in front of the house of the hospital of St John in Old Sarum was called '*le Furlong*'. Plots in this furlong held by the Glendy and Everard families were bounded by lands of Helene Glendy and Mabilie Stretend. Lands associated with St John's Hospital included St John's croft, with its half-acre of headland, and half an acre of land opposite St John's Hospital.

Old Sarum's western suburb dated from the time of the foundation of the first cathedral in 1091, when the canons were allotted land outside the west gate of the castle, on either side of the road, for their gardens, houses, courtyards and barns.[16] Recent archaeological investigations demonstrated the presence of high-status stone-built houses of the 11th and 13th centuries, constructed on chalk platforms, flanking the road leading west from Old Sarum's west gate.[17] The settlement was delineated by surrounding earth banks and ditches of a 12th-13th century date.[18] Newton's bounds were known to the compilers of the *Registrum* deed of 1284, which refers to 1¼ acres of land in 'La Gore' beyond the Ville of Newton. 'La Gore' probably lay to the north, behind Newton, since those drawing up the deeds took a Stratford-centric view. After the departure of the clergy to Salisbury in the 1220s, permission was granted to demolish the structures, so that the stone could be used to build the new cathedral, but the demolition only occurred in the 14th century.[19] The dovecot in Newton (Westgate) was not demolished, and *Registrum* deeds recount its transfers of ownership from the late 12th century until the mid 15th century, when it was held by Richard and Edith Maywardyne, of Maywardyne Court. Three places associated with Newton were *Colemansmill* on the River Avon, a plot near it called '*Colmanthesacre*,' and a field called '*Binethetown*', which lay opposite the mill, seemingly to the west of Newton. The *Registrum* deeds record that for 250 years Newton's dovecot descended to landholders who also held the mill, so it seems likely that the mill lay near the settlement.

Agricultural lands

The deeds indicate that the major agricultural lands were Middlefurlong, located to the north of Old Sarum, Medefurlong, which flanked the River Avon in Stratford sub Castle, and Orchard Furlong, located to the south of the city. Middlefurlong, traversed by the road to Amesbury, seems to have contained both pasture and arable lands, since deeds mention the 'arable parts of Middelforlong'. The name Middlefurlong occurs in a 1536 survey of lands in the Stratford sub Castle and Old Sarum area: 'in the feld of midyll furlong upon Ambresbury Way ... in the myddyll furlong by the lynche towarde the north syde.'[20] The toponym Middlefurlong also appears on 19th century tithe maps.[21] Both *Registrum* deeds and later maps indicate that each furlong contained numerous small plots, of varying sizes and shapes, held by a range of individuals.[22]

Orchardfurlong, probably named because of its proximity to the King's garden and orchard towards the south end of Stratford sub Castle, must have been quite large, for it was subdivided into fields, such as Southfield. The Glendy and Everard families, Walter de la Stratende and Henry Welbonde held land in Orchardfurlong. Southfield is further attested both in 15th century deeds and in the 1536 terrier: 'in the felde callyd South Felde at the South ende of the same felde in Red Land i acre ... in the same South feld in the furlong next Stratford Way i acre'. Southfield also appears on tithe maps.[23]

Medefurlong, indicating meadowland, flanked the river Avon in Stratford, and one rod of land in it was bounded by the Dean's land on one side, and by a paling, or fence, on the other. Perhaps this fenced land enclosed the king's mill, garden and pond, which were sited by the river at the south end of Stratford, for only high-status individuals were likely to enclose land with fences. Features located along the river included a meadow called Gooseham, presumably an enclosed area where geese were raised, and an adjoining meadow called Millham, its name signifying an enclosure including a mill.[24] Both the Succentor and Helen Glendy held land near Goosham and Mulham. The westernmost of the braided river channels in the valley must have been known as WestheWater, since a cultivated meadow, or field, subdivided into a number of plots, called 'BiWesthewater' lay by it. A meadow called Cherlinmede lay adjacent to the Succentor's meadow to the west of Westhewater.

One sizeable sheep-related valley feature was the Pentslade, with its neighbouring area 'binethpentslade'. The Pentslade seems to have been a place for penning sheep prior to shearing, butchering or skinning. In tithe maps, a spacious area called The Pennings, probably formerly the Pentslade, was located flanking the river Avon, on the north-west side of Old Sarum, north of Stratford Bridge. The Pentslade occurs in the 1536 terrier: 'in Long Penslade iii acres ... in the Shorte Penslade iii acres.' The Bishop, Michael le Scot, William and

Bartholomew Glendy and William Everard all held land in the Pentslade during the 13th century, which suggests these protagonists' involvement with wool and sheep processing.

Routeways

The *Registrum* deeds mention three different types of routeways traversing the Old Sarum landscape, the 'street', '*vicus*' and 'weye'. The main roads across the landscape were regarded as '*vicus*'; a '*vicus*' lay to the north of Old Sarum, probably the road from Old Sarum to Amesbury. Stratford sub Castle's street is embodied in the name of an inhabitant, Walter at the Stratend, who held land near the south end of the street, indicating that Stratford's main thoroughfare had a defined end. Various dwellings, such as the '*Domus de Matilda la Wise*' and the messuage called '*Thestresake*' of the 1284 deeds lay along Stratford Street. The cottage and curtilage which Robert Hering '*Le Messer*' granted to John Everard in 1333 (*Registrum* deed 7), which were bound by the tenement of Adam de Kibbell on the south and the land of the Succentor on the north, probably also stood on Stratford's street, which has a north-south axis.

The third type of routeway, the 'weye', occurs in the toponym '*La Borwe*', which may be the road, now track, leading south west from the east gate of Old Sarum to Stratford. This *Borwe*, or *Burway*, may be the highway of the former Anglo-Saxon burh, deemed to have been sited south of Old Sarum; the Bishop, the Dean and the Succentor all held land beside it. Folk-memory of the burh may also be indicated by the toponym '*Boreshalve*' for half an acre of land mentioned in the deeds, and by the place-name '*binethburwey*,' probably an area on the sloping land to the south of the trackway. Another way place-name, '*le Greneweye*', was perhaps an ancient trackway flanked by thick vegetation; land either side of the *Greneway* was held by the Dean.

THE COMMUNITY

The lands with which the *Registrum* deeds are principally concerned were held by the Bishop. The deeds of 1284 and 1292, however, mention many neighbouring lands held by the Dean, including land in Witfurlong, lands in le Myddilforlong, land in the Staple and land in Denefurlong. Following the dissolution of the Prebend of Stratford/Old Sarum in 1226, many former prebendary properties, including mansions and messuages inside the city, and meadows and lands in Stratford sub Castle, were granted by Bishop Richard Poore to the Dean and Chapter.[25] Some of the Dean's lands mentioned in the *Registrum* deeds may have been former prebendary properties. The Dean and Chapter are also known to have held land by the river in Stratford, alongside land and mills, including a fulling mill, held by St Denys Priory, Southampton.[26] Bishop Richard Poore had also granted one hide of land to the Succentor, about the year 1215.[27] The *Registrum* deeds of 1284 and 1292 list several properties of the Succentor, neighbouring those of the Glendys and Everards, including land at the Burway in Eastfield, in Medefurlong, near Gooseham, in Orsland, in '*la Bongake*', in the '*Furbrodeneland*', in the Forestaple, four plots of land in Myddelforlang, a plot against the castle ditch, and a meadow located to the west of the river. Some of these lands may have been part of the 1215 grant.[28]

The *Registrum* deeds people the late 13th century landscape of Old Sarum and Stratford sub Castle with ordinary residents and land-holders, including the Mylford, Glendy, Everard, le Scot, Upton, Ceresey, Severe, Bouche, Pachet and Hering families. The Glendy family were established residents in Stratford from the early 13th century, since in 1240, Hugo Glendy, his wife Agnes, and their heir William granted half an acre of land adjacent to a house in Stratford, called '*Hevedhalve in Rottuk*' to St Denys Priory.[29] The *Registrum* deeds record that the bundle of properties Hugo Glendy acquired from Richard de Mylford around 1240, included dairy farms, fisheries, and a sandpit acre, the latter suggesting extractive industries, so it is clear the Glendy family were economically active in a number of areas. We hear the voice of William Glendy in 1284 referring to 'my arable lands' and that of his son, Bartholomew Glendy, in 1292 speaking of 'my pastures'. Chaplain Bartholomew Glendy's grant of the lands to William Everard, son of Everard de Stratford, in 1292 meant that the Glendy family lost these particular lands, but the family retained others.

The *Registrum* deeds show that, in or after 1292, Helen Glendy, whose exact relationship with other Glendys is unknown, held land near the Staple, near a meadow called Gooseham by the river Avon, at 'Grenemantel' (possibly the wooded slope on the west side of Old Sarum), in Medefurlong, in Middlefurlong, at Woddych, in Le Rontland, in Cardmere, in Dunlond, and a plot, where she may have lived, in the furlong in front of the House of the Hospital of St John's. Bartholomew Glendy's brother, Stephen Glendy, was resident at Stratford sub Castle in 1332, as he paid 12d tax there that year.[30] But Stephen and his wife Anne also held property in Salisbury, since a charter dated February 1316 records them holding a tenement and site of land extending between Brown and Gigor (i.e. Gigant) Street.[31] In April 1348, Stephen and Anne Glendy's three daughters, Christina, Joan and Matilda, each held tenements in Martinscroft and Salisbury.[32] Thomas Glendy, 'son Stephen Glendy of Stratford', held land called '*la Stonyacre*' in the field of Stratford in 1353.[33] By the 14th century, the Glendy family's property and commercial interests spanned Old Sarum, Stratford and Salisbury.

The Everard family were likewise long-term residents in Stratford sub Castle, having probably moved from the Sarum Bishops' manors of Potterne, Cannings, Lavington and Ramsbury, where they had been present in the time of Bishops

Jocelin and Hubert in the 12th century.[34] Located closer to Old Sarum by 1201, Everardus de Durnford visited Old Sarum resident Alice de Cormelies on official business of the King's court that year and declared the woman to be sick.[35] Ebrard de Gardino occurs in *Registrum* deed 4 in 1284 as having paid 21 pence rent to William Glendy for property in Old Sarum or Stratford sub Castle. The properties William Everard acquired from Bartholomew Glendy in 1292 included ponds and fisheries, so these were probably managed commercially. The dealings of William's son John Everard and his wife Beatrice with Bishop Robert Wyville over the properties seems to have commenced around 1336.[36] John Everard also held, in 1331, messuages, land, meadows and rents in Stratford, and, in 1338, a croft of arable land on the west side of Stratford street, on which he was to construct a house, as well as a meadow to the west of the croft, which extended to the river.[37] In 1339 John possessed land in the west side of the castle (i.e. the city), bounded by land of the cathedral community to the north.[38] In 1345, John Everard and his wife Beatrice's daughters, Christine and Isabel, each held one messuage and one acre 'all in the same township land of Stratford'.[39] Succeeding generations of the Everard family held property in the area.

The le Scot family, Anthony and Michael, appear as substantial landowners in the deeds. In 1284, Michael le Scot held land in 'Cardmere', possibly a locality within the city of Old Sarum, as well as plots in Medefurlong, in Pentslade, near Colmansmylle in the field called 'Binethetown', land near Hedhalve, and land against the ditch of the castle. Antony le Scot, a dyer of Salisbury, held lands beneath the Burwey, in Shulflode, and near Cattesbraune, the latter being cultivated land with a headland, seemingly located near the river towards the south of Stratford. 'Cattisbrain' occurs in the 1240 charter of Hugo Glendy and St Denys Priory, and 'one acre of arable land in CatysBrayne' also appears in the 1536 Stratford sub Castle terrier.[40] A probable relative of Anthony and Michael, John le Scot, a citizen and wool trader in Salisbury, held a virgate of land in Stratford, which included trackways, waterways, fields, meadows and pastures, granted to him between 1252 and 1280 by Prior Nicholas of St Denys.[41] John le Scot is called the reeve in a Salisbury deed dated 23 May 1255, and a medieval street in Salisbury, Scot's Lane, was seemingly named after him - he had a house at the west end of the street, on the corner, in 1269.[42] William le Scot, a dyer 'tinctor', was one of the 300 Salisbury citizens who signed the agreement with the bishop after the bitter disputes of 1306.[43] William is listed as an Alderman of the Market in Salisbury in 1306, as are William le Scot, junior, and Anthony le Scot.[44] In the same year, a Petronella Scot appears in a list of inhabitants of St Martin's and Fisherton in Salisbury.[45] The Scot family, like the Glendys, had property and economic interests in Old Sarum, Stratford sub Castle and Salisbury.

The Upton family were long-term inhabitants of Old Sarum, and the *Registrum*

Fig 6: View of Old Sarum from present day Stratford-sub-Castle (*Roy Bexon*)

deed of 1284 records that Walter Upton, an Old Sarum burgess, held land near the east gate of the city, as well as a burgage plot, for which he paid rent of a pair of leather gloves. In 1270 and 1271 Walter Upton and his wife Laurencia, and John Upton and his wife Agnes held property in Old Sarum.[46] At Michaelmas 1321, a John de Upton, his wife Matilda, John's son John, John junior's brothers Walter and Alan, and Alan's sister Christine were all named in a dispute over property in Old Salisbury and Laverstock.[47] John of Upton was bailiff of the liberty of Old Sarum in 1327, and was a taxpayer of Old Sarum in 1332/3, when he paid subtax of three shillings.[48] John Upton witnessed *Registrum* deed 7, Robert Hering's 1333 charter about property in Stratford. A John Upton, coroner of Salisbury, held cottages in Gygorstreet (Gigant Street) and Mulmongerstreet (Mealmonger Street, now Greencroft Street) in the 1360s.[49] But Uptons remained active in urban life in Old Sarum, too, for a Walter Upton was elected as a parliamentary burgess to represent Old Sarum in 1386 and 1388.[50]

One prominent individual mentioned in the *Registrum* deeds, Stephen de Reigate, who paid half a pound of wax as rent for property in Old Sarum or Stratford sub Castle in 1292, was a wool merchant involved in international trade. In 1275, an inquiry into the export of wool in disobedience to a Royal Council embargo, noted that among the 15 Salisbury merchants who had exported wool through Southampton or Lymington were Thomas de Reigate and Stephen de Reigate, who exported 40 sacks and 6 sacks respectively via Lymington.[51] Several individual women, while not directly involved in the wool trade, feature in the deeds as substantial land-holders, including Matilda la Wise, who had held a messuage with croft adjacent, called '*Domus Matilda la Wise*' in Stratford sub Castle prior to 1284, Dionisia (Denise), daughter of Elias Bouche, who paid rent of half a pound of wax for a property in Old Sarum or Stratford sub Castle in 1284 and Margareta Lamiel, widow of Lammiel, who paid three shillings rent for property or land either in Old Sarum or Stratford sub Castle in 1292.

CONCLUSIONS

The *Registrum Rubrum* deeds demonstrate that Old Sarum, Newton Westgate and Stratford sub Castle were closely inter-connected, economically and socially, in the late 13th century. Here was a medieval landscape of fulling and water mills, dairy farms, sheep-pens, arable, pasture, and meadow-lands, of fisheries, mineral extraction and trade in wool. The abundance of named plots, fields, roads, landscape features and places in the deeds, together with detail of many of their locations, greatly increases understanding of the topographical layout of the area, drawing a virtual medieval map of the city of Old Sarum and its surrounding landscape. The spatial layout of the city of Old Sarum has become clearer, informed by newly-discovered place-names, including the market area of the city, '*La Staple*,' and the western residential area in 'the castle.'

Long after the departure of the clergy in the 1220s for their new cathedral and city in Salisbury, the Dean, the Bishop, and the Succentor continued to be involved, both economically and socially, with Old Sarum, including the Staple market and its wool trade. The deeds have enabled the partial reconstruction of the population of the area, which was comprised of ordinary individuals, such as Mabile Streetend and Margareta Lamiel, and of prominent land-holding families, such as the Glendys, Everards, Scots and Uptons. Many people were active in both Old Sarum and Salisbury; the two cities were closely linked socially and commercially in the late thirteenth and early fourteenth centuries.

Perhaps the most significant discovery in the *Registrum Rubrum* deeds is that Old Sarum had a Staple market in the late 13th century. This commerce in wool linked the city economically to Europe and involved the leading Florentine merchant bankers of the day. The history of Old Sarum is thereby changed, utterly.

Notes

1   Wiltshire & Swindon Archives (WSA), *Registrum Rubrum*, WSA D1/1/3, folios 108-112
2   Draper, Simon, 2011, 'Language and the Anglo-Saxon Landscape: Towards an Archaeological Interpretation of Place-Names in Wiltshire', in Nicholas J Higham and Martin J Ryan, *Place-names, Language and the Anglo-Saxon Landscape*, The Boydell Press; Field, John, 1967, *A History of English Field Names*, London
3   Langscape website www.langscape.org.uk, accessed 12/19
4   Salisbury Museum, Hawley Site Diaries, Old Sarum Excavations 1909-1915; McNeill, John, *Old Sarum*, English Heritage, 2006
5   Powell, Andrew, 2008, 'A Possible Site for the Hospital of St John the Baptist and St Anthony at Old Sarum, Salisbury', *Wiltshire Archaeological and Natural History Magazine (WANHM)*; Rahtz, Philip, and Musty, John, 1960, 'Excavations at Old Sarum, 1957,' *WANHM*, 57, 353-370; Toulmin Smith, Lucy, 1964, *The Itinerary of John Leland*, vol 1, Centaur Press, 260-1; Salisbury Cathedral Archives (SCA), *Liber Evidentiarum* C, folio 251
6   Musty, John, and Rahtz, Philip, 1964, 'The Suburbs of Old Sarum', *WANHM*, 59, 130-154
7   Strutt, Kristian, Barker, Dominic, Langlands, Alex, Sly, Timothy, (The Old Sarum Landscapes Project), *Research Report No.3 on the Geophysical Surveys at Old Sarum, Wiltshire, April and July 2016 and April and July 2017*
8   Crittall, Elizabeth, 1959, 'The woollen industry before 1550', in *A History of the County of Wiltshire: Volume 4*, VCH, 115-147
9   Jenckes, Adaline, 1908, *The Origin, organization and the location of the Staple in England*, University of Philadelphia, 10-11
10 Bell, Adrian, 2006, *Advance Contracts for the Purchase of Wool c. 1200-1327*, List and Index Society; Jenks, Stuart, (ed), 2004 and 2005, *The Enrolled Customs Accounts, Parts I and II*, List and Index Society, 306, 958
11 Ruddock, Alwyn, 1952, *Italian Merchants and Shipping in Southampton, 1270-1600*, Southampton University College Southampton Press, 120-1
12 WSA D1/1/3, folio 118, letter, Pope Clement V, 1305
13 Edwards, Kathleen, (ed), 1959, *The Registers of Roger Martival, Bishop of Salisbury 1315-1330, Vol. I The Register of Presentations and Institutions to benefices*, Diocese of Salisbury, Canterbury and York Society, (LV), OUP; Sapori, Armando, 1929, *La Compagnia dei Frescobaldi in Inghilterra*, Florence, 79
14 SCA, Osmund Register, D/1/1/1, folio 37, no. 29, Old Sarum Cathedral foundation charter, 1091; Mynors, Roger A B, Thomson, Rodney M, and Winterbottom Michael, (eds), 2007, William of Malmesbury, *Gesta Pontificum Anglorum, Volume I: Text and Translation*, (Rolls Series lii), Oxford, vol I, 288; Torrance, W J, 1960, 'Henry of Avranches *De Translatione Veteris Ecclesie Saresberiensis et Constructione Nove*', *WANHM*, 57, 242-6
15 SCA, Press I, Box 28, bundle 1/17, 24 October 1339.
16 Jones, William Henry Rich, (ed), 1883, *Vetus registrum Sarisberiense, alias dictum Registrum S. Osmundi episcopi*, Longman, I, 198; WSA D1/1/3, folios 114-5. Letter of Pope Eugenius III, 1146; Jones, William H Rich and MacRay, William D, 1893, *Charters and Documents of Salisbury*, Spottiswode, 13, 147-8; '*decano autem et capitulo Sarum omnes domos*

quas inhabitabat dictus canonicus, cum horreis et area in qua sitae sunt dicte domus'.

[17] Langlands, Alex, July 2018, Lecture 'Old Sarum, New Perspectives: Excavations in the Western Suburbs,' Salisbury Museum

[18] Strutt, Kris, July 2019, Personal Communication

[19] Royal Commission on the Historical Monuments of England (RCHME), 1980, *Ancient and historical monuments in the City of Salisbury*, HMSO, 1-24; Dean and Chapter, Press IV C2/18, 16th December 1276, Letters Patent of Edward I

[20] WSA, *Liber B*, D1/1/2. Terrier, May 1536

[21] WSA, 1843 Tithe Map Survey, Old Sarum and Stratford sub Castle

[22] WSA, Map of Stratford sub castle prebend estates in Stratford parish, CC Map 47 (4674)

[23] Crittall, Elizabeth, (ed), 1962, 'Stratford-sub-Castle', in *A History of the County of Wiltshire: Volume 6*, VCH, pp. 199-213; WSA, *Liber B*, D1/1/2. Terrier, May 1536

[24] Draper, 'Language and the Anglo-Saxon Landscape'

[25] Jones, Register Osmund, I. 259; WSA, *Liber B*, D1/1/2, no. 557 '*praebenda Veteris Sarum in Stratford*,' 1225; Crittall, 'Stratford-sub-Castle'

[26] Blake, Ernest O, 1981, *The Cartulary of the Priory of St Denys near Southampton*, Vol II, Southampton University, pp. xxxiii, xxxviii, 4, 127-128. Walter Nontal de Wilton held the fulling mill from St Denys Priory in 1275-1277; British Record Society, *Wiltshire Inquisitiones Post Mortem Temp. Henry III to Edward II*, 118-19, 28 April 1277, 246, 330

[27] WSA, *Liber B*, D1/1/2, 521, 557

[28] Crittall, 'Stratford sub Castle.' The Succentor's land is mentioned in 1328 and 1336, when said to be in '*le Ridelonde*'.

[29] Blake, *The Cartulary of the Priory of St Denys near Southampton*, 130 no 407. Hugo Glendy sued Prior Wakelin regarding land in Stratford in 1227; see Fry, Edward A, *Wilts Feet of Fines*, folio 17, 86

[30] Crowley, David A, (ed), 1989, *The Wiltshire Tax List of 1332*, Wiltshire Record Society, XLV, p. 9

[31] SCA, Press I Boxes 9-10, Salisbury 1/16, 4th Feb 1316

[32] SCA, Press I Boxes 9-10, Salisbury 1/43a, 23rd April 1348 (Joan); Press I Boxes 9-10, Salisbury 1/43b (Matilda); Press I Boxes 9-10, Salisbury 1/44, (Christina)

[33] The National Archives (TNA), WARD 2/5/21/2. 13 October 1353

[34] SCA, Press IV, C3: Lavington/10, 1142-1174; SCA, Press IV, C3: Potterne/16, 16th October 1173; SCA, Press IV, C3: Potterne/1, Roger, son of Everard; SCA, Press IV, C3: Royal Grants to Bishop/24 = FG/2/8, Charter of Henry II, 1174-1176

[35] Clay, Charles, (ed), 1922, *Curia Regis Rolls of the Reigns of Richard I and John, preserved in the Public Record Office*, HMSO, 423, 1201

[36] SCA, Press IV, E1 Stratford sub Castle/12, Indenture Bishop Robert Wyvill and John Everard, 10 July 1336

[37] Elrington, Christopher R, (ed), 1974, *Abstracts for the Feet of Fines Relating to Wiltshire for the reign of Edward III*, Wiltshire Record Society (XXIX), 31; SCA, Press IV, E1 Stratford sub Castle/13, 5 October 1338

[38] CA, Press I, Box 28, bundle 1/17, 24th October 1339

[39] Elrington, *Feet of Fines Wiltshire*, 76

[40] Blake, *The Cartulary of the Priory of St Denys near Southampton*, vol II, charter 405, 26 June 1240; WSA, Liber B, D1/1/2. Terrier, May 1536

41 Blake, *The Cartulary of the Priory of St Denys near Southampton*, 130, no 407

42 SCA, Press I, Boxes 9-10, Salisbury 1/1, 23 May 1255; RCHME, *City of Salisbury*

43 Crittall, Elizabeth, 1959, 'The woollen industry before 1550', in *A History of the County of Wiltshire: Volume 4*, VCH, 115-147

44 Inner Temple Library, London, Salisbury Cartulary, Petyt Collection MS 511.18 folio 149, 1306

45 WSA, G 23/1/222, 1306

46 Fry, Feet of Fines 1270 and 1271, Case 252 file 22 no 13, no 25

47 Pugh, Ralph B, (ed), 1939, *Abstracts of the Feet of Fines of the reigns of Edward I and Edward II relating to Wiltshire,* 109 no 36. 1321

48 Crittall, Elizabeth, 1962, 'Old Salisbury: The borough', in *A History of the County of Wiltshire: Volume 6*, VCH, pp. 62-63; TNA, 179/196/8 1332/3

49 WSA, G23 212, folios iii v, 4r, 13, 18, 20; SCA, Press I, Boxes 9-10 Salisbury 1/71; Crittall, Elizabeth, VCH vol VI, 179; Benson, Robert, and Hatcher, Henry, 1843, *The History of Old and New Sarum or Salisbury*, Nichols and Son, 68, 742-3

50 Kightly, Charles, 1993, 'Old Sarum' in Roskill, Clark and Rawcliffe, *The History of Parliament*, Boydell and Brewer

51 Crittall, Elizabeth, 1962, 'Salisbury: Economic history to 1612', in *A History of the County of Wiltshire: Volume 6*, VCH, 124-129

Why Move Salisbury Cathedral?
A Tale of Hill and Vale

Emily Naish

On 28th April 1220 a crowd gathered in modern day Salisbury Cathedral Close to witness the laying of the foundation stones of a new cathedral. This crowd included not just the great and the good but also 'a great multitude of the common people who came from everywhere around.'[1] This new cathedral building was not an entirely new Salisbury Cathedral but was the relocation of an earlier Salisbury Cathedral, founded in 1091, located two miles away within a Norman castle on the hilly exposed site of an iron age hillfort known today as Old Sarum.[2] (Figs 1 & 2)

What prompted and motivated the bishop, dean and other church dignitaries to make the momentous decision to move an entire cathedral – a task which would seem daunting to us in the 21st century let alone to people without the benefit of modern technology in the 13th century. This article will seek to explore the reasons why Salisbury Cathedral moved as recorded in the manuscripts written by our thirteenth century ancestors. Alongside the 'facts' as recorded in these ancient documents there is also the 'fiction', legends which have grown up over the centuries since 1220; legends including dreams, an errant bishop, an archer, a brindle cow and a deer.

There can be no doubt that the most important surviving account of the move is that residing in the cathedral archive. This is the Register of St Osmund, a cartulary, that is a collection of important documents bound together in one volume.[3] At first glance the Register appears a relatively unassuming volume being approximately A4 in size covered by a nineteenth century leather binding. Miraculously an earlier binding made of parchment, (animal skin) has also survived. The Register's 91 folios are also made of parchment with the text having been written by several different scribes using a quill and ink made from oak galls. Altogether its pages contain a wealth of information about the cathedral's earliest history; without it we would be much the poorer.

Fig 1: The footprint of the cathedral at Old Sarum (*Roy Bexon*)

Fig 2: The new cathedral of Salisbury viewed from Old Sarum (*Roy Bexon*)

Fig 3: Papal Bull issued by Pope Honorius III as recorded in the Register of St Osmund giving the cathedral permission to move (*Wiltshire and Swindon Archives*)

St Osmund was bishop of Salisbury between 1078 and 1099. His reputation and popularity were such that after his death a cult quickly developed, and Salisbury soon became a place of pilgrimage although Osmund was not officially canonised until 1457. Over time the Register was named after Osmund not because it was written or compiled by him but because it contains the statutes, rules and customs made and prescribed by him to be observed at Salisbury Cathedral. The name may also have been bestowed in his memory to honour his place as the perceived greatest of the earliest bishops of Salisbury.

The Register is arranged into seven main sections which might have originally been written separately and subsequent bound together. One section, the narrative or chronicle written by Dean William de Wanda, is our key source for why the cathedral was moved and the only source for the date that the foundation stones were laid. Not much is known about William de Wanda. He was elected Dean of Salisbury in 1220 a post he held until his death in 1236. Before he was dean Wanda held the post, also at Salisbury, of precentor with responsibility for music and he had also carried out a visitation (inspection) of the properties, estates and churches held by each cathedral prebend.[4]

William de Wanda begins his account with the words 'Temporibus Herberti'. This is a reference to an earlier bishop, Bishop Herbert Poore (died 1217), who together with the canons of the time first discussed the idea of moving:

> In the time of Herbert of good memory, formerly bishop of Sarum, the question of moving the church there to a less enclosed and more convenient site was discussed often and at length by the canons of the church of Salisbury. For the church was within the ramparts of the king's castle and was in consequence exposed to many injuries and daily harassments and great and grievous wrongs.

Here, in the very first paragraph, Wanda is keen to record the difficulties for the cathedral authorities of living side by side with the castle garrison: difficulties which he will later elaborate on. On Herbert's death in 1217 his brother Richard Poore was appointed bishop in his place. Poore would have been familiar with the cathedral, its organisation, life and people as he had previously been dean. He was extremely well-educated, and 'a man of the highest principles', who had also fought faithfully and well against the son of the king of France. Wanda observes that the bishop 'was greatly moved by the sword of compassion over the sufferings and harassment of the church of Salisbury, his new bride, and was deeply anxious for its liberation.' Bishop Poore lost little time and in 1218 envoys were sent to Pope Honorius III in Rome with a report from Gualo, the papal legate in England. This report was an investigation Gualo had made, on the Pope's instructions, into the problems experienced by the cathedral and its people at Old Sarum. The envoys were successful, permission to move was granted, and Gualo returned to Salisbury triumphantly bearing the papal bull confirming Pope Honorius III's agreement. This papal bull (addressed to the cathedral authorities and copied directly into the Register) elaborates not only on the difficulties with the castle garrison but also provides further reasons for the move (Fig 3):

- 'it is subject to so much inconvenience and oppression that you cannot live there without great danger to life and limb'
- 'it is continually buffeted by the winds, so that you can scarcely hear each other speak while you are celebrating divine offices'
- 'the place is so damp that those who live there are subject to constant illness'

- 'the population is scarcely sufficient to provide for repairs to the roofs of the church which are constantly damaged by storms'
- 'they are obliged to buy water at as great a price as would elsewhere be sufficient to buy the common drink of the country,[5] nor can they have access to it without the permission of the castle guard'
- 'the faithful who wish to visit the mother church on Ash Wednesday and Maundy Thursday, or for…other festivals are refused entry, the guards giving as an excuse that some danger threatens the defences'
- 'you do not have sufficient houses for yourselves there, so that many are obliged to rent houses from laymen'.

These reasons expand on what Wanda highlighted in the introduction to his account - the problems of living in such proximity to the castle. But there are other reasons too: scarcity of water, noisy winds: undoubtedly all good grounds for complaint but which overall cannot have been persuasive arguments on their own. Reading the papal bull one has the impression that the cathedral authorities were trying to boost their case as much as possible.

Once the Pope's permission was received Bishop Poore immediately convened a meeting of all the cathedral dignitaries and canons at which it was decided that the cost of the relocation and construction of the new building would be shared amongst themselves: each canon contributing a share from their own income for the next seven years[6]. A wooden chapel was erected on the new site and the foundation stones laid on 28th April 1220. What does the Register of St Osmund tell us about the events of that day?:

> In the year of Grace 1220, on the feast of St Vitalis the Martyr, which then fell on 28 April, the foundation of the new church of Salisbury was laid. The Lord Bishop had expected the Lord King and the papal legate and the Archbishop of Canterbury to come there on that day, together with many of the nobility of England, and in anticipation of their coming had prepared a great store of provisions, as a solemn feast was to be held for everyone who came. In the event the Bishop's hopes were dashed because negotiations were being conducted with the Welsh at Shrewsbury at the time.

The unavailability of the Archbishop and of King Henry III must have been a bitter disappointment to Poore not least because he had obviously made great preparations to impress his guests. The date could not be rescheduled as the ceremony had already been widely advertised. In the end on the day itself few members of the nobility attended but there was 'a great multitude of the common people who came from everywhere around' and who hopefully would have been able to enjoy the feast. Wanda tells us that Bishop Poore laid the first

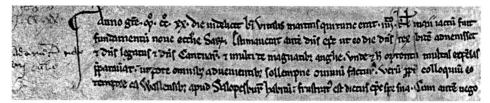

Fig 4: Laying of the foundation stone entry from the account of dean William de Wanda in the Register of St Osmund, Salisbury Cathedral Archives, image reproduced by permission of Wiltshire and Swindon Archives.

stone in the name of the Pope, the second in the name of the Archbishop and the third in his own name. William Longespée, Earl of Salisbury and his wife Ela Devreux Countess of Salisbury 'a woman truly worthy of praise for she was filled with the fear of the Lord' laid the fourth and fifth stones followed by an unspecified number of nobles and cathedral dignitaries also laying stones. Again, Wanda mentions the multitude of common people who 'shouted and wept for joy and freely made their offerings for the work according to the means which God had given them'. Even without an Archbishop and King it must have been a magnificent and unforgettable occasion! (Fig 4)

Wanda's account in The Register of St Osmund is mostly a record of practical steps taken to obtain permission to move and the stages in which that was achieved. Probably he would only have intended it to be read by his fellow priests at Salisbury both at the time of writing and in the future. Another surviving 13th century manuscript concurs broadly with Wanda's account but was intended for a different audience and is written in an entirely different style. In this manuscript the move from Old Sarum to the current site is portrayed as a symbolic undertaking from which can be drawn parallels with events in the Bible; this is the theme of a poem by 13th century poet Henry of Avranches.[7] (Fig 5)

Henry of Avranches (1190/99-c1260) was a poet in the court of King John and King Henry III. His job was not dissimilar perhaps to that of poet laureate today and his audience would have been a public one: members of the King's court and nobility. The Salisbury poem is one of about 160 poems which have been attributed to him and collected together in one volume now residing at Cambridge University Library. In total the poem consists of just over 200 lines and can be dated with some degree of accuracy to having been written around the time of the cathedral's consecration on 28th September 1225.[8] The poem's emotive final lines suggest that not only was construction underway when the poem was written but that Avranches himself had visited Salisbury and seen the work with his own eyes:

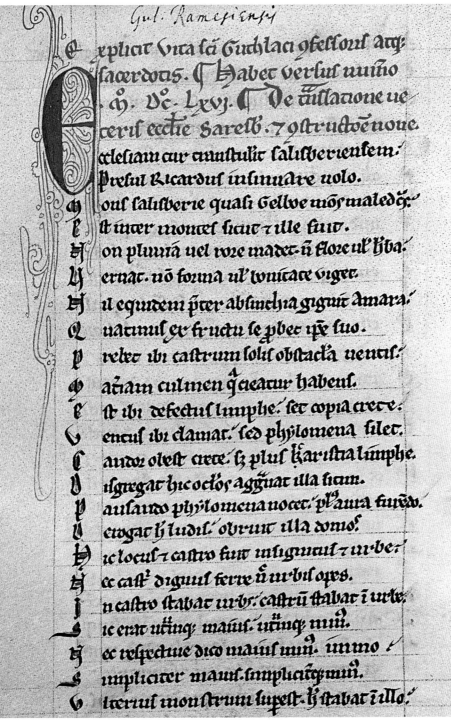

Fig 5: The beginning of the poem by Henry Avranches (*Cambridge University Library*)

> Happy the man who lives to see this Cathedral finished! It will be glorious after such pleasant labour. Let the King give the materials: the bishop his aid: and the masons their skill. All three are needed for the work to prosper. For in this great work will be seen the charity of the King, the love of the bishop and the faith of the craftsmen…Here busy workmen build a new church, remarkable in its beauty, and outstanding in position.

To return to the beginning of the poem Avranches starts by speaking directly to us 'I propose to explain why Bishop Richard moved Salisbury Cathedral.' The next hundred lines are taken up with a description of the problems of Old Sarum - problems which mostly agree with those recorded in the Register of St Osmund, but which are described in far more romantic and 'poetic' language. Avranches doesn't paint a very attractive picture of Old Sarum or 'Sarum Hill' as he calls it:

> It was covered with neither grass nor flowers. It was sodden with rain and dew. Nothing beautiful nor useful could grow there… Little water was to be found: but chalk in abundance. The winds howled, but no nightingale ever sang. The chalk soil was bad enough, but the shortage of water worse. The former dazzled the eyes, and the latter provoked thirst…The steep ascent to the city was tiring, whether going up or down. It was slippery and dangerous.

Particular emphasis is put on the effects of the shortage of water:

> Nothing can be worse for the inhabitants of a city. Water quenches thirst, and extinguishes fires… It gives life to grass and flowers, and new life to birds and little fish…To the taste it is sweet and refreshing. Water re-invigorates old men and women. It cleanses from guilt and sin and drives away the plagues of the devils… What then will be the state of a city which lacks water for its people? When that which is more beneficial is absent, then the greatest harm must ensue. There can be no greater evil for a city than drought.

Avranches describes the problems of Old Sarum as recorded in the Register of St Osmund. Avranches also mentions some other problems: lack of birdsong, the dazzling chalk, the cathedral authorities being compelled to feed the soldiers, the poor being hounded by the castle guards, and the steep, slippery and dangerous route up the hill. Maybe Avranches wanted to increase dramatic effect or perhaps he had had a personal opportunity to mix, and talk with, those living and working at Old Sarum and therefore had a greater understanding of what life was like at Old Sarum for the less well off.

He is also eager to draw parallels between the cathedral's circumstances and events in the Bible, starting by comparing the useless and barren landscape of the hill of Old Sarum with Mount Gilboa, a mountain range which today overlooks northern Israel and the state of Palestine. It was here, the Bible tells us, that Saul and his three sons were all killed in battle. When King David learns of this tragedy, he curses the mountain:

> Ye mountains of Gilboa, let there be no dew or rain upon you, nor bounteous fields! For there the shield of the mighty was defiled, the shield of Saul, anointed with oil no more.[9]

Avranches described the House of God – the cathedral – as imprisoned within the castle grounds just as the Ark of the Covenant was in the Temple of Baal:

> Freedom is Nature's universal bounty, the gift of God…how serious it is to lose the privileges of former freedom, and to be forced to submit to slavery. To the clergy, especially, who are accustomed neither to inflict nor to suffer harm, how grievous the bondage must have been!

Avranches, by comparing the move to biblical events, gives it a symbolic purpose which is of greater significance than the purely practical purposes of requiring additional space, a better water supply and peaceful life. He goes further and portrays the move as the fulfilment of biblical prophecy. Drawing on the prophecies of Isaiah in the Old Testament Avranches sees the decline of the old order (Old Sarum) and a vision of the rising of the new (the Cathedral and City in the valley). Although Old Sarum was abandoned and allowed to fall into ruins this enabled the cathedral to live again in the new site:

> The old church was allowed to fall into ruins, so that the clergy should not be able to return. But while it crumbled into decay it is preserved as it were and stands again in a new site. Oh, wonder of renewal! It died that it might live; fell that it might stand; was abandoned to be found again; was distant to be here!

Avranches was not the only person to compare the building of the new Salisbury Cathedral with biblical events and prophecies. Peter de Blois (c1130–c1217) like Avranches a French poet, but also a theologian and diplomat, wrote a letter to the dean and chapter of the cathedral when Herbert Poore was Bishop. In this letter Blois compares Old Sarum with Noah's Ark:

> The Arc of Noah…seeing that it had saved the last of the human race, later resided amidst the mountains of Armenia, being suitable for no further use. Let us therefore in God's name…go down on to the level, where the valleys will yield much corn, where the fields will become especially fertile, where each person, beneath their own fig tree, will be inspired by their own life, and a day in thy courts will be better than a thousand.[10]

Both Avranches and Blois make the same point: the cathedral founded by Bishop Osmund at Old Sarum had a purpose but that purpose was no longer relevant just as the Ark having saved Noah, his family, and the animals was then redundant.

Unfortunately, there are no surviving documents which tell us <u>how</u> the cathedral was built as opposed to why, but at the end of his letter Blois also portrays the move as the fulfilment of biblical prophecy, this time to events in the book of Ezekiel[11]. Unwittingly Blois here gives us maybe an insight into, if not the details of, how the construction was approached.

> I recall the man in Ezekiel…with a line of flax in one hand, and a measuring reed in the other hand, measure the length, breadth and height of the building, the walls, doors, halls, lintels, altars, tables as well as the Holy of Holies and the chambers and windows. I appear to see Solomon fretfully exhausted over the building of the temple, Hiram providing the wood and the quarrymen, stonemasons, bookkeepers and porters pressing on to make a more elaborate building…the work ought to be urged on as quickly and as vigorously as possible, let there be no disappointment with delays.

Peter of Blois is saying this is a great idea, don't delay, get on with it!

Returning to Henry Avranches and his poem. He also finishes with enthusiasm and optimism promoting the beauty and bountifulness of the new site in the valley:

> All sorts of trees grow there and all kinds of animals will be found. Many of the trees were fruit-bearing, and none of the animals was fierce…In the orchards and meadows by the river-side birds were seen vying with one another in song…Better in this place than the flocks of birds, the wild animals and the dense woods, are the fields of fertile soil. In them are to be found the yellow crocus, the white lily, the blue violet and the red rose. The valley is rich with springs and streams…here, busy workmen build a new church, remarkable in its beauty, and outstanding in position. What was formerly built on the hilltop is now on low-ground. Humble may be its situation, but its importance is high…Happy the man who lives to see this Cathedral finished!

And the final accolade:

> If Adam had come here when driven out of paradise, he would have preferred exile to his native Eden.

So, the 13th century Register of St Osmund, Henry Avranches' poem and, to a lesser extent, Peter de Blois' letter, together with a few shorter references in other documents[12] are our sources for the 'facts' for why the cathedral moved. But what about the fiction? – the legends that have grown up and been handed down over last 800 years culminating today in the story of an arrow and a dying deer.

John Chandler, in *Endless Street*, his comprehensive history of Salisbury, comments that 'Over the years details in the legends have been changed for various reasons; and although it is usually the innocent desire to improve a good story, sometimes there is a hint of propaganda to help a long-forgotten argument.'[13] Political relationships between cathedral and castle, king and bishop, are likely to have continued well after the move and building work had finished. Today a visitor taking a guided tour to the base of the cathedral spire, 225ft from ground level, can see for themselves (as long as the weather is good!) how direct the sightline is between Old Sarum and the cathedral. No doubt the Bishop, by building a huge building surrounded by a large area of land on which there were large and commodious houses for the clergy, was deliberately sending a message to his previous adversaries at the castle.

The legends that have developed are not interested in the reasons why the move was necessary but essentially how the new site was chosen. One legend is recorded in another manuscript in the cathedral archive, written in the 1600s some 400 years after the event, by Dean Thomas Pierce.[14] Not unexpectedly Pierce begins by explaining the conflict between cathedral and castle:

> It chanced that on one Rogation-tide[15], all the canons, together with their attendants, went in procession from the close of Sarum to the church of St Martin, and the Rogation-office being completed, were returning in due time to the castle, but the officers of the King closed the gates against then, and would allow none of them to enter. The bishop's advice (in tears) to the canons was: When they persecute you in one city, flee ye into another.

Pierce's account then goes on to describe how the new site was chosen: a quite extraordinary tale of how the Bishop had initially planned to use land belonging to nearby Wilton Abbey. However, the Bishop overhears 'a certain old seamstress' gossiping about his frequent visits to the Abbess of Wilton speculating that he might be planning to marry her. The seamstress' companion puts her right regarding the true reason for his visits whereupon the seamstress declares: 'Hath not the Bishop land of his own, but that he must needs spoil the Abbess?' This sets the Bishop thinking…On the following night the Virgin Mary appears to him in a dream instructing him to build at a place called Myrfield. Where Myrfield is the Bishop only later discovers when he overhears one of his servants talking about a herd of oxen in a meadow called Myrfield which he interprets as Mary-field (the cathedral is dedicated to the Blessed Virgin Mary).

A new twist on the legend appeared less than fifty years later in the Salisbury

Ballard a 164-line poem written around 1713 by Dr Walter Pope. Pope introduces a few new elements to the legend's cast including an archer, an arrow and an animal – in this case a brindle cow. Before the archer and arrow are introduced the scene at Old Sarum is set:

> 'Old Sarum was built on a dry barren Hill,
> A great many Years ago,
> 'Twas a Roman Town of Strength and Renown,
> As its stately Ruins show.
>
> Therein was a Castle for Men of Arms,
> And a Cloyster for Men of the Gown,
> There were Friars and Monks, and Liars and Punks[16]
> Tho' not any whose Names are come down.'

The Bishop's dream is introduced…

> 'One time as the Prelate lay on his Down-Bed,
> Recruiting his Spirits with Rest,
> There appear'd, as 'tis said, a beautiful Maid,[17]
> With her own dear Babe at her Breast.
>
> To him thus she spoke, (the Day was scarce broke,
> And his Eyes yet to Slumber did yield)
> Go build me a Church without any Delay,
> Go build it in Merry-field.'
>
> 'Full early he arose on a Morning grey,
> To mediate, and to walk,
> And by chance overheard a Soldier on the guard,
> As he thus to his Fellow did talk
>
> I will lay on the side of my good Yewen Bow,
> That I shoot clean over the Corn,
> As far as that cow in Merry-field
> Which grazes under the Thorn.
>
> Then the Bishop cry'd out, Where is Merry-field?
> For his mind was still on his Vow:
> The Soldier reply'd, by the River-side,
> Where you see that Brindle-Cow.'

Over a century later, in 1844, the legend appears again in another poem, by Miss Child.

> '... the Bishop was visited thrice in one night
> By a beautiful figure in luminous white,
> Who enjoined him to build (where no mortal had kneeled)
> A Gothic Cathedral in the rich Merrifield.
> Not knowing the place, after much deep reflection
> He sought the fresh air to soothe moody dejection:
> And as musing he slowly pursued his lone walk,
> He passed two of the guards – while, in sociable talk,
> One said to the other "I would wager this bow,
> That 'twill send forth an arrow to reach yonder cow
> Which in Merrifield now chews her cud by the thorn,
> On the banks of the river that waters the corn.'[18]

Today the most common version of the legend has transformed Dr Pope's and Miss Child's archer, arrow and cow into archer, arrow and deer. It goes like this: an archer shot an arrow from the embankment at Old Sarum so that wherever the arrow fell there the new cathedral would be built. One indisputable fact is that Salisbury Cathedral today is located about two miles from Old Sarum and therefore it is impossible that anyone could shoot an arrow that far. The legend gets around this problem by claiming that the arrow hit and embedded itself into deer which then (conveniently for Bishop Poore) wandered about for a few miles before lying down to die.

However appealing tales of dreams, brindle cows, archers and deer may be they have no factual basis. To find out the truth about the move we can only rely on the written evidence of the 13th century and in particular the Register of St Osmund and Henry Avranches' poem. Of the two the Register presents a more chronological and factual account, although it is important to bear in mind that it is likely to have been influenced by both the local politics of the day and the practical difficulties of living and working at Old Sarum. The poem seeks biblical precedent and authority to validate the move. To those living in the 13th century it is likely that both views would have been of equal importance. Salisbury Cathedral has now stood in its fertile vale for over 800 years, its predecessor stood on the hill of Old Sarum for less than 150 years. For this reason alone, it seems reasonable to conclude that the move was a success. Today we are fortunate not only to live to see the cathedral finished, as Henry Avranches wished, but to live to see it thrive.

Notes

1 Register of St Osmund (RSO), Salisbury Cathedral Archives FG/1/2. All translated excerpts quoted in this article are from f60–62 and are the work of Daphne Stroud.

2 The 1075 Council of London had decreed that the sees of Sherbourne and Ramsbury should be united and moved to Salisbury (Old Sarum).

3 In recent years the Register of St Osmund was in the custody of the Wiltshire & Swindon History Centre. In 2015 it was transferred to Salisbury Cathedral Archives.

4 Prebends are land or property owned by the Cathedral. Many of these were given to individual canons (priests) to provide them with a personal income.

5 ie beer

6 Indulgences were also issued to raise money.

7 Cambridge University Library Dd XI f92–96. The poem is printed together with a translation by W J Torrance in WANHM vol 57 (1960), 242–246 from which quotes in the article are taken.

8 Frost, Christian, 2005, 'The Symbolic Move to Old Sarum', *WANHM* vol 98 158

9 2 Samuel 1:21, New Revised Standard Version

10 Peter of Blois, 'Letter 104', written between 1182 and 1206 and translated in Frost, 2005.

11 Ezekiel 40–42

12 Other sources are: William of Malmesbury 'Gesta Pnotificum Anglorum', ii.83 and The Tropenell Cartulary published in Davies, Silvester, 1908, 'The Tropenell Cartulary, contents of an old muniment chest', WANHM, vol 35.

13 Chandler, John, 2001, *Endless Street*, 12

14 Salisbury Cathedral Archives FG/8/1/1 'De prima fundacione Sarisberiensis Ecclesiae'. A translation (excerpts from which are quoted in this article) can be found in Jones, W H, 1879, 'Fasti Ecclesiae Sarisberiensis', 47–50.

15 Rogationtide is a religious festival during which prayers are made to God against plagues and natural calamities and particularly for God's blessing on the growing crops. Also during Rogationtide elaborate processions would take place to mark the boundaries of a parish.

16 Much poetical license has been taken here. Salisbury was never a monastic cathedral so there would never have been any friars or monks. Pope explains in a footnote that 'Liars' are tradesmen and 'Punks' are harlots.

17 Pope's footnote reads 'Who that Maid and Babe were, the Learned and Devout understand.'

18 Child, Miss, 1849, *The Spinster at Home in the Close of Salisbury Together with Tales and Ballads,* Frederick A Blake, Salisbury, 6th edition, 27

Reading the Architecture

John Elliott

Salisbury's cathedral is architecturally important because it has a unity of style that most other cathedrals lack. This article attempts to explain what is unique about Salisbury and to also give an outline explanation of the differing architectural styles that have existed.

The Gothic style majors on the pointed arch, which provides structural stability and enabled the medieval masons to achieve great heights in their buildings. An arch of stones has a smaller surface area on the inside of the arch than on the outside. Hence the stones interlock, providing structural strength when the final key stone is inserted.

Gothic predominated in the 13th, 14th and 15th centuries. It had been preceded by the Norman or Romanesque style (Fig 1) which used round arches and depended upon the wall mass for much of its structural strength. Gothic was followed by several centuries of classicism which relied upon columns and beams for much of their strength and were based on precedents derived from ancient Greece and Rome. In the 19th century Gothic returned to dominate architectural style, and especially that used in churches. This renaissance of Gothic was a reaction against the effects of industrialization and was based upon a desire to return to the style of a pre-industrial medieval age. In addition, many argued that as the classical style was based on the pagan temples of Greece and Rome it was inappropriate for use in Christian churches, whereas Gothic was derived from a pre-Reformation Christian era.

Most cathedrals are a mix of architectural styles. There may be traces of the Norman style, then various Gothic additions and later evidence that the building was partly modified and upgraded by the addition of window tracery in a later style. Exeter Cathedral is an excellent example.

The English form of Gothic was a fusion of stylistic ideas that existed in France and various local English traditions.[1] A separate chapter in this publication addresses these influences.

In 1817 Thomas Rickman attempted to classify Gothic into three forms.[2] The earliest of these is what we now call Early English (Fig 2) which was popular in

Fig 1: A Norman style, round arch, doorway at St Mary, Breamore (*Roy Bexon*)

the thirteenth century, or more precisely from *c*.1180 to *c*.1280. This was a much lighter structure than the preceding Norman one and, in addition to the pointed arch, was based on rib vaulting, and narrow lancet windows as you can see in the nave of Salisbury cathedral.

The Decorated style (Fig 3) followed in the 14th century, or from *c*.1250 to *c*.1350, and is noted for its larger windows with tracery, lierne vaulting and the addition of more decoration. The medieval builders had learnt how to make larger apertures in the walls for windows without endangering the stability of the building. The best example in Salisbury is the United Refformed Church in Fisherton Street, though this dates from the 19th century Gothic Revival period rather than from the medieval. The great west window at Exeter is also an excellent medieval example.

Finally, came the Perpendicular style (Fig 4) in the 15th century, or *c*.1330 to sometime after 1485. Here there is an emphasis on strong vertical lines, fan vaulting, often lower roof lines and a use of crenellation. Many of the windows in St Thomas's church at the northern end of the High Street are in this style and were part of a restoration of a church that was originally built in a much earlier style. The best national example is most probably St George's Chapel, Windsor where the western end is a complex mix of masonry and glass in the perpendicular style and a celebration of the amazing structural progress made by the medieval masons who could now create such large decorative features without threatening the structural stability of the building – something that would have been unheard of when Salisbury's cathedral was built.

However, architectural style never changed in a regimented manner and the process of developing a new style is always accompanied by a period of transition when some new elements are mixed with older stylistic manifestations.

Because the main body of Salisbury Cathedral was built between 1220 and 1258, the architectural style which was used is Early English. The windows are simple lancets, or tall narrow lights which can be used singly or in groups of two, three or five, the arches are pointed, there is much rib vaulting in the nave and aisles and the columns supporting the triforium and clerestory are a compound mix of shafts.

The tower and spire were added in the early 14th century and so fall into the transitional period between the Early English and Decorated styles. The main architectural evidence of this is the use of ball-flower (Fig 5) as a form of decoration, something that was very popular in the early years of the 1300s and the tower and spire are peppered with it.[3]

The Cloisters were added around 1240-66 and the Chapter House most probably between 1248 and 1266. Both illustrate how the Early English style

Fig 2: Early English lancet windows in the nave of Salisbury Cathedral. These are in pairs but they could also be arranged in singles or larger multiples, especially at the east end of the church (*Roy Bexon*)

Fig 3: The west window of the United Reformed Church church in Fisherton Street with a geometric patterned Decorated window. which almost fills the west wall. (*John Elliott*)

Fig 4: Perpendicular windows from the 15th century at St Thomas's church. Note how much larger the window openings are than with either the Early English or Decorated style. (*John Elliott*)

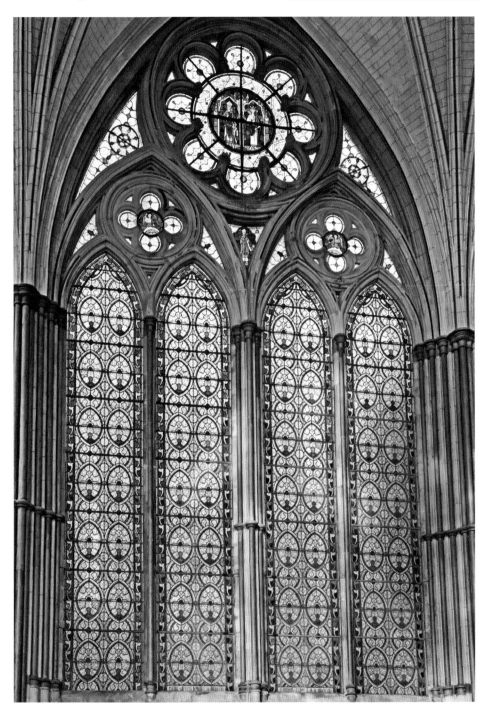

Fig 6: Chapter House windows and a slightly later development. Notice how the simple lancets are now paired and each topped by a quatrefoil and the whole thing topped by an octofoil round light. (*Roy Bexon*)

Fig 5: An example of ballflower. The tower and spire are highly decorated with ballflower and there is even evidence of it in the plinths of some statues on the western end from where this photograph was taken. (*Roy Bexon*)

Fig 7: Strainer arches at the crossing which were inserted to support the tower and spire. Note the more vertical, or perpendicular, emphasis of the architectural style from the styles that went before. (*Roy Bexon*)

Fig 8: Crossing vault which was inserted in the 15th century to seal off the tower. Before the tower and spire were erected the crossing extended upwards to the top of the lantern. Once ironwork started to be introduced to stabilise the tower this became unsightly and the vault was erected. (*Roy Bexon*)

developed towards the Decorated style with groups of lancets separated by slim columns and topped by circular foiled tracery. That in the Chapter House (Fig 6) is especially notable with each bay being illuminated by groups of four lancets which are topped by two quatrefoils and all topped by an octofoil.

There is also evidence of the Perpendicular style inside the cathedral. The two great strainer arches (Fig 7) which span the area between the columns where the transepts emerge from the crossing are of this style. Here the decoration is more fulsome and the architecture lighter and more confident. The vault (Fig 8) above the crossing which was added in 1479-81, to hide the stabilizing ironwork which had started to be inserted in the tower, is also in this style. It is the only non-thirteenth century vault in the cathedral.[4]

So, while it is not completely inaccurate to claim that Salisbury Cathedral was built in the Early English Gothic style, the statement ignores the fact that the tower and spire were added some 50 or so years after the main structure was completed, and exhibit elements of the Decorated style, while even later additions inside the cathedral which were added in the 15th century have traces of the Perpendicular style in them.

Notes

1   For a full discussion of this topic see Draper, Peter, 2006, *The Formation of English Gothic* and especially the Introduction

2   The terms Early English, Decorated and Perpendicular were invented in the late eighteenth century – see Rickman, Thomas, 1825, *An Attempt to Discriminate the Styles of Architecture in England, from the Conquest to the Reformation*

3   There is also ballflower on the plinths of some statues on the western front

4   A vault above the crossing was originally at the top of the lantern and considerably higher than the current vault. Once the tower and spire were added, the structural problems which followed necessitated the use of ironwork inside the old lantern. To hide this from view the current tower vault was erected

Vive La France,
not forgetting Wells and Lincoln!

John Elliott

It is easy to think of the construction of Salisbury Cathedral in isolation from all the other cathedral building that was taking place at the same time (Fig 1). Without any doubt the medieval period was one of great devotion with many new churches, abbeys and cathedrals - just as today we build office blocks, high rise flats and car parks so they built places of worship, castles and palaces. Of these it is often the churches that have survived and many of the results are still around us.

Even before work started on the cathedral the bishop started to plan the creation of the city which in effect became a by-product of the cathedral project. By creating a market-town the bishop generated a vast income stream that underpinned the church's ambitious plans. I believe that it is true to say that the cathedral would never have been as grand if it had not been for the income flowing from the city where the first market became established in 1219.

However, Salisbury was not alone in the creation of grand cathedral buildings – it was happening all over northern Europe as well as in England. and most of it was also associated with the use of a new architectural style – the Gothic.

It is hard to identify exactly where any new development started, but in this instance the initial impetus almost certainly came with the revival of church building in the Ile-de-France during the 1130s. Then came the work of Abbot Suger at St-Denis, just 11 kms north of Paris (Fig 2).[1] It is generally accepted that it was the work at St-Denis, a church that originally dated from around 775, and especially the rebuilt choir which was constructed between 1140-44, that established a new form of architecture, the Gothic, which then spread rapidly throughout northern Europe and Britain.[2] Much cathedral building, or rebuilding, followed in France with Chartres in *c*.1194–1220, Bourges c1195, Reims from 1211,[3] and Amiens 1220.

Fig 1: Salisbury Cathedral from the north west. (*Ash Mills*)

Fig 2: St-Denis in the northern suburbs of Paris where Abbot Suger played a major part in developing a new form of architecture. (*John Elliott*)

Fig 3: Lincoln Cathedral, like the earlier cathedral at Old Sarum was built on the top of a steep hill adjacent to a castle. It is considered to be highly important in spreading the new architectural ideas, though its ornateness was most probably responsible, at least in part, for the much simpler lines of Salisbury Cathedral. (*John Elliott*)

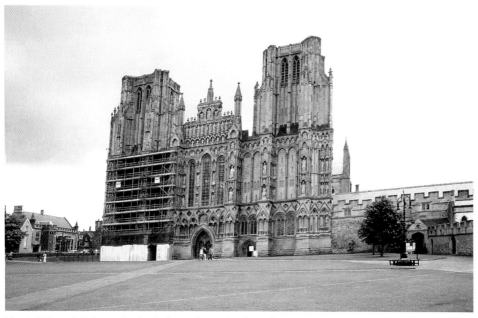

Fig 4: When Salisbury Cathedral was being built Wells Cathedral was being rebuilt on a site adjacent to earlier buildings which had been an Anglo-Saxon and then a Norman cathedral. It would have provided a direct stylistic comparison with the cathedral being built at Salisbury. (*John Elliott*)

There had been a tradition of church building in England, and especially after the Norman Conquest when, during the 11th and early 12th centuries, almost every English cathedral and abbey church was rebuilt on a massive scale, though with the exception of Salisbury almost all the gothic additions to these churches had to be extensions or re-buildings of earlier structures and styles. The rebuilding of York started in 1160 but this was mainly due to the inadequacy of the existing Romanesque structure, and most of the precedents were continental; this was also true of the rebuilding of the choir at Ripon in *c*.1160-70. The theory is that the Cistercians brought French stylistic ideas with them and these were used at Byland Abbey and then York and Ripon.[4] The work at Canterbury towards the end of the 12th century was very much influenced by French ideas.[5] The first architect was William of Sens who was building on a Romanesque crypt, and the stained glass that goes with this building is obviously French and almost identical to that at St Remi in Reims. He was succeeded by William the Englishman who, despite his name, was even more French than William.

As Christopher Wilson says, it was the 'Cultural affinity with northern France [that] was the key factor in England's very early receptiveness to Gothic architecture'.[6] French was the language of the ruling elite; from 1135 England was ruled by kings who held land in both France and England and many of the clergy either came from France or were trained there.

Following the murder of Thomas Becket in 1170, Canterbury became a place of pilgrimage as Becket was seen as having protected the church from a tyrannical king. In the process Canterbury gained power, prestige and riches. Seeing the benefits which Canterbury had gained, the other English cathedrals started looking for somebody from their past that they could elevate into a state of sainthood and create a shrine for pilgrims to visit.

Hence the cult of Osmund, whose body was transferred from Old Sarum and reinterred in the new cathedral to create a focus for pilgrimages, as with pilgrims came money.[7] At the same time there was a growing sense of national identity, which was sometimes assisted by Papal attempts to exploit the revenues of the English church and clergy, and a resentment towards French power, and particularly the power of Philip II after his conquest of Normandy in 1204 and an attempted invasion of England in 1216. As a result, while cathedral building continued apace on both sides of the channel, the influence of French architectural thinking started to decline in England and was replaced by domestic ideas.

A cathedral was built at Lincoln after 1072 inside a walled town, and so more easily defended. An earthquake mostly destroyed the Norman building in 1185 and rebuilding work started almost immediately. The eastern transept and St Hugh's choir were begun in 1191, the western transept, nave, crossing tower and the Angel Choir all followed (Fig 3).[8] Peter Draper claims that Lincoln was the most influential building in the process of disseminating the new architectural ideas, though 'Extravagance on the scale of Lincoln could also provoke reaction and that, surely, is how the architecture of Salisbury needs to be read.'[9]

A Saxon church had existed at Wells since the 8th century and it became the see of a bishop in 909. This was replaced by a Norman building which was consecrated in 1148. Work on the current building began c.1180, including rebuilding the choir, crossing tower, transepts and nave. (Fig 4) Then came work at the western end, the Lady Chapel, ambulatory and eastern part of the choir, plus construction of the Chapter House.[10] Like Lincoln and Wells, Salisbury was built in the English tradition and combined regional and wider influences, though the two sets of transepts were probably derived from Canterbury, as was the arrangement of lancet windows, with two in the aisles and three in the clerestory. It was Wells that provided the influence for the exterior with clean external contours, which were not dominated by

Fig 5: Like Salisbury, in 2020, Amiens Cathedral also celebrates 800 years since work started on its construction. It represents the French variant of the new Gothic style while Salisbury represents one of the English variants. (*John Elliott*)

buttresses.[11] The retrochoir at Winchester was an influence but other design elements used at Winchester were not emulated in the Salisbury design.[12] Likewise, the Lincoln apsidal eastern end,[13] was rejected in favour of an English rectangular ambulatory.

Meanwhile on the continent cathedral building continued apace, especially at Amiens (Fig 5). There have been several cathedrals in Amiens, most of which were destroyed by fire. A Romanesque style building was erected around 1152 but this soon proved too small after the acquisition of what was supposed to be the skull of John the Baptist in 1206.[14] The acquisition of such a high-ranking relic made Amiens a major pilgrimage destination. Then in 1218 a lightning strike destroyed much of the cathedral and the decision was made to rebuild on a much grander scale in the Gothic style. The foundation stone was laid in 1220 and the choir added in c.1236-67. It therefore shares an 800th anniversary with Salisbury in 2020.[15]

The thirteenth century was a period of rapid cathedral building in England and on the continent. After the Norman Conquest the style in England shifted to a replication of buildings in Normandy (eg Durham and parts of the current Winchester cathedral). In addition, the Cistercians brought with them plans of churches in Burgundy, and within a generation a distinctly English version had become dominant. It was Lincoln and Salisbury that started to mark this individuality of English architecture. However, the building of Salisbury cathedral did not happen in a vacuum, but was just one of many cathedral building projects that existed in England and northern France at that time. What was unique about Salisbury is that it was built on a 'virgin' site without any need to modify or add to a pre-existing building, though the pre-existing cathedral at Old Sarum and the need to accommodate the new Use of Sarum liturgy must have placed constraints on the design.[16] The speed of construction was also rapid, though most probably not as rapid as Chartres cathedral, which is bigger, and was built between 1194 and 1220. Salisbury represents one very important strand of the English variety of Gothic, though it is just one amongst many cathedrals that were being built or rebuilt around that time.

Bibliography

Wilson, Christopher, (1990), *The Gothic Cathedral*

Draper, Peter, (2006), *The Formation of English Gothic: Architecture and Identity, 1150-1250*

Acknowledgements

I would like to thank Dr Brian O'Callaghan, Ruth Newman and Steve Dunn for reading versions of this text and for making comments and suggestions.

Notes

1   Today St-Denis is a northern suburb of Paris and close to the Stade de France. It is the historic place of burial for the kings of France

2   The western block had previously been rebuilt in 1135-40 and a nave extension in 1140 before work started on the choir

3   Part completed by c1250. The west towers were designed in c1255, though not begun until 1435

4   The choirs of York and Ripon would seem to have been built to an almost identical design. This design shares many details with Byland Abbey. This opens up the idea of the Cistercians and 'Missionaries of Gothic' (article by Christopher Wilson with this title), the broad idea being that Cistercian Monasteries founded at this time brought with them French gothic ideas. Cistercian houses are to be found in the less well-developed parts of the country (West Country, Welsh Marches, Yorkshire) thus regional versions of gothic start there as well as direct influence via Canterbury

5   The choir was remodelled in 1175-7, the eastern transept remodelled in 1177-9, the presbytery rebuilt in 1179-84 and the Trinity Chapel in 1180-4

6   Wilson, Christopher, 1990, *The Gothic Cathedral*, 72

7   He was not canonised until 1457. Pilgrimage is important because it brings in revenue to those with a successful cult. It is architecturally important because along with the cult of the Virgin Mary (many Lady Chapels) it resulted in the rebuilding of the east ends of major churches. It is usually these new east ends that have the characteristic English squared off end. Their predecessors were almost always apsidal.

8   The western transept in c1200-20, the nave c1220-35, the crossing tower after 1237 and the Angel Choir from 1256

9   Draper, Peter, 2006, *The Formation of English Gothic*, 149, 152

10 Further work at the western end was undertaken between c1230-40 and the Lady Chapel, ambulatory and eastern part of the choir in c1320-40. Additional work, plus construction of the Chapter House, was undertaken in c1285-1345

11 Such buttresses that now exist were added later to stabilise the tower and spire which were added after the initial construction

12 See Draper, Peter, 2006, *The Formation of English Gothic*, 155

13 Note how the cathedral at Old Sarum had an apsidal eastern end as did all the churches that were built after the Norman Conquest

14 The skull was supposedly captured when the crusaders raided Constantinople in 1204 and was then brought back to Amiens

15 Building work continued for much longer than at Salisbury. For instance, the south tower was completed in 1372, the north tower in 1401-2. There were major restorations in 1482-1510. The spire was destroyed by fire in 1528 and a new one built in 1528-33, but then shortened in 1628. There have been significant restorations and re-orderings in the eighteenth, nineteenth and twentieth centuries. The world-famous choir stalls were erected in 1508-22

16 See Draper, Peter, 2006, *The Formation of English Gothic*, 152-3

Fig 1: An inscription of 1610 in the Cathedral. (*Steve Dunn*)

Conversations with the Past: Graffiti in Salisbury Cathedral

Stephen Dunn

Graffiti is part of the modern landscape, its presence ranges across the whole spectrum of the human condition, from political slogans, angry statements from the disaffected, those who feel that there is no other outlet for their protest, expressions of love, prayer, and simple 'signatures' or 'tags' to show that someone felt the need to express their attendance at one location or another. Graffiti has also become accepted within artistic circles as a new genre of art within pop culture, and increasingly this high-end art is created by street artists made respectable by their notoriety. Graffiti can be seen as something beautiful and enhancing therefore, or creating a sense of menace, violence or discomfort in the observer. This is not a new phenomenon. There is a vast amount of evidence to show that graffiti is so ancient that it is hard to decide quite when its origins were; certainly Greek and Roman societies abounded with graffiti. Perhaps most surprisingly it is in places of worship that we find some of the longest standing graffiti in this country. The 21st century notion of church in Britain has been heavily coloured by the palette of religious Reformation[1] in the 16th and 17th Centuries, with the tearing down and reordering of altars and associated furniture, glazing styles and the subsequent liturgical impact on ecclesiastical art. Walls that were once covered in painted illustrations of biblical events, saints and moral lecturing are now scraped bare, or overpainted with thick limewash. The effects of a return to a more colourful environment in the period of revival instigated by the Oxford Movement in the 1830s did little to highlight the existence of graffiti and it has mostly lain unseen, little noted or recorded from the day that it was made until modern times.

What is graffiti?

Oxford dictionaries[2] define graffiti as 'Writing or drawings scribbled, scratched, or sprayed illicitly on a wall or other surface in a public place.' This definition reinforces the view that graffiti, must be something that is done clandestinely and without approval from the church authorities. This is an erroneous view, however, as not only was graffiti tolerated by the clergy prior to the English Reformation, but also there is evidence in the Cathedral, and other churches, to suggest that they were complicit in its manufacture and it takes many forms.

Prior to the 19th century little attention was paid to the subject of church graffiti, and though occasionally noted by antiquarians and historians, no particular thought was given to its study. In fact the first book solely devoted to the subject does not appear until 1966, when Val Pritchard wrote a book that considered graffiti in parish churches primarily in Cambridgeshire and 'within 60 miles of Cambridge.'[3] Her work considers graffiti in its two commonest manifestations: drawings and textual inscriptions. She quotes M R James, writing about the Lady chapel at Ely cathedral: 'the more closely we study the remains of early sacred art the more frequently do we detect that the smallest details have a meaning.' She suggests that this is equally true of graffiti, where even the tiniest mark has the potential to have meaning. Not until 2010 does graffiti receive a serious study with the formation of the Norfolk Medieval Graffiti Survey by Matthew Champion, an archaeologist, who decided to conduct an in depth community based research project to survey and record the myriad of graffiti that can be found in Norfolk, and later Suffolk, churches. Champion published his own book, 'Medieval Graffiti'[4] in 2015, which is now regarded as a primary reference and handbook of the many regional based graffiti surveys around the country. In a recent essay Champion writes: 'The largely volunteer led county based surveys of England and Wales have recorded tens of thousands of new inscriptions in the last decade, the vast majority of which have never been documented.'[5]

Churches are undoubtedly focal points for communities. Almost every village, and certainly every town in the country, has a church that is a common element of the landscape. Church towers and spires are taken for granted, yet they provide an often unique site for us to discover those who lived in these places in the centuries before us. Whilst the graveyards provide, in some cases, a dynastic record of certain families, they usually shed no further light on the lives of the people commemorated beyond their inscriptions on the tomb stones. The evidence as we move into the chapel, church, abbey, minster or cathedral of those who visited becomes more obvious the more we search the walls of these places and Salisbury Cathedral is no exception.

Graffiti Surveying in Salisbury Cathedral

The Salisbury Cathedral Graffiti Survey follows on in the tradition of community based volunteer led graffiti survey projects. Founded by the author in 2017 it seeks to survey and record graffiti found in the Cathedral as well as architecture marks and mason marks. A total of sixty-one volunteers stated their interest, approximately half were drawn from Cathedral guides and the others from The Arts Society Sarum, many of whom had just completed a church recording project in St John the Baptist, Bishopstone. The Survey is to report in 2020 as a part of the Cathedral's 800th Anniversary programme, although it is likely that there will be more work to be done into the future, especially in the Tower and roof spaces where there is a prolific amount of post 18th Century graffiti. (See Fig 1)

Aim

The Survey has three aims: to record the variety of accessible graffiti and analyse where possible. To provide a publicly accessible record and to provide a record to the Wiltshire Historic Environment Record (HER) and the corpus of graffiti nationally.

Methodology

Whilst there is much obvious graffiti in the Cathedral, a great deal more has been hidden under paintwork, the detritus of centuries of dust and wear and lost beneath later graffiti as in a palimpsest. The latter examples are more difficult to see and require careful teasing out from the overlays of later inscriptions. However, the basic essential tools are simple and easily available: a torch, measuring scale and a small handheld camera, even a modern mobile phone camera manages quite adequately provided that it can record in .jpg format. Recording can be achieved by a single surveyor; however, it is better for two or three to act as a team; one to hold the torch, another to operate the camera, and the third to line the scale up against the graffito being recorded. The method of recording is by the use of 'raking light'. The torch shone directly onto a flat surface can act to bleach out any graffiti; far better to angle it at up to 90° so that the beam runs perpendicular to the surface being inspected. This has the effect of highlighting inscriptions enabling very lightly inscribed graffiti to be seen. With the light trained on the graffiti the surveyors can then apply the measuring scale and torch to best effect. The image is saved, the type and location of the graffiti then logged for entry to a master spreadsheet. Ultimately it is intended that all the data collected will form a single, searchable database available either within the Cathedral's own website, or a separate standalone website.

The Graffiti

The evidence for graffiti and wall inscriptions found thus far seems to be based around the building design in the form of architectural marks, the marks of the builders – masons marks for example - apotropaic marks (Greek meaning to 'ward off 'or 'away') sometimes, and erroneously, called 'witchmarks'; devotional marks, votive inscriptions and memorial marks. Unsurprisingly, there are also many name inscriptions left by visitors over the past two hundred years. Additionally, although not graffiti and outside the scope of this paper, there are engravings made as a result of 20th century fund raising activities when members of the public were given the opportunity to record personal names, occasions, obituaries, etc, as a commemorative memorial onto diamond shaped glass set into windows in the tower.

Dating

Dating graffiti is not straightforward and harder to establish when surveying a single building with no ready comparisons against which to establish commonalities. In order to make a 'best guess' recourse is made to the existing data available in the public domain, of which, fortunately, there is an increasing amount. Additionally, specialist websites and publications, such as Matthew Champion's book mentioned above, provide an extremely helpful guide to some of the possible meanings of the inscriptions and drawings. Of particular assistance has been the published findings of other great churches and the work of individual scholars. Champion writes 'The dating of the graffiti inscriptions we find in English parish churches is, in many cases, difficult to do with any degree of accuracy. Whilst it is possible to ascribe a period, era or century to some individual inscriptions, many others remain enigmatic. In many cases the best that can be done is to describe an individual graffiti inscription as either pre- or post – Reformation. Even then, particularly with some of the simpler pictorial images, the borderline is distinctly hazy'.[6]

This view is one that has been borne out time and again during the progress of the Salisbury survey. The sheer variety of inscriptions found make it attractive to imagine that much is pre-Reformation, however, the likelihood is that the overwhelming majority of inscriptions are more recent with the majority being concentrated into the 17th, 18th and 19th centuries. Examples made in the 20th and 21st centuries are less common, although they most certainly do exist.

Who made the Graffiti?

Cathedrals have always been places of memorialisation for the senior members of society both spiritual and temporal. We are familiar with the pyramids of the Egyptian pharaohs and the elaborate mausoleums of the Romans, therefore, it comes as no surprise that Christians wished to follow suit. Monumental commemoration in churches was initially reserved for the clergy. However, as churches flourished under the patronage of secular sponsors the desire for them to be similarly remembered followed quickly. The first people to be buried at the Cathedral at Old Sarum were bishops[7] and shortly after the consecration of the Trinity Chapel at the east end of the new cathedral in 1225, their tombs were relocated into the new building and elements in respect of all three, at least by attribution, exist still in the nave and Trinity Chapel. However, the first man to be interred in the new Cathedral was not a priest but William Longespée, the half-brother of King Richard I and King John. He was a major benefactor of the cathedral and Earl of Salisbury. The following centuries saw an influx of memorials that commemorated only those with the means to fund them, but what of the ordinary man and woman, how and where might they too make their mark?

Graffiti is often attributed to 'bored choir boys', however, there is little evidence for this – for example there is no graffiti in the Choir stalls. Evidence of concentrations of graffiti is chiefly found in the areas where the public gathered, and it is here that we must start the exploration. The urge to leave a mark behind to show that we have visited remains as strong today as ever, however, the reasoning behind this urge is more complex. The church was central to the lives of most people and it saw the principal events of religious life: baptism, marriage and funerals, as well as routine worship. The church acted as a safe place for people to socialise and many inevitably wished to leave their mark. Something that cannot be overlooked is what today we might dismiss as superstition but before the Reformation, and beyond, there was by popular acknowledgement the recognition of the existence of supernatural forces. Witchcraft was an accepted aspect of life and whilst not condoned, permeated secular life and was normalised at every level of society. Witchcraft was primarily a matter for the ecclesiastical courts until the 16th Century, with one exception, that was the use of witchcraft against the King's body, and his immediate family which is dealt with under the Treason Act of 1352, and remains valid in English law today. Cunning folk were employed by communities to provide a range of powers from healing to love magic. Some, no doubt for a high price, could also be called upon to provide darker services. Generally, they were seen as a force for good by the public, a fact that exasperated the church; George Gifford, vicar of Maldon in Essex writing in 1597, complained that his parishioners went to the cunning man 'as if they were his (their) god'. The desire to protect the sacred space of a cathedral from external malevolent forces is understandable therefore, and most likely accounts for the origin of several genres of symbols inscribed into the interior stonework. Cathedrals were built for God, and the splendour that we see may reflect man's ambition to design perfection in architecture and art. However, it was not humans that they were trying to impress; God Himself was the audience and it was essential that the space was maintained untrammelled by those intent on evil.

The section of a Cathedral west of the Quire, where the crossing is in Salisbury, would primarily be an area for personal prayer with worshippers scattered around the central area beneath the Rood (cross). The main entrance for most visitors today is on the south side of the nave through the former Consistory Court. In the late middle ages, there were two principal entries, both on the north side. The existing north porch enters directly into the nave, the former St Thomas's porch gave access though the north transept. The latter porch and doorway were removed in the late 18th century; prior to this, visitors would have made a beeline for the crossing in the centre of the Cathedral and for access prior to the Reformation to the altars that were in this vicinity. Here are also found the strainer arches that support the tower; and on their western columns is found the largest concentration of graffiti in the Cathedral other than in the tower. The graffiti here are many and varied, however, one consistent theme is

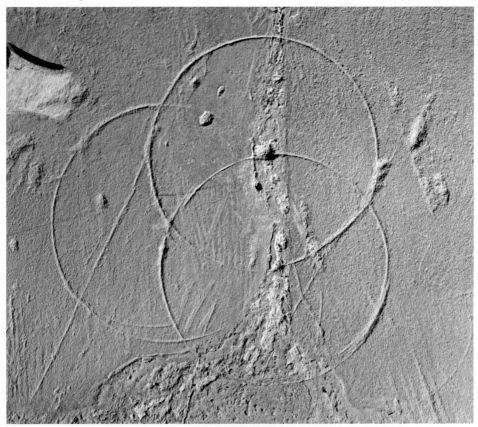

Fig 2: Compass drawn circles on the Mitford tomb (*Roy Bexon*)

Fig 3: Compass drawn inscription on the south west crossing column (*Roy Bexon*)

that of devotion through ritual protection marks. Compass drawn circles are in abundance [Figs 2 & 3], as are Marian marks, overlaid letter Vs that are reputed to signify devotion to Mary, Mother of Christ as 'Virgo Virginum' (Virgin of the Virgins). The circle is a common theme in both devotional art and architecture and in respect of the former has a far longer history than its adoption by Christians. The medieval church enabled worshippers to engage with altars and shrines outside the Presbytery in an almost constant flow of human traffic. We find isolated areas of intensity of inscriptions around the tombs of two significant 14th century bishops, Simon of Ghent and Roger de Martival. Both men had

Fig 4: Inscribed text on column in south choir aisle (*Roy Bexon*)

a role in the erection of the tower and spire and the latter also drew up the Statutes of the Cathedral in 1319. The graffiti is mostly devotional in nature with crosses in abundance. There are also signatures, and several complex and currently unidentifiable inscriptions in the vicinity of the tombs.

Another significant group of likely graffiti makers were Cathedral staff, both clerical and lay. The tower in particular provides a rich selection of inscriptions, mostly 18th and 19th centuries that frequently include reference to the employment status as 'mason', 'bellboy', and more from the 20th century – 'steeplejack' and 'electrician'. Another example appears to have been made either by a member of clergy or a member of the choir. [Fig 4] Written in an early 16th century Gothic hand in Latin, it appears to have been penned by a Henry Webster. Precisely who Henry was is unknown, however, he is clearly literate albeit his hand is extremely difficult to read. The initial text reads – 'alma salve regina mea beata…' – the remainder has proved unintelligible. Clearly it is invoking the Virgin and may possibly be a short stanza from a Marian hymn dating from the early 16th century, or perhaps the final prayer of the Rosary. Something that perplexes many is that graffiti was tolerated in a way that is not the case today. The graffiti was made in a public area and was generally overt. The walls of the Cathedral were painted in a masonry style, that is, lines in red to imitate rows of ashlar masonry into which the graffiti was incised and no objection seems to have been made to its existence. Later, when iconoclasm came to bear in the 16th and particularly 17th centuries there is evidence that some graffiti was painted over and some probably lost when plasterwork was removed in the latter half of the 18th century, but by no means all and much is still very clearly visible.

The earliest inscribed marks are probably those made by masons, the builders of the cathedral. Masons marks are widely reported to be ubiquitous in medieval churches and the Cathedral is no exception. The conventional view of these marks is one related to payment. Masons were reputed to have their own symbol, or 'mark' which would be recognised from the work that they did and were paid accordingly. These symbols [Fig 5] are usually fairly simple and could be made quickly by the mason using a straight wedged tool such as a chisel. The same or similar marks are found all over Britain and Northern Europe and across all time periods. The evidence for payment by piecework is sparse; masons guilds do not seem to have maintained master lists of ownership of marks and it is most likely that masons were paid on a weekly basis.

Probably, masons were provided with an individual or project mark to apply to their work. There is a suggestion prevalent currently that the marks would be used for productivity or quality assurance purposes by the Clerk of Works, rather than as always a means for an individual to prove their work for remunerative purposes.

Fig 5: Mason's mark in the Chapter House (*Roy Bexon*)

Consecration

The official consecration of a church is an essential part of establishing the building in its new sacred form. Salisbury Cathedral saw at least two consecration ceremonies, in the 13th Century. Firstly, the Trinity Chapel was consecrated in 1225, and then in 1258 the whole, now completed, main body of the Cathedral with the exception of the later additions of Chapter House, cloisters and tower and spire.

The consecration service is deeply formal and ritualistic. Laura Varnam explains 'The consecration begins with the detachment of the church from the surrounding space'.[8] The formal blessing of consecration crosses, twelve of them inside the church and twelve on the outside, is an essential element and, she continues 'secures the physical foundation of the church just as it symbolically encompasses the foundation of Christianity.'

The Cathedral's consecration crosses are evident as mostly brightly painted and situated in the geographical extremities of the church and both sets of transepts.

Fig 6: Consecration cross in the north transept (*Roy Bexon*)

However, two very much smaller ones have also been found, carved at about 1 metre from the ground in both the Trinity Chapel and the north transept. [Fig 6]

Possibly, these were added prior to the formal crosses as a way to mark the newly built sacred space. Jacobus de Voragine later in the 13th century wrote that the function of the crosses is: 'to frighten the demons who, having been driven out of the building, (by the consecration service) see the sign of the cross and are terrified of it, so they do not enter there again'.

This apotropaic (ritual protection) function is common amongst early graffiti and explains a great number of the inscriptions and markings that are found. This is especially, although not exclusively, the case in areas of liminality, doors and windows in particular.

Circles

The circle is the perfect shape and thus deeply significant. Consisting of a never ending line it resonates strongly with both religious and pagan beliefs and

Fig 7: Cross in north choir aisle (*Roy Bexon*)

cultures. The circle is also a common architectural form, together with triangles and squares which have been found in the Cathedral. St Augustine is believed to have written that 'the nature of God is a sphere whose circumference is nowhere and whose centre is everywhere', to him it was a deeply significant shape and one that was a symbol of virtue. We see the circle in windows and other church architecture and art. The circle is deeply symbolic therefore, and the adoption of the shape in graffiti is not too surprising.

The south western column at the central crossing is a riot of circle emblems. There are plain circles, concentric circles and hexfoils or 'daisy wheels' as they are known sometimes. All of them are thought to be apotropaic.

Medieval men and women were as familiar with the concept of demons and malevolent spirits as they were with the concept of Christian religion. They felt it important to keep evil forces away from sacred spaces and used these symbols as a means of protection. The prevalence of this graffiti at the crossing and elsewhere around the quire and chancel reflects the inherent sanctity of this space. Members of the public, whilst not admitted to these areas, would have flowed around the aisles visiting the altars and chapels in the transepts and aisles; and after 1457, the shrine of St Osmund in the Trinity Chapel. A small protective hexfoil has been inscribed into the marble top of the foramina tomb shrine base that is still a fixture of the south side of the chapel. Curiously there are also board games alongside the image, perhaps as will be seen later, these were also apotropaic, or possibly the tomb plinth was used for gaming purposes in the years after the Reformation or Civil wars.

Crosses [Fig 7]

The cross is the commonest symbol associated with western Christianity, and there ought to be no surprise about finding the emblem as graffiti in the Cathedral. However, unlike parish churches, where they may commonly be found in porches, all the crosses that have been encountered in the Cathedral are either on the western crossing columns or in the north and, to a lesser extent, south quire aisles. For a long time the thought behind these symbols as graffiti was that they were made by pilgrims or those going on crusades. There seems little evidence to support either notion and the crusader theme seems to be relatively modern; there is no mention of this prior to the 19th century. Instead, it seems that crosses might form a kind of formal agreement between contracting parties, evidenced by their common appearance in porches, a well known site for negotiations and deals to be struck. However, this theory is less convincing when the cross is found inscribed into the stonework of the tombs of Bishops Ghent and de Martival and lend themselves more convincingly as devotional marks. Whether these marks are evidence of a minor cult of bishops has not been proved and is a work in progress.

Marian Marks

Perhaps the commonest of all inscribed marks are 'VV' marks. [Figs 8 & 9]

Fig 8: Marian symbol in the north choir aisle (*Roy Bexon*)

Fig 9: Cross and Marian symbol in the north choir aisle (*Roy Bexon*)

Usually they appear as 'W' and span a time period from the Cathedral's foundation until well into the 18th century. It would be no exaggeration to state that these marks are those most frequently found as graffiti in churches. The Cathedral is no exception. Many of these are undoubtedly post-medieval, appearing in large numbers incised into alabaster effigies, columns, the benches around the walls and the walls themselves. 'VV' is widely accepted in the church context as meaning 'Virgo Virginum' translated as 'Virgin of the Virgins'. Inverted, the letters form the letter 'M', shorthand for 'Mary'. Thus, this may have a connection originally to the cult of Mary, which was at its height during the early part of the Cathedral's existence, and are symbols calling on her for protection of both the individual and the cathedral space. However, post Reformation this explanation is hard to justify, especially as the inscriptions continue for at least the following 200 years. The sheer frequency with which these symbols appear suggests that they are more than simply initials – as Brian Hoggard says: 'If it were all just initials, the population would be full of William Wilberforces, Wally Winterbottoms and Willemena Wileys – but this is improbable'.[9]

Whilst the explanation may be unclear, there is no doubt that these series of letters were popular and had special meaning for the inscriber. The view that we have developed is that they were initially prayerful in nature and invoked the protection of the Virgin. Later perhaps, the meaning may have changed. In the case of certain effigies, it may even be that there was a degree of mocking of the effigy of the commemorated, perhaps as a political and anti-Catholic statement.

Games Boards [Fig 10]

Perhaps the next largest set of inscriptions are those that appear to be board games. Primarily they are found outside of the main body of the Cathedral in the cloisters along the east and south walks. The games are mainly dice games based on the morris format - nine mens morris for example, that are first recorded in the earliest compendium of games - Alfonso's 'The book of games', published in 1283. Salisbury's cloisters were completed around 1266 so it is possible that some of the game boards found may date from the latter part of the 13th century.

Inscribed onto the top of the tomb shrine plinth of St Osmund in the Trinity Chapel there are two games, both are thought to be the game of Fox and Geese.

Fig 10: Game board in the east range of the cloisters (*Roy Bexon*)

This is a game based on 'the hunt' with a single fox and thirteen geese, the latter being permitted free movement around the boards. The aim of the game is for the geese to trap the fox and until a rewrite of the rules in the 17th century this seems to have been the usual outcome. The puzzle in respect of the shrine tomb plinth is who might have inscribed the games.

St Osmund was the second Bishop of Sarum, who died in 1099. From the outset, canonisation was wished for him. Osmund was not finally canonised until 1457 after which a new shrine was constructed. After the Reformation, his shrine tomb plinth, now effectively redundant, must have attracted some interest during periods of iconoclasm. Possibly this was the time that it gathered the game inscriptions.

A curiosity is the discovery of game boards appearing on vertical planes. This would not have lent itself to the use of dice or markers. Unless there is evidence of the re-use of stone from a horizontal level, then the change may reflect an apotropaic function, a view that has gained some traction in recent years.

There is also a well known chequer board design on the bench of the inner east walk adjacent to the cloister garth. The board is too small to be a chess board or for draughts. Popularly thought to have been inscribed by prisoners of war in the late 17th century it may well be earlier. There are other small inscriptions along that bench, one of which appears to be a blocking game called 'Hare'. Three hunters are set against a single hare who has the task of breaking through their line to reach the other end of the board. Salisbury lacked a monastic house based on the Cathedral, so the likelihood is that the makers of these games were either minor clerics or more likely, visitors with time to spare.

Modern Graffiti

Finally, the graffiti that has been found in the Cathedral clearly demonstrates that the desire to leave a mark has been a continual obsession for centuries and probably right from the earliest days of its existence. However, whilst this chapter has focussed mainly on the early evidence, the majority of inscriptions are post Reformation with many made within the last three hundred years but especially in the 18th and 19th centuries. The move to an increasingly literate population may be reflected by this graffiti. The earliest date that can be reliably evidenced – via its style compared to the inscription of a contemporary tomb – are two small inscriptions on the north west column at the crossing. The date '1554' is recorded although there is nothing to show the significance of that year. Fifty years later we see many names, some dated, appearing on tomb chests. Memorial inscriptions, usually initials enclosed within a square box start to appear, some of which are dated. The current view of these is that they are a poor man's equivalent of the wall mounted memorials, particularly in the nave, of the wealthier members of, chiefly, the Close. The instance of dating graffiti by its maker grows and by the 19th century the marks reflect the increasing numbers of tourists who start to visit. Interestingly, once into the 20th century graffiti seems to reduce, with the exceptions of the two world wars when military personnel appear to have visited. The face of Mussolini appears in the glasswork of the Parvis Room over the north porch, but otherwise there are few carved inscriptions. Pencil and chalk graffiti, especially in the roof spaces, increase however. The nave roof space has a large list of visitors, some from Canada. The stairwells commonly used by guided tour groups reflect modern inscriptions and in one window recess a very obviously false date '1496' – the numeral shapes are inconsistent with the number forming of that time. A fine profile carving of a man is to be found in the northwest turret and further down from him another profile, this time of a bishop. In the south nave aisle there is a recent graffito – 'MMC Buck II' in a memorial box. The inscription is modern and amply displays that the desire to leave our mark remains as much today as ever in the past.

Bibliography

Champion, Matthew, 2015, *Medieval Graffiti – The Lost Voices of England's Churches*, Ebury Press

Champion, Matthew,, 2018, *Church Monuments, Journal of the Church Monuments Society Volume XXXIII,*

Hather, Jon, 2018, *Historic Board and Dice Games*, Gothic Green Oak

Hoggard, Brian, 2019, *Magical house protection : the archaeology of counter-witchcraft*, Berghahn Books

Pritchard, Val, 1967, *English Medieval Graffiti*, Cambridge University Press

Varnam, Laura, 2018, *The Church as sacred Space in Middle English Literature and Culture,* Manchester University Press

Notes

1　For this purpose the Reformation is deemed to be between the dates of 1533 and 1560
2　https://www.lexico.com/en/definition/graffiti accessed 9.12.2019
3　Pritchard, 1967
4　Champion, 2015
5　Champion, *2018*
6　Champion, 2015, 15
7　Bishops Osmund, Roger and Jocelyn
8　Varnam, 2018
9　Hoggard, 2019

Fig 1: Memorial to Gilbert Kymer at entrance to north choir aisle (*Roy Bexon*)

Medical Men and their Monuments in Salisbury Cathedral

Alastair Lack

There are more than 1300 memorials in Salisbury Cathedral; some are in the windows, some in sculpted images, many are on grave slabs, and some are just a number which is referenced in the Cathedral records. There are clergy, members of the armed forces, and notable locals. And there is a handful of medical men of interest.

Dean Gilbert Kymer
died 1463

Gilbert Kymer was Treasurer of Sarum from 1427-1449, Chancellor of Oxford 1431-4 and 1447-53, and Dean of Salisbury 1449-1463.[1] He received his DM (Doctor of Medicine) in about 1423, and a law degree ten years later. He held senior university administrative posts in Oxford University, before moving to London. There he presided over a case where a patient sued a colleague, ruling that 'malign astrological influences' had caused the patient's misfortune.

As a leading royal physician he wrote a regimen for health for Humphrey, Duke of Gloucester and held a licence from Henry VI to practice alchemy. Some of his writing on medical matters was later reprinted by Thomas Hearne who died in 1735. Kymer died on 16 May 1463 and asked to be buried in the cathedral.

His elegant tomb chest of Purbeck marble was once adorned with stone shields and brasses beneath a canopy. (Fig 1) The tomb was formerly ascribed to Lionel Woodville, Bishop 1482-84, but is now thought to be that of Gilbert Kymer.

Dr D'Aubigny Turberville
1612 -1696

D'Aubigny Turberville was the most famous oculist in England in the mid/ late 17th century with an international reputation and a successful practice in Salisbury. His biographer, Dr Walter Pope, had been treated very successfully by Turberville. He wrote

> *'.... him, to whom, under God, I owe my sight, a blessing, in my opinion, equal, if not preferable, to Life itself, without it. It was he, who twice rescued me from Blindness, which without his aid, had been unavoidable, when both my Eyes were so bad, that with the best I could not perceive a Letter in a Book, nor my Hand with the other, and grew worse and worse every day.'[2]*

Dr Turberville was born in Wayford, Somerset in 1612, of a reputable family.[3] He was admitted to Oriel College, Oxford and took the degree of Doctor of Physic; his mother had advised him to make diseases of the eyes his principal study. When the Civil War broke out, he left university and joined the Royalist forces. He was in Exeter when it was besieged in 1646, until it surrendered to Parliament. Under the terms of surrender he was able to return to his home in Wayford, where he married.

He set up his ophthalmic practice at his home and at Crewkerne, the next adjacent market town, but 'finding that those places could not provide accommodation for his patients', he moved to London for a short while, but found that the air did not agree with him.

He therefore left London and moved to 17 The Close, Salisbury, before 1671, from where he made numerous journeys to London to treat 'persons of quality' who sought his advice.[4] On one occasion, he was summoned to treat the young Princess of Denmark, later Queen Anne, 'labouring under a dangerous inflammation in her eyes.' The court physicians had tried in vain, and demanded to know what the doctor would use, wanting to approve or reject his medicines before he applied them. Turberville refused, saying that if she was committed to his sole management, he would attempt to cure her, but he would have nothing to do with the court physicians; he had expected to learn something from them, but to his amazement he found them wholly ignorant. They were duly dismissed, and his patient perfectly cured, to Turberville's great reputation and profit. The Duke ordered that he be paid £600, but he never received more than half of it.[5]

Another patient was Samuel Pepys, the great diarist. On the 22 June 1668, Pepys wrote in his diary 'my business was to meet Mr Boyle, which I did, and discoursed about my eyes: and he did give me the best advice he could, that refers me to one Turberville of Salsbury (*sic*), lately come to town'.[6]

Pepys took Boyle's advice, and saw Dr Turberville the next day. A week later he

Fig 2: Monument to D'Aubigny Turberville. North side of West Door (*Roy Bexon*)

was prescribed some physic and eyedrops. However his confidence in Turberville was somewhat shaken four days later, when they met in an alehouse with some other medical men to dissect several eyes of sheep and oxen; he thought it strange that Turberville, 'so great a man, and yet to that day had seen no eyes dissected.'[7] Pepys had every reason to be surprised since at that time Turberville was 56 years old and had been practising medicine and ophthalmology for some 28 years!

However, it is clear that Turberville knew his limitations, turning down patients whom he did not believe he could help. He 'generally prescribed to all, shaving their heads and taking tobacco, which he had often known to do much good'.[8]

He is described as 'Loyal, a pious man and a good Christian. He was far from being covetous; he cured the poor without fee, and received from others donations as they pleased'.[9]

Dr Turberville died in Salisbury in 1696, aged 84. He left a considerable estate, part of which went to his sister, Mary Turberville, who continued his practice in London with good reputation and success.

His memorial is on the north side of the west door. (Fig 2) A plain black wall tablet of Purbeck marble or slate with gold lettering is surmounted on the right by 'a sorrowing cherub' holding a skull.[10] Beside the memorial is a charming translation of the Latin verse: –

> 'Alas! Alas! He's gone forever
> And left behind him none so clever;
> Beneath this stone extinct he lies,
> The only doctor for the eyes.'

Henry Hele
c1689 – 1778

Henry Hele practised successfully as a physician in Salisbury for over 50 years.[11]

At a meeting on 24 September 1766, he was nominated as one of the first two physicians of the new hospital that became the Salisbury Infirmary. Towards the end of his long life, in 1776, he became involved in a scandal concerning an alleged conspiracy by one Mary Bowes to have her sister Diana forcibly incarcerated in a lunatic asylum. Hele signed the certificate of lunacy that made the committal possible and was indicted by a grand jury.

From 1744, he lived in Myles Place, one of the finest houses in the Cathedral Close in Salisbury.

His memorial, (Fig 3) a white marble wall tablet, surmounted by an urn and foliage, has an inscription which reads:

> 'M.S. [Memoriae sacrum] Henrici Hele qui rem medicam in hoc clause & civitate adjacenti per quinquaginta Annos probe & feliciter exercuit'.
> 'Sacred to the memory of Henry Hele who conducted a medical practice in this Close and adjoining city for fifty years with integrity and success'

Fig 3: Henry Hele. South Nave Aisle (*Roy Bexon*)

William Long
16 June 1747 – 24 March 1818

William Long was born in Salisbury, the youngest of ten children of Walter Long of Preshaw, Hampshire (1690–1769).[12] He was eminent in his profession of surgery and for 33 years, from 1784 to 1807, was a surgeon at St Bartholomew's Hospital in London. He was appointed Master of the Royal College of Surgeons in 1800 and was among those who gave a donation to help fund their new surgical library. He was also on the College's list of first Governors, first Examiners of Surgeons and the first Court of Assistants. He wrote several papers, including one (unpublished) entitled *The Effects of Cancer*.

He lived in London's Chancery Lane, and later at Lincoln's Inn Fields, and developed close friendships with the painter George Romney, sculptor John Flaxman and the artist William Blake. Long sat for Romney as his first subject for a portrait for his friend William Hayley. Subsequently Long acquired many of Romney's paintings.

After his death on 24 March 1818 his collections of preserved medical specimens and surgical instruments were donated by his executors to the Royal College of Surgeons' Museum in London.

Fig 4: William Long. St Thomas's Chapel, east wall (*Roy Bexon*)

He was a man of compassion and generosity, and when resident at his country seat away from London, always gave his advice and medicine freely to the poor of the surrounding neighbourhood.

William Long is buried in St Thomas's Chapel, with a large monument flanked by figures of learning and charity, with his coat of arms above, probably designed by John Flaxman. (Fig 4) His widow erected the monument to 'perpetuate the memory of a much esteemed husband'. Part of the epitaph, written in Latin, says:

> *He improved the natural powers of the mind, by various extensive learning. To the poor in sickness, his advice, his skill, and his purse were ever open, and he administered to their wants with a most liberal hand. He added a suavity of manners, to a firmness of expression, which was at once perspicuous and convincing, steady in his friendship and inflexible integrity, he was warmly and firmly attached to his relations, no less by the bond of love and affection, than by the natural impulse of his heart and feelings.*

Richard Brassey Hole
1818 – 1849

Richard Brassey Hole was born in 1818 in Devon, and studied medicine in Edinburgh, where he married Anne Burn.[13] He died of cholera in Salisbury on 24th July 1849, in his house in the Close. His obituary in the *Salisbury Journal* wrote of 'a spirit of active benevolence and self denial. . . unhappily most fatal to

TO THE MEMORY OF
RICHARD BRASSEY HOLE MD
WHO DIED OF CHOLERA 24 JULY 1849
AGED 30 YEARS
MINISTERING WITH UNTIRING ENERGY
AND IN A TRUE SPIRIT OF CHRISTIAN
LOVE TO THE NECESSITIES OF HIS SICK
& DYING FELLOW CITIZENS DURING THE
SAD SEASON OF THAT PLAGUE HE COUNT
-ED NOT HIS LIFE DEAR UNTO HIMSELF
BUT NOBLY SPENT IT FOR HIS BRETHREN

Fig 5: Richard Brassey Hole. South Nave Aisle (a modern, simple stone tablet) (*Roy Bexon*)

himself'.[14] He was a contemporary of Andrew Middleton (see below) and they worked briefly together before his early death.[15]

His monument (Fig 5) records that he had been 'ministering with untiring energy and in a true spirit of Christian love to the necessities of his sick and dying fellow citizens during the sad season of that plague'.[16]

William Martin Coates
1812 - 1885

Martin Coates, as he was known, was one of a long line of surgeons appointed to Salisbury Infirmary, including his father and sons. In 1837 he married Caroline Kelsey (1816-1897), and they went on to have seventeen children.[17] He was obviously of an enquiring disposition, as evidenced by his paper 'Observations on Chloroform and its administration' in which he describes his experience of the use of chloroform in childbirth, and refers to his use of John Snow's apparatus.[18] He was on the staff of Salisbury Infirmary from 1847-1885, and his name can be seen on the lists of staff boards at Salisbury Hospital. Four of his sons studied medicine.

His memorial window in the south nave aisle, (Fig 6) erected by 'friends and grateful patients', depicts the healing of the centurion's servant, the healing of the widow of Nain's son, the healing of the woman with an issue of blood, and the healing of Jairus's daughter.[19]

Prince Leopold, Duke of Albany
1853 - 1884

Although Prince Leopold was a royal prince, not a medical man, the manner of his birth revolutionised the view of the public with respect to pain in childbirth.

In those days, the pain of childbirth was seen as ordained by God, who said 'In pain you shall bring forth children'.[20] Queen Victoria did not enjoy the experience of childbirth (she had suffered severely during her first labour) and asked Dr John Snow, a London anaesthetist to administer chloroform to her for the birth of her last two children - Prince Leopold in 1853, and Princess Beatrice in 1857. From then on, analgesia in childbirth became respectable – 'Chloroform a la Reine'.

Dr Snow had also been thinking about the spread of cholera in London, in what is now Southwark.[21] In 1854 he persuaded officials to remove the handle from the Broad Street water pump, so arresting the cholera epidemic in that vicinity and proving the mode of its transmission. Snow is now recognised as one of the pioneers of epidemiology.

Prince Leopold was a highly intelligent and accomplished man – though cursed by the haemophilia from which he died in 1884 at the age of 30, whilst on holiday on the Riviera.[22]

Fig 6: Memorial window, by Clayton and Bell, to William Martin Coates South Nave Aisle

The memorial window to Prince Leopold, (Fig 7) who rented Boyton Manor, near Warminster from 1876-1882, is in the South Choir aisle. On the left is Jacob's dream, and on the right the sealing of the servants of God with St John writing what he heard.[23]

Andrew Bogle Middleton, MRCS
1819 – 1879

Andrew Middleton was Salisbury's great champion of sanitary reform. He perhaps did more than anyone to improve living standards and people's general health in the city in the second half of the 19th century. The 1849 cholera epidemic in Salisbury is well documented but Middleton's two memorials in the Cathedral are not generally known and his memorial window rightly reflects his pioneering work.[24]

Middleton was a surgeon, trained at St. Bartholomew's Hospital, who moved to Salisbury in 1842. For a while he was assistant to Mr Henry Coates (1779-1848), surgeon to the Infirmary, whose daughter Sarah he married.[25] Sarah was William Martin Coates' cousin. Middleton was sure that the saturated soil under the city was the cause of many of Salisbury's ills. He was principally concerned about consumption but the cholera epidemic of 1849 when nearly 200 people died in Salisbury in just a few months, added strength to his argument. No other town in England of comparable size suffered to the same extent. Middleton worked tirelessly to eliminate Salisbury's open water channels which ran through most streets giving the city the dubious title of 'The English Venice'. By the 19th century they were little more than open sewage channels meaning that cholera was given every chance to spread rapidly. Middleton was convinced of the need for a deep drainage system to dry out the soil and petitioned successfully for a full enquiry which took place in 1851.[26] Following its damning report Middleton further published three pamphlets to convince the authorities of the need to eliminate Salisbury's canals.[27] Eventually, with his tireless pressure, a deeper sewerage system was installed, and a fresh water supply.

Looking back on his work towards the end of his life he wrote: I shall always be happy to plead guilty to any charge of having caused the destruction of "the English Venice", since by that destruction a "New Salisbury" has been created, and very many hundreds of human beings saved from untimely death'.[28] His obituary described him as 'dogmatic in character' whilst admitting that Salisbury 'has lost a real benefactor who laboured . . . energetically for the real interests of the city.'[29]

Middleton and his first wife, Sarah (died 1872) share a tablet on the wall of

Opposite Fig 7: Memorial window, by Clayton and Bell, to Prince Leopold, Duke of Albany. South Choir Aisle (*Alastair Lack*)

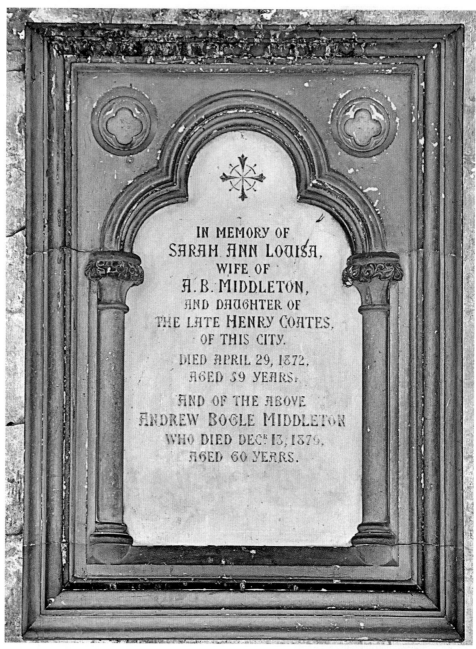

IN MEMORY OF
SARAH ANN LOUISA,
WIFE OF
A.B. MIDDLETON,
AND DAUGHTER OF
THE LATE HENRY COATES,
OF THIS CITY.
DIED APRIL 29, 1872,
AGED 59 YEARS.

AND OF THE ABOVE
ANDREW BOGLE MIDDLETON
WHO DIED DEC. 13, 1879,
AGED 60 YEARS.

Fig 8: Andrew Bogle Middleton and his wife Sarah. North Cloister (*Roy Bexon*)

the North Cloister. (Fig 8) The monument is by William Osmond, a prolific 19th century mason in the Cathedral and friend of A W N Pugin.

Middleton also has a memorial window in the east of St. Thomas's chapel,

Fig 9: Memorial window, by Ward and Hughes, to Andrew Bogle Middleton. St Thomas's Chapel, North Transept. (*Alastair Lack*)

in the North Transept, (Fig 9) reflecting the major part he played in providing a fresh water supply to Salisbury.

It is in two parts; the top panel shows King Hezekiah, who cut the Siloam tunnel to provide water to Jerusalem during the siege by the Assyrians. The bottom panel depicts Jesus meeting the woman of Samaria at Jacob's well at Sychar, when he said 'whosoever drinketh of the water that I shall give him shall never thirst; but the water that I shall give him shall be in him a well of water springing up into everlasting life'.[30]

The memorial window, as reported in the *Salisbury Journal*, was dedicated just ten years after his death, presumably by his widow and second wife Adelaide, née Stockwell, who was still living in the West Walk of Salisbury Close in 1891.[31]

Since these eminent men of medicine, Salisbury has continued to have a long and distinguished history; from the plastic and burns surgery of the post-war years at Odstock Hospital, to the continuing specialist and compassionate care of present-day healthcare professionals.

Notes

1   Kymer, Gilbert in *Oxford Dictionary of National Biography* (ODNB), 2020, OUP; on line at https://bit.ly/36ShyVw, accessed Dec 2019 (registration required)

2   Pope Walter, 1697, *The life of the right reverend father in God, Seth, lord bishop of Salisbury,* William Keblewhite, London, 98. Dr Walter Pope was Bishop Seth Ward's Chaplain.

3   Although he was born in Somerset, Pope incorrectly connected him with Beer, and there is in Bere Regis a vast vault where many of the Turbervilles are buried, later immortalised by Hardy.

4   Royal Commission on the Historical Monuments of England (RCHME), 1993, *Salisbury: The Houses of the Close*. HMSO, 105

5   James, R R, 1926, 'Turberville of Salisbury', *British Journal of Ophthalmology*, 465-74

6   Pepys' Diary. https://www.pepysdiary.com/diary/1668/06/22/

7   https://www.pepysdiary.com/diary/1668/06/29/; https://www.pepysdiary.com/diary/1668/07/03/ accessed Dec 2019

8   Pope, Walter, 1697: https://bit.ly/33OpZPN,103 accessed Dec 2019

9   Pope, Walter, 1697: https://bit.ly/33OpZPN,104 accessed Dec 2019

10 Brown Sarah, 1999, *Sumptuous and Richly Adorn'd*. RCHME,135, 150

11 https://en.wikipedia.org/wiki/Henry_Hele; also at https://bit.ly/2R6HjMS, accessed December 2019

12 https://en.wikipedia.org/wiki/William_Long_(surgeon), also at https://bit.ly/34Hbfme, accessed December 2019

13 ODNB on line (free); https://doi.org/10.1093/ref:odnb/100749. This relates to his son, William, but includes biographical detail about Richard Brassey Hole. See note 16

14 *Salisbury and Winchester Journal*, 28 July, 1849, 3

15 *SJ*, 21 July, 1849, 2

16 After his death, his wife and son moved back to Edinburgh. William Fergusson Brassey Hole (1846-1917), became a fine artist, with many works in the National Gallery of Scotland.

17 www.johnfamilyhistory.esco.net.au/Coates.htm, entry for William Martin Coates in John Coates' Family History Pages, online at https://bit.ly/38gerra, accessed December 2019

18 Coates Lancet https://bit.ly/38i7ndw (registration required)

19 Brown Sarah, 1999, 109.

20 Genesis 3:16

21 Snow on Cholera: https://bit.ly/2rClieV, accessed Dec 2019

22 Haemophilia is an inherited disease in which a protein deficiency in the blood means that it does not clot; victims may suffer from bleeding from any injury. If the bleeding is internal (as in Leopold's case – he tripped and hit his head), the damage may be fatal.

23 Spring, Roy, 1997, *Stained Glass Salisbury Cathedral*, R L Smith & Associates, 13

24 Lack, Alastair, 2012, *Cholera, the Canals of Salisbury and Andrew Bogle Middleton*. Lulu.com; Chandler, John, 1983, *Endless Street, A history of Salisbury and its people*, Hobnob Press; Newman, Ruth, 2006, 'Salisbury in the age of cholera', *Sarum Chronicle* 6

25 Middleton's obituary, *Salisbury and Wiltshire Journal*, 20 Dec, 1879, 8

26 Rammell, Thomas W, 1851, *Report to the General Board of Health on a Preliminary Enquiry into the sewerage, drainage, and supply of water and the sanitary condition of the inhabitants of the city and borough of Salisbury, in the county of Wilts*, HMSO

27 Middleton, A B, publications, 1852, 1864, 1868. Reprinted Lack, Alastair, 2012, *Cholera, the Canals of Salisbury, Lulu.com*

28 Middleton, 1868; Lack, 2012, 113-4

29 *SJ* 20 Dec, 1879, 8

30 John 4:14

31 *SJ*, 1 Dec, 1889, 5

The Consistory Court

John Elliott

As you enter the south-west corner of the cathedral from the cloisters, you are walking through what used to be the consistory court. A consistory court was a diocesan activity rather than a cathedral one,[1] even though it was located adjacent to the cathedral, or in some cases within; no doubt because the cathedral was the bishop's seat, and it was the bishop who was ultimately responsible for the administration of the court.

Such courts were established shortly after the arrival of William the Conqueror and were little affected by the Reformation.[2] The Salisbury court would have handled matters throughout the diocese which has varied in size over the last 800 years. Initially the court covered cases relating to the probate of wills, matrimony, defamation and the moral behaviour of both clergy and laity. It also dealt with matters relating to church buildings and graveyards. Cases were often brought as a result of matters raised at visitations or by individuals seeking resolution of a problem.

The court was, and still is, headed by a chancellor who was appointed by the bishop. Appeals against its decisions in the area covered by the Archbishop of Canterbury were to the Court of Arches. Before 1532 there was a further appeal to Rome, but after the break with Rome the supreme head of the church became the king and so appeals were to the crown.

Much of this responsibility was lost in the nineteenth century as power passed to civil bodies. This was all part of the growth of civic government and a decline in the relative position of the church, which in turn was a consequence of the rapid social changes which followed the industrial revolution. The religious census of 1851 showed that about half the population did not go to church on census Sunday, and of those who did, about half went to one of the non-conformist chapels. Salisbury had a higher church attendance than most other parts of the UK, and the Church of England in Salisbury was stronger there than

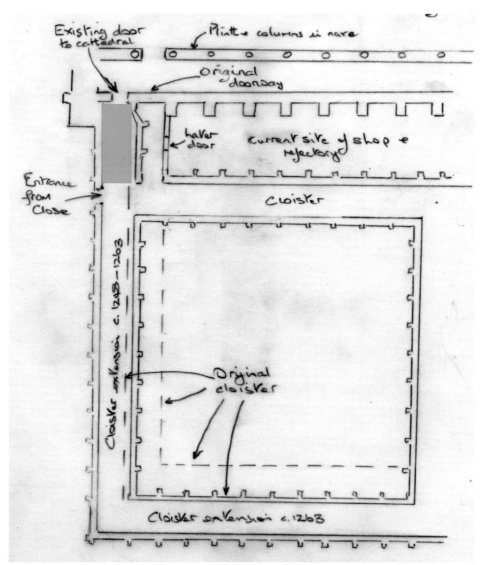

Fig 1. A reconstruction of how the cloisters and Consistory Court may have looked, showing the original cloisters and the enlarged ones which still exist. The Consistory Court was in the coloured area.

elsewhere, though overall church attendance was less central to people's lives than it had been before.[3] In these circumstances it was inappropriate for the church to continue to judge on many of the matters that affected secular people.

In 1855 the court lost control over defamation and in 1857 it lost probate which was from then on dealt with by the Court of Probate, and matrimonial cases passed to the divorce courts. It retained control over ecclesiastical property (churches and graveyards), and over serious acts by members of the clergy (immoral conduct, neglect of duty or doctrinal and ceremonial matters) until 1963 when matters of doctrine, ritual and ceremonial were transferred to the Court of Ecclesiastical Causes Reserved, and in 2003 when clergy discipline passed to bishop's tribunals. Today most of the court's activities are related to church property and administration of the faculty system which controls changes that are made to parish churches and church land. The Salisbury court was removed from the cathedral in 1863.

No records of substance on the consistory court activities have survived in the cathedral archive though some limited material is held by the Wiltshire & Swindon History Centre. However, one very high-profile case which happened in the Exeter Diocese will give some insight into the sort of doctrinal issues that the church courts were asked to handle during the feverish religious atmosphere which pervaded much of the nineteenth century.

In 1847 the Rev George Gorham was hoping to be appointed to a living at Brampford Speke near Exeter. He was interviewed by the bishop, Henry Phillpotts, and a debate ensued about baptism. Gorham was an evangelical and believed that baptism was a *symbol* of spiritual regeneration and so depended on the willing receptiveness of the baptised. This meant adult rather than infant baptism. Phillpotts was a 'High' church man and believed that baptism was a *means* of spiritual regeneration and did not need the consent of the baptised, so infant baptism was completely valid.

The bishop refused to appoint Gorham and the latter eventually took the case to the Court of Arches who rejected his appeal. He then went to the Judicial Committee of the Privy Council where the Archbishops of Canterbury and York, plus the Bishop of London, sat as non-voting advisors. The Privy Council supported Gorham and this caused additional tension as the Privy Council's involvement was seen as a civil court interfering in church matters. Despite the courts Gorham was not appointed.

Chester Cathedral has the best surviving consistory court whereas architecturally what was the Salisbury version has been changed considerably since its original conception.

The Salisbury court was created as a self-contained space at the northern end of the west range of the cloisters from which it was entered. The original cloisters did not extend as far to the west or south as the current ones (see Fig 1), and there is much debate about when the original cloisters were erected, and again when they were extended to their current size. It is possible that the western arm was enlarged around 1248,[4] and on 15 June 1263 the bishop granted a plot of land 16 ft wide on the south side of the cloisters so that they could be enlarged in that

Fig 2. The traces of where the original door from the Cathedral was located are still visible on the left and right of this image. (*Roy Bexon*)

direction. The enlarged cloisters were almost certainly finished by 1266.[5] The consistory court then became the extension towards the north of the western arm of the cloisters.

Originally there was no doorway into the cathedral from the court, perhaps illustrating its separate function. Access to the cathedral from the south-west was through a doorway which was located just a few metres to the east of the current door and the traces of where it used to be are still visible inside the cathedral (Fig 2). This doorway led into the original unenlarged cloisters, and its location was most probably driven by the liturgy of the cathedral – the Use of Sarum – which required wide aisles and passageways for processions. The original doorway aligned perfectly with the gap between the nave arcade columns at the western end of the cathedral. On major feasts the clergy assembled in the

Fig 3. The curremt door into the cathedral from the Consistory Court. The doorway was originally located a few metres to the east (see Fig 1). Note how the doorway mouldings cut into the arcading. (*Roy Bexon*)

Fig 4. The dootway into the shop which is of a much later style than that into the cathedral. (*Roy Bexon*)

choir and incensed and sprinkled all those attending with holy water. They then proceeded to process around the eastern end, down the nave, and during the summer out into the cloisters. Along the way they incensed and sprinkled all the altars. The most elaborate procession took place on Palm Sunday when the procession around the cloisters met up with another one which had processed around the town and together they entered the cathedral through the great west

Fig 5. The modern wood and glass wall and dootway into the Consistory Court from the cloisters. (*Roy Bexon*)

doors, while choristers sang from the western gallery in imitation of angels. The position of the south-western door was not just a matter of convenience it was central to the cathedral's ritual.[6]

However, by 1863 the consistory court had ceased to be located adjacent to the cathedral. Presumably as part of George Gilbert Scott's great restoration, it was reordered as a porch and entrance to the cathedral.[7] Today it is an entrance room giving access to the cathedral and to the shop and refectory – a place to shake off the rain; to make a donation towards the cost of running the cathedral, or to adjust to the different atmosphere that awaits you.

The current door from the court into the cathedral is clearly a later insertion when the door was moved from its original position a few metres to the east. While the door surround is clearly from the thirteenth century,[8] the fact that it was not part of the original cathedral is clearly evidenced by the way it cuts through the blind arcading and the 6-foil above the doorway (Fig 3).

The doorway to what was a workshop or plumbery and is now the shop is of a later style, and more Perpendicular in its elements. Cocke and Kidson date it as of the 19th century when it replaced an earlier doorway a little to the south Fig 4). There is also some uncertainty whether there was a wall separating the consistory court from the cloisters. Most authorities suggest that there was no wall, though a plan appended to a reprint of *Vetus registrum Sarisberiense alias dictum registrum S. Osmundi Episcopi: The Register of S. Osmund* of 1883 by W H Jones shows a wall. The glass wall and doorway with its fabulous engraving which now separates the consistory court from the cloisters is of more recent origin and dates from the twentieth century (Fig 5).

The consistory court was formed after the cloisters were extended to the west around 1248 and occupied an extension towards the north that was enclosed on at least three sides. The original south-western door into the cathedral was at some time relocated inside the consistory court and the cathedral wall filled in. In the nineteenth century, when the consistory court lost most of its powers and was relocated out of the cathedral, a doorway was created between the consistory court and what is now the cathedral shop, and in the twentieth century the southern end of the court was glazed and doors provided. The Court was then converted into the main visitor entrance to the cathedral, which it remains today.

Notes

1   The cathedral is the bishop's teaching seat though the day-to-day management of the cathedral rests with the Dean & Chapter and not with the bishop. The Consistory Court was a diocesan activity even though it was located in the cathedral.

2   The church courts operated on the basis of Canon Law and ran in parallel with the temporal courts and were part of the King's judicial system and were based on Common Law, which was, and still is, created by precedent. While those who ran the Church courts were generally educated at Oxford and Cambridge, the Common Law court officials formed a separate profession which were educated at the Inns of Court. Inevitably there was some rivalry between the two. For more information see MacCulloch, Diarmaid, 2018, *Thomas Cromwell*, 160-161, Hey, David (ed), 2010, *Oxford Companion of Local and Family History* and Traver, Anne, 2008, 'English Church Courts and their Records', in *The Local Historian* 38, 4-22.

3   For details on Salisbury Church attendance in 1851 see *Sarum Chronicle*, 2006, 47-57.

4   Cocke, Thomas & Kidson, Peter, 1993, *Salisbury Cathedral: Perspectives on the Architectural History*, 8.

5   Tatton-Brown, Tim and Crook, John, 2009, *Salisbury Cathedral: The Making of a Medieval Masterpiece*, 82 & 84.

6   See Baxter, Philip, 2008, *Sarum Use: The Ancient Customs of Salisbury*, 69-73.

7   Cocke, Thomas & Kidson, Peter, 1993, *Salisbury Cathedral: Perspectives on the Architectural History*, 29. However Thomas Cocke provides no information on his sources, and despite extensive searches I have not been able to find any corroborating evidence of this date in the cathedral archive.

8   This dating is supported on stylistic grounds but also see the drawing at the back of Cocke, Thomas & Kidson, Peter, 1993, *Salisbury Cathedral: Perspectives on the architectural History* which dates the doorway as *c.*1250-80.

Restorations of Salisbury Cathedral 1220-2000

John Elliott

Foreword

This chapter aims to provide a comprehensive overview of the various restoration works that were undertaken on the cathedral between its original construction and the year 2000, though where specific aspects of this work have been published elsewhere they are not repeated here, but a short summary provided.[1]

Construction of the current cathedral started around 1220, and the first service was held in the eastern end in 1225. The building was mostly finished and consecrated in 1258, with the construction of the cloisters and chapter house continuing until 1266. The tower and spire were added in the early 1300s. There were periods when the cathedral appeared to receive little restoration effort, and as a result it deteriorated significantly before a major restoration was launched to correct matters. In contrast, there were other periods when regular restoration work was undertaken.

The internal arrangements of the cathedral have been altered many times as liturgical preferences changed. A screen between the nave and the choir came and went as liturgical preferences changed during and after the Reformation, as did a reredos behind the altar. At one stage there were galleries in the choir, and the division between the choir and what today is called the Trinity Chapel was removed to create a large space for the celebration of liturgy.

Many of these liturgically driven changes were analogous to those which affected most English medieval churches. The medieval separation of choir and nave with the provision of a separate Lady Chapel at the eastern end gave way to an arrangement which was more concerned with creating an inclusive liturgical space east of the crossing. Then, as part of the nineteenth century Gothic Revival, there was an attempt to sweep away all of these later changes and return the internal arrangement to something more like it would have been when the cathedral was constructed. Since then many of the nineteenth century changes have been removed and today the worship space is focused either within the choir or at a separate nave altar which is placed under the crossing.

Where the cathedral is different from most other buildings is in its scale and the massive costs associated with maintaining it. However, because of its status as one of the finest medieval cathedrals in Britain, if not the world, it has also been fortunate in being able to attract the support of the famous and wealthy. Perhaps the best recent example of this was the 'Save our Spire' appeal that was launched by Prince Charles in 1985 and the giant concert - called 'Symphony for the Spire' - which was held in the Close on 8 September 1991 and attended by Prince Charles and Princess Diana, Kenneth Branagh, Phil Collins and Placido Domingo.

Early structural problems

The addition of a large structure on top of a building that was never designed to support such weight caused problems right from the start and has challenged cathedral architects and clerks of works ever since. In addition, the tower and spire are subject to significant weather wear, especially from the prevailing wind on the south-west face.

It seems likely that as a result ironwork was added at the top of the existing lantern, some wall passages were blocked up and buttressing was added as the new upward extension was undertaken.[2] Tim Tatton-Brown points out that:

> a very elaborate series of iron tie-bars (at two levels) were put in to bind up the critical area at the base of the new tower. These long iron bars run through the masonry walls (where they were set in lead) to external tie-bars, while inside they are joined together by elaborate braces and ties, which in places have decorated ogee elements ... This is the most elaborate example of medieval structural ironwork known in Britain.[3]

Above this, two stages; of a new 80 ft masonry tower were created.[4] Four squinch arches were built on top plus a pair of doors on each face which led to a parapet walk. The corner turrets were topped by seven sided spirelets all covered in ballflower.[5]

The extra weight of the tower and spire forced the four crossing piers downwards, an effect that is evidenced in the moulding that runs along the top of the south and north arcades. The settlement was not uniform and produced a lean of 2 ft 7 ins. A series of flying buttresses were added internally and externally around the base of the tower at the triforium and clerestory levels. Stylistically the mouldings suggest that some of these date from the late fourteenth century (probably 1398-9). Further buttresses were added slightly later (1481) over the

Fig 1: Looking up the wooden scaffold inside the spire (*John Elliott*)

nave aisles and the eastern arm of the roofs. This process of adding buttresses over a lengthy period indicates an anxiety about further settlement.[6]

Internally there remains evidence of this structural movement with distortion in the north transept where the Purbeck shafts are set askew of their bases. There is also damage to the eastern transept where the vaulting of the south bay on the north side is fractured.

The inside of the spire is dominated by a large timber structure. (Fig 1) This internal scaffold joins with a vertical iron bar which runs up through the capstone to the very top of the spire. The iron bar is connected to the wooden scaffold by an adjustable threaded nut that needs to be checked and tightened periodically so as to maintain the stability of the spire.[7] It also enables the spire to move in a controlled way during strong winds.

There has been much debate about the age of the timber structure, some claiming that it was erected when the spire was built to provide a form of scaffolding, citing the putlog holes as supporting evidence. Others claim that it was built somewhat later, around 1362, when a lightning strike destroyed the upper part of the spire and some form of access to the top was required to enable rebuilding to take place. The scaffolding has 9 stages, the three lowest are in the form of a timber tower but with a central mast,[8] constructed almost entirely of oak.[9]

English Heritage has undertaken a major survey of the cathedral roofs and a more limited one of the spire scaffold.[10] Using the technique of dendrochronology they collected core samples of the timber to examine the tree ring pattern, and through this analysis estimate a felling date for the timber. They took 11 samples, nine were considered to have been new timber at the time they were used. Four outer braces rising from the corner posts at the first stage of the scaffold were dated, and at least two originated from the same tree. The results suggested that the most likely felling date between 1344-76.[11] One of two reused timbers from the fourth stage was also dated. It had a felling date of 1210-44 and the timber was possibly originally used elsewhere in the cathedral roof and transferred to the scaffold much later as part of a repair.[12]

English Heritage suggests that the scaffold was erected to aid repairs following a great storm in mid-January 1362: 'It is clear that the scaffold was built because of damage to, or concern about, the steeple following the storm' when it is likely that '30 ft … or more of the spire was rebuilt'.[13]

The sampling and associated dating work indicate that the scaffold was erected between 1344 and 1376 after 'the spire must have been completed for a generation or two'. Historical and architectural evidence supports this contention, suggesting that the spire was constructed between 1310 and 1330, and that the scaffold was most probably erected after the spire was built.[14] The occurrence of ballflower decoration indicates construction in the earlier part of the 14th century.

Two large strainer arches across north and south sides of the great crossing are datable by style to the first quarter of the fifteenth century and may be the result of a contract with Robert Wayte who made repairs in 1415-20.[15]

Wren to Wyatt

Christopher Wren (1632-1723) visited bishop Seth Ward (bishop 1667-89) during 1668 and carried out a survey of the cathedral. The results were reported to the Dean & Chapter in 1669 and Wren's report is held in the cathedral archive.

The work undertaken following Christopher Wren's inspection included that carried out by Francis Price (c1704-53) who worked on restoring the cathedral between 1734 and 1751; Edmund Lush (c1722-95) after 1734, and James Wyatt (1746-1813) who undertook major changes to both the close and cathedral between 1789 and 1792. The latter is well documented by me in *Sarum Chronicle* 19 so will not be repeated here; instead just a summary follows providing a link with what went before and after.[16]

Wren summarised what was required in 1668. Much work was required on the spire, which needed bracing with iron towards the top as well as replacing some damaged stone. A broken pinnacle needed to be repaired and the timber scaffold inside the spire also required some attention. He suggested that the tower and spire should be plumbed at regular intervals to check if any movement had occurred.[17] New timber needed to be spliced into the roof at the west end and some new timber added at the eastern end of the crossing.[18]

It is unclear how much of this work was carried out. The perceived wisdom is that Bishop Ward failed to raise the necessary funds to undertake the installation of an iron brace at the top of the spire.[19] The cathedral archives have little material that helps form a view. In 1691 Thomas Naish, the Clerk of Works, suggested adding certain ironwork which was similar to that which Wren had proposed.[20] However, in 1700, when advising on how to brace the Bodleian Library, Wren claimed that the work had been carried out at Salisbury, writing: 'I braced the lofty Spire of Salisbury, after the Lightening [*sic*] had rent it with Cracks of 200 feet long'.[21]

After this little else of great substance seems to have happened until Francis Price was appointed Clerk of Works in 1737. He had completed a survey in 1734 and that led to a series of works; chiefly an extensive programme of repairing and renewing the roofs that was undertaken between 1736 and 1751. He also measured the declination of the spire in 1737 and found that there had been no significant movement since Wren's earlier measurement.[22]

Fig 2: A view of the Close looking north from the top of the spire (*John Elliott*)

In 1777 the cathedral was closed for two years, and services transferred to St Thomas's church while Edmund Lush undertook a major interior restoration. His objective was to create a larger choir area so that services could be held there, whereas from about 1660 it had been the practice for the sermon to be delivered in the nave. He removed the pulpit and pews from the nave and much of the choir paneling,[23] including the screen separating the choir and Lady Chapel – both of which had been erected by Wren and Alexander Fort – because they were considered too gaudy. He then created additional congregational space by constructing galleries behind the choir stalls and added some new paneling in imitation oak.

With the arrival of Bishop Shute Barrington (bishop 1782-91) it fell to James Wyatt (1746-1813) to carry out a more extensive restoration of the cathedral and close between 1789-92.[24] He completed a survey in 1787 and, like Wren, plumbed the tower and spire. The cathedral was closed from 1 October 1789 for almost three years. Externally, Wyatt created a large underground drain that was three feet in diameter and ran west to east to take all the surplus water from the north side of the cathedral. He created a plan of the graves and then removed the grave stones, raised the ground, leveled it and created gravel paths.[25] (Fig 2) In addition, Wyatt supervised the demolition of the bell tower and adjacent buildings which were located on the north side of theclose. (Fig 3)

Fig 3: The original belfry that stood in the Close to the north of the cathedral, adjacent to the current Belfry Tea Rooms. Photograph taken from item in Cathedral Archive. (*Roy Bexon*)

Wyatt's work on the interior of the cathedral was no less comprehensive. In 1789 the Dean & Chapter approved his proposals, which included the making of new canopies for the choir stalls, creation of a new pulpit, bishop's throne and a Morning Chapel. He planned to erect an iron communion rail and coping and two wainscoted screens across the aisle and varnishing all the choir stalls. Perhaps most controversially he suggested laying blue stone paving in the Lady Chapel, cleaning and colour washing the church from the east end to the transept to remove the medieval decoration, while most of the remaining stained glass was to be replaced by plain.

In November 1789 the Dean and Chapter further approved lime-washing the remainder of the cathedral and removing the late medieval Hungerford and Beauchamp chapels.[26]

There was opposition, chiefly from those who favoured the medieval, and only 50 years later the changes made by Wyatt would be condemned as destructive and inappropriate by the Gothic Revivalists, and in the mid nineteenth century they would be largely swept away by the restoration of George Gilbert Scott.

The nineteenth century changes

While in 1829 some work was carried out on the capstone of the spire, nothing substantial happened until towards the middle of the century, after which a number of architects worked, almost continuously, planning and overseeing major periods of restoration.

In 1849 the lightning conductor that had been installed was inspected by Charles Walker, and in his report of 3 October he declared that the existing conductor was 'very inadequate … being defective both in mass of metal, and its general arrangements'.[27]

Prior to the installation of the conductor the spire had been struck by lightning on a regular basis. There were strikes in 1431 which set the spire alight, 1560 which left a rent 60 ft from the top,[28] 1641 when the spire was set alight again and in 1741 when it also caused an internal fire.[29] Prior to the installation of a lightning conductor around 1800 the normal practice was to insert a holy relic in the spire, and Salisbury relied upon a supposed piece of the Virgin's veil to perform this role.[30]

When Walker inspected the spire in 1849 he found that at the top there was an iron vane which was connected to the wooden scaffold by a 25 ft long and 2-inch square iron post. In addition, the tower and spire had been strengthened from time to time with bands of iron. There were seven bands that 'adds a most excellent bandage of iron to the upper part of the arcade', though 'Without a Lightning Conductor this arrangement of detached metal contains in itself the very elements of destruction', as a lightning strike would pass from one metal element to the next, causing an explosion at each level.

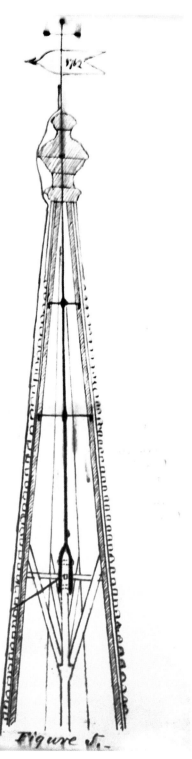

Fig 4: Suggested arrangement for ironwork and lightning conductor at the top of the spire. Note the iron rod that runs down from the capstone to join the wooden scaffold and the lightning conductor that runs outside the capstone and spire. Photograph of drawing in Scott Papers Bundle 3 in Cathedral Archive. *(Roy Bexon).*

Walker suggested certain changes, namely that the top of the vane should have a rod of copper attached to it. This would be at the top of the vane and pass through the ball at the base of the cross. The copper rod should have no acute angles or bends as it proceeds downwards. (Fig 4) All the other metal objects like the clock, bells and gutters should also be earthed into the conductor. At its base, where the conductor enters the earth, a hole should be dug until water appears. The conductor should be terminated with a copper ball from which three small pointed copper rods reach into the water. The hole would then be filled with graphite.[31]

In his *Recollections*, George Gilbert Scott (1811-78) wrote that 'I was appointed to this work [the restoration of Salisbury cathedral], I think, about 1859'.[32] As well as taking on the work Clutton had started in the Chapter House,[33] Scott surveyed the cathedral and started a restoration programme that was going to occupy a major part of the remainder of his life. He was the most active cathedral architect during the nineteenth century. He also oversaw restorations of the cathedrals at Bangor, Canterbury, Chester, Chichester, Durham, Ely, Exeter, Gloucester, Hereford, Litchfield, Peterborough, Ripon, Rochester, St Alban's Abbey, St Asaph, St David's, Southwell Minster, Westminster Abbey and Worcester.

At Salisbury his priority was the exterior of the cathedral, where 'The stone, though generally in fair preservation, was partially decayed, and the whole building was gone through carefully and conservatively, replacing such stones as were irrecoverably perished'.[34] The cathedral archives hold a copy of the contract that was signed in 1863 between the Dean & Chapter and George Peter White, a London builder, to undertake these initial works,[35] namely:

Foundations, drainage and underpinning
> A trench was to be taken out 18" wide from the walls and filled with concrete to a depth of 3' 3", which was also the depth of the foundations. An open drain would run along the outer edge of this plinth. (Fig 5)

Plinth and base moulds
> Any stone that needed to be replaced was to be Chilmark stone.

Flying buttresses and pinnacles
> The north east flying buttress against the nave and clerestory was to be taken down and rebuilt, as was the second from the tower on the north side, the buttress on the north side of the choir and that on the east side of the north transept. The remainder of the buttresses on the north side were to be repaired as were the buttresses in the north transept and a flying buttress on the south side. Most of the pinnacles were to be rebuilt.

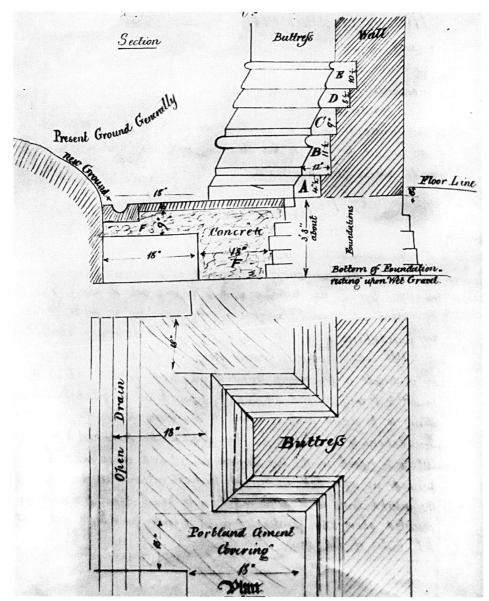

Fig 5: Plan of the foundations showing the depth as 3' 3". Photograph taken of drawing in 1863 Contract book in Cathedral Archive CH/13/24 p142. (*Roy Bexon*)

Parapets, finials and buttress cappings

Many were to be taken down and rebuilt in part.

Purbeck marble shafts

Where Purbeck Marble shafts were damaged they were to be removed and

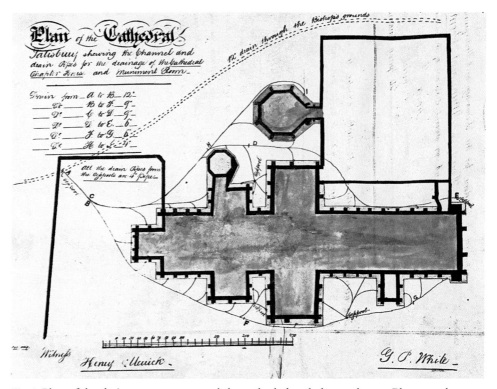

Fig 6: Plan of the drainage system around the cathedral and chapter house. Photograph taken from Contract book in Cathedral Archive CH/13/25 page 1. (*Roy Bexon*)

new shafts supplied in one length, which would be pointed at both ends and the face rubbed ready for polishing.

Roof repairs

Much of the flashing was to be removed and recast, the wall plates and rafters repaired by splicing in new English Oak to the sound older timbers. The roof boarding should be repaired as needed with 1000 feet of Baltic boards. Many of the gutters were to be replaced. In addition certain roofs to be re-leaded with newly cast lead.

Glazing and joinery

Reglaze 16 lights in the north aisle and nave, and 3 clerestory windows on the north side. Any damaged window tracery was also to be replaced.

The archives hold a copy of a further contract dated December 1863 between the Dean & Chapter and White concerning additional drainage works which Scott had specified.[36] This contained a detailed drawing which shows the installation of a 12 inch drain which would run underground around the cathedral and be connected to drainage points at the edge of the concrete plinth which was to be created along the outside of the cathedral. These drainage points would be fed by downpipes from the roofs. (Fig 6)

One part of this drain started at the north west corner of the cathedral and ran down the north side. It was joined by another arm which started at the south west corner of the cathedral and ran down the south side with an addition spur feeding in from the Chapter House. Four cesspools where to be built where there were multiple adjacent drainage points, such as between the transepts, or between the north transept and the north porch, and where the drain from the Chapter House joined. This system of drains would connect to a main drain that ran past the eastern end of the cathedral and into the Bishop's Palace grounds. This drainage system and the cesspools still exist.

In his *Recollections* Scott states that having started the work restoring the exterior 'Our next great work was strengthening of the tower'.[37]

Shortly after starting work at Salisbury Scott had been appointed to oversee the rebuilding of the tower and spire of Chichester cathedral. At Chichester the cathedral was being restored by William Slater, and specifically the Arundel screen between the nave and choir was being removed, when it was noticed that the columns supporting the tower and spire were in a poor condition. The Dean & Chapter called in a surveyor who declared the structure safe and work recommenced. However, it soon became clear to the architect that things were not as they should be and the structural engineer was called again. He again declared the structure safe. A few nights later, on 21 February 1861, in the midst of a gale, the tower and spire collapsed into the cathedral.[38] Scott was called in to supervise the rebuilding and on 16 March 1864 reminded the Salisbury Dean & Chapter that they should take the advice of the architect and not that of an engineer as 'It was this fallacy which destroyed Chichester Cathedral'.[39]

Scott's report on the Salisbury tower and spire concluded that the:

> great piers which sustain the Tower will naturally appear to be the main seats of failure; as they are evidently out of the perpendicular. This deflection [sic] arises partly from the outward pressure on the heads of the piers [?] the great arches of the Tower and partly from the inward pressure in the middle of their height caused by the greater compression at that level of the backs of the piers which are of rougher stone work than their fronts, these being built of closely bedded marble.

He added that the 'thrust of the arches of the aisles and the partial subsidence of the foundations' adds to the problem.[40] However, he was sure that the piers had not moved since the start of the eighteenth century, and not moved seriously since the close of the fifteenth.

Fig 7: Ironwork inside the tower (*John Elliott*)

Key to Scott's approach was the insertion of a number of large scissor beams within the tower. These would join opposing corners of the tower and continue around the outside so as to pull the structure together. In planning this work Scott called upon the structural ironwork expertise of F. W. Sheilds. Sheilds produced a report in 1865 which concluded that the fault with the great piers was caused by their slightness, with a pressure of 6 tons per square foot of their section, and this had caused them to sink 'very considerably'. Also, the structures were inadequate to resist the thrust of the arches, that from the aisle and transepts pressing inwards, while those above pressed outwards. The solution to these problems was to use iron ties where the arches spring so as to reduce the thrust. In the lantern he suggested the use of strong iron bands connected to the four angles and covered to protect them against any corrosion, and changes in temperature which would alter the length of the bars.[41] Further iron work was to be added in the nave and aisles, and a substantial iron member was to be erected across the choir arch.

Fig 8: Ironwork around the exterior of the tower which connects to the iron beams within (*Roy Bexon*)

However, he reported that Mr Hutchins had suggested an alternative solution that Mr Sheilds may 'be disposed to substitute' as the ironwork across the choir would have been unsightly and something that would have interfered with the organ. This avoided the 'great beam across the Choir Arch and the ties across those from the Aisles'.[42]

There clearly were some differences of opinion. FR Fisher suggested that the bending of the piers was caused by the yielding of the mortar in joints of irregular stonework, and that the solution was to use ties at the point of weakness.[43]

There was also much debate about the number of scissor beams that would be inserted in the tower. (Figs 7 & 8) It seems that the initial plan was for four. This was reduced to three and this is what is shown in the Sheilds drawings which survive in the cathedral archive.[44] Later a fourth scissor beam was reinstated.[45]

In 1866 work started on the West Front, and the contract was again with George Peter White.[46] Those responsible for more recent restorations have concluded that Scott's work was 'remarkably conservative in extent and nature'.[47] This work was to take place in two stages, initially on the central screen and buttresses, but followed by work on the western ends of the nave and the stair turrets.[48] There are two drawings in the cathedral archive which show the extent of the works which were undertaken.

An earlier study of the west front by Professor C.R.Cockrell, suggested that there had originally been 123 statues on the west front which were arranged in a Te Deum Laudamus scheme,[49] and a further 37 elsewhere. The plan was to replace those which were not salvageable and repair the remainder. The work of creating the statues was passed to J F Redfern and continued until 1873.[50]

Restoration work continued and in 1869 White was again given a further

Fig 9: The Skidmore screen – since removed. Photograph in the Cathedral Archive. (*Roy Bexon*)

Fig 10: Reredos by Farmer & Brindley – since removed. Photograph in the Cathedral Archive. (*Roy Bexon*)

contract to restore the area beyond the choir which comprised the chancel and Lady Chapel and involved removing the altar and reredos which Wyatt had introduced,[51] repairing the stonework and removing the whitewash that had also been added by Wyatt.[52]

Work on the choir followed, including extensive work to the woodwork and to the desks of the choir stalls, removing Wyatt's screen and replacing it with an iron one which was to be made by Francis Skidmore of Coventry (since removed),[53] (Fig 9) further enclosing the choir by erecting a giant reredos (Fig 10) which was created by Farmer & Brindley (since removed),[54] recreating the tomb on the north which Scott believed to be that of Bishop Poore and creating a new tomb as a memorial to Bishop Hamilton on the south side. In addition, a marble choir pulpit was added (since removed), the pavement was relaid with tiles which were produced by Godwin (since removed) and he commissioned Thomas Earp to create a splendid wooden bishop's throne. The vault medallions were repainted by Clayton & Bell,[55] supposedly from drawings of what had been there before Wyatt obliterated them, though Scott later discovered that at least some of the medallions were not based on any historical evidence.[56]

Three other contracts were issued during this period covering repairs to the inside of the cathedral. The first was in July 1873 when White was asked to restore the eastern transept and the choir aisles.[57] Then in 1875 White received another contract to restore the interior of the great transepts.[58] Finally in 1877 White was commissioned to restore the nave and nave aisles.[59] The work involved removing whitewash which had been applied by Wyatt, polishing all the Purbeck marble shafts, and adding new stone to bases, shafts and capitals of the columns.

Scott died in 1878 and was succeed by George Edmund Street (1824–81) who had worked for Scott between 1844 and 1849. His most notable building is the Law Courts in The Strand (c1868), though he was also architect to the diocese of Oxford, York, Ripon and Winchester and published a number of books, chief of which was his text of 1855 on the use of brick and marble in Italy.[60]

The first job that Street handled was the repaving of the nave and aisles. Again, White was the contractor with the contract dated May 1878.[61] While Street oversaw the work the specification had been prepared by Scott and his son John Oldrid Scott (1841-1913). The task was to take up all the paving apart from a small section of the original diagonal paving which was located in the north aisle east of the porch. The paving was to be relaid on a bed of concrete, with any spaces above the various tombs being filled with rubble which was to be well rammed. If there was a shortage of paving then the deficit was to be made good with Purbeck stone. The stones were to be laid in bands of varying lengths but of equal width throughout each band.[62]

Then in 1880 it was decided to restore the north porch. Street prepared the plans and this time the work was given to a Salisbury firm – Thomas, Henry and Robert Soper of 14 St Martin's Crescent. The work was to be completed by March 1881.[63] The specification is detailed. All the stonework was to be cleaned, many of the columns and capitals needed to be replaced or repaired, a new central shaft was needed at the doorway to the cathedral, along with new mouldings. The pavement was to be relaid with marble and stone and the steps were to be of Purbeck marble. Some 28 ft of stone seating was to be provided inside the porch. Most of the wooden doors were to be replaced with English Oak, and with new hinges, latches and bolts.[64]

Just before his death in December 1881, Street produced designs for an organ case that was added in 1882 when Alfred Robinson of Bloomsbury carved cases for the organ on the north and south sides of the choir.[65]

Despite Scott's work restoring the spire and tower there was only a short gap before further work was required. In 1895-7 Arthur Blomfield (1829-99),[66] undertook a series of works to stabilise the foundations and replace shattered stonework in the tower and spire. An inspection was carried out by a structural engineer, a Mr Thompson of Peterborough, on 20 June 1895. Thompson wrote to Blomfield declaring that 'I think there can be no doubt that "Dangerous" is a correct application'. He pointed out that much of the stonework was 'insufficient for such a structure' and that there were problems with the north west and south west corners and cracks in the tower and squinches. He also said that he would like to see some of the ironwork removed.[67]

Blomfield produced a report on 29 June, noting that there was 'something seriously amiss' with the upper part of two western stair turrets. Scaffolding which had been erected around the north-west turret had shown that the stonework was in a worse state than had been feared as the external stonework was split and fractured, loose and unsafe. He was unable to give any assurances 'of security from disaster' as there were cracks that showed there had been recent movement. Blomfield cited the corrosion of iron bands, rods and ties as the cause plus the action of rain and frost and the great thrust of the spire. He concluded that there was a need to stabilise the angle turrets, starting with that on the north west corner.[68]

An undated report from Blomfield then records that they had found further problems, this time with the foundations. Excavations had revealed that the solid chalk bed was 33 ft down, that there was 4 ft of alluvial soil on the surface and then a stratum of 15 inches of thick white clay with gravel and flints below this down to the bed of chalk. The 28 ft gravel bed was full of water and the foundations were of unsquared stones with little by way of footings and so were unstable and insufficient. Blomfield suggested that a concrete bed was introduced.[69]

Work started and the Dean made an appeal for funds in the *Times* during 1897. He reported that the foundations had been strengthened and shattered stone in the tower and spire had been replaced. In July 1898 Blomfield reported that the work had been completed at a cost of £12,993.[70]

Into the twentieth century

In 1912 the cathedral architect was Charles Edwin Ponting (1850-1932). Ponting said that he had inspected the spire in 1868, or perhaps 1867, during the Scott restoration, and he noticed that there had been serious deterioration since then.[71]

The Dean & Chapter considered a report that had been prepared by Frankland & Phillips in July. They reported that the lightning conductor was satisfactory, though some of the fixings needed tightening. However, there was decayed stonework on the spire from the vane to 8-Doors which are at the base of the spire. It had been repointed 10 years previously but there was 'further and marked dilapidation'; too much ironwork had been used previously and this was now causing the stonework to burst – the problem was very obvious about 20 ft up from 8-Doors; much stonework has either fallen or is about to fall – this could be prevented by using 'copper pins or studs'; parts of the crockets, and ridges had fallen. They recommended that the stonework be scraped and brushed and then at least two coats of fluate be applied.[72]

Then in September Ponting made a further inspection of the exterior. He reported that the iron cramps, both original and more recent, were doing considerable damage – 'all the Iron cramps have seen their lifetime'. He suggested that they be removed and replaced by copper.[73] The Dean & Chapter accepted the recommendations and recorded that work had already commenced.

After the end of the First World War a minimal amount of restoration was undertaken. In 1921 the spire was repaired above the weather door,[74] and a year later repairs were carried out to the west window and the two windows on either side of it, and the lightning conductor was inspected.[75] In 1935, W A Forsyth surveyed the cathedral and reported a need to replace iron supports with copper, and that the tracery in the cloisters needed attention.[76] The Dean & Chapter launched an appeal to raise £5,000.[77]

In 1937 WA Forsyth, and a consulting engineer, Charles Freeman, inspected the cathedral, and especially the tower and spire. Their recommendation was to repair the cathedral roofs with some re-boarding and re-leading, to fill in the eight single lancet lights within the lantern as well as the four spiral staircases at this level so as to strengthen the tower.[78] A wooden staircase and iron ladder was to be built to replace the filled in staircases, brick corbels were to be erected to support the squinches and a stainless-steel ring was to be placed at the base of the spire. Metal ties were added to the nave arches to provide additional support.[79]

The aftermath of the Second World War created a groundswell of renewed interest and enthusiasm in many areas of the cathedral's life which had of necessity been suspended during the war. This included the need to resume a repair and maintenance programme.

A new survey of the whole cathedral structure was undertaken by Forsyth in 1946. His report concluded that work was needed to replace the corroded ironwork in the tower and spire.[80] A further more detailed inspection followed in 1949 which revealed that not only did the ironwork need replacing but also the cross at the top of the spire.[81] In addition, the top 29 ft 6 ins of the spire needed to be replaced because the masonry had been damaged by the corroded ironwork and the next 25 ft needed to be repaired.[82]

On 9th February 1950 a special meeting of the cathedral's chapter was held to discuss and plan for the repair work. At the meeting Forsyth reported that the spire was not really dangerous but that the effects of weathering and corrosion meant that the proposed repairs were essential.[83] Clipsham stone would be used in place of the more local Chilmark. A large amount of ironwork had been placed in the tower and spire in the 18th and 19th centuries, and while much had been removed in the 1920s, that in the top 20 ft of the spire had not been removed or replaced.[84] In addition, more general repairs were required to the pinnacles and other areas of masonry,[85] and aircraft warning lights were to be installed.[86]

At this time the cathedral did not employ a substantial team of stone masons so the work was undertaken by two contractors JW Gray & Son Ltd and The Wandsworth Stone Masonry Works. Work began and an appeal was launched to raise £100,000, both for the immediate repair work and then for ongoing maintenance.[87] Six stages of steel scaffolding were erected at the top of the spire and a specially constructed double rail track was fixed to the spire's north face to enable masonry and other materials, including a new cross, to be transported to the top of the spire.

Unfortunately, that winter turned out to be one of the most severe on record and work was hampered, but not halted, by several inches of snow. Disaster struck in July when a broken cable resulted in the hoist plummeting uncontrollably part way down the rail track on the side of the spire. In August the Dean & Chapter heard that work removing the capstone was half complete, and that a plate dated 1867 had been found which recorded what had been done at that time.[88] Work continued, the Clerk of Works reporting in September that they were ahead of schedule, and in October that the non-ferrous metal had arrived, reconstruction work had begun and a record of the work undertaken had been placed in the capstone on 15 November.[89] In the following September the Clerk of the Works reported that the work had been completed.[90]

Just 15 years later, in 1967, yet more work was needed, though not on the same scale. The cathedral architect, Lawrence Bond, completed a survey and wrote to the Dean & Chapter on 29 July. He reported that work was required on the top of the tower, where some iron bands just below the parapets were heavily corroded and damaging the masonry, as was another iron band a bit lower down which had been inserted by Wren, and another at the base of the spire close to a squinch arch. Again there was much masonry that needed to be repaired. Nothing much seems to have happened though some minor repairs were carried out in the 1970s and the tower and spire were checked annually for signs of movement.

A survey of the structure was undertaken in 1980 which recommended a comprehensive list of works to the tower, west front, roof and roof timbers plus reroofing of the cloisters, repairs to the glazing and rainwater pipes and cleaning the masonry, whitening the vault and polishing the marble.[91]

In 1983 a progress report was produced by Peter Taylor,[92] which summarised all the previous findings and specified a programme of major repairs which became the essence of the SOS – Save Our Spire appeal which was launched by Prince Charles on 10th April 1985 with the aim of raising £6.5m to cover work on the spire, tower and west front.

In the spire the main focus was preserving the decorative bands where the

Fig 11: The tower and spire covered in scaffold during a twentieth century restoration.
Photograph in the Cathedral Archive. (*Roy Bexon*)

stonework was only 5 ins thick and was much decayed. The plan was to insert a steel frame on the inside of the spire behind each of the decorative bands which would enable damaged stones to be replaced and also reduce the vertical pressure. This work was estimated to cost £1m, work on the pinnacles £263,000, that on the tower £3.8m, the west front, and the replacement of 90 statues, £1.3m.

The appeal was so successful that work on the tower and spire was completed and the scaffolding removed as early as May 1993, though that on the west front continued until 2000. About 90% of the lead on the roofs was replaced in 2005. Since then work on the external fabric has continued at a steady rate, and is currently concentrating on the eastern end where the level of masonry decay was found to be worse than in other parts of the cathedral.

Salisbury cathedral is one of the great medieval cathedrals and of special importance because of its architectural unity and its very dramatic tower and spire. Unlike most cathedrals that have been developed over many centuries, Salisbury is unique in that the main building was completed in a single phase and the tower and spire were added shortly afterwards. The addition of its tower and spire have always caused architectural challenges and will no doubt continue to do so, though ironically it is the spectacular spire that makes Salisbury stand out from all the other English cathedrals. The weather and acid rain have caused ongoing problems and eroded the stonework, while the use of iron to aid stabilisation has caused as many problems as it has solved as rust damages the adjacent stonework. However, despite all these problems the cathedral and its spire stand spectacularly as signs of Christianity and a living church, and the enthusiasm to keep both in a good state of repair remains undiminished.

Bibliography

Ayres, Tim (ed), 2000, *Salisbury Cathedral: The West Front*, Phillimore

Brandon, Mark, unpublished recording of the main events recorded in the Dean & Chapter minutes between 1741 and 1834

Brown, Sarah, 1999, *Sumptuous and Richly Adorn'd: The decoration of Salisbury Cathedral*, HMSO

Cocke, Thomas and Kidson, Peter, 1993, *Salisbury Cathedral: Perspectives on the Architectural History*, English Heritage

Dale, Anthony, 1936, *James Wyatt Architect 1746-1813*, Basil Blackwell

Dodsworth, William, 1782 & 1814 editions, *A Guide to the Cathedral Church of Salisbury with a particular account of the last great improvements made therein under the direction of James Wyatt Esq*, Brodie and Dowding

Elliott, John, 1995, *The architectural works of Richard Cromwell Carpenter (1812-55), William Slater (1819-72) & Richard Herbert Carpenter (1841-93)*, unpublished doctoral thesis.

Elliott, John, 2017, *The Restoration of the Chapter House of Salisbury Cathedral*, Spire Books

Elliott, John, 2019, 'From Wren to Wyatt', in *Sarum Chronicle*, 19, 41–59

Ferry, Benjamin, 1861, republished 1978, *Recollections of Pugin*, Scolar

Frew, John, 1984, 'James Wyatt's choir screen at Salisbury Cathedral reconsidered', *Architectural History*, **27** 481-7

Jardine, Lisa, 2002, *On a Grander Scale: The Outstanding Career of Sir Christopher Wren*, Harper Collins

Little, Bryan, 1975, *Sir Christopher Wren: A Historical Biography*, Hale

Macey, Chris, unpublished catalogue of all references in the Dean & Chapter minutes to work done on the tower and spire between 1946 and 1952.

Martin Robinson, John, 2012, *James Wyatt, 1746-1813 - Architect to George III*, Yale

Matthews, Betty, 1983, *The Organ and Organists of Salisbury Cathedral 1480-1983*, Salisbury

Miles, D W H, 2002, *The Tree-Ring Dating of the Rood Carpentry of the Eastern Chapels, North Nave Triforium, and North Porch, Salisbury Cathedral, Wiltshire*, English Heritage

Miles, D W H, Howard, R E and Simpson, W G, 2004, *The Tree-Ring Dating of the Tower and Spire at Salisbury Cathedral, Wiltshire*, English Heritage

Price, Francis, (1753), *A Series of particular and useful observations made with great diligence and care, upon that admirable structure, the Cathedral-Church of Salisbury*, privately published

Scott, Sir George Gilbert, 1879 reproduced 1995, *Personal and Professional Recollections*, Paul Watkins

Tatton-Brown, Tim and Crook, John, 2009, *Salisbury Cathedral: The Making of a Medieval Masterpiece*, Scala

Tatton-Brown, Tim, Lepine, David and Saul, Nigel, 2013, '"Incomparabilissime Fabrice": The Architectural History of Salisbury Cathedral *c.*1297 to 1548', *Journal of the British Archaeological Association*, **166** 51-98.

Wren, Christopher, 31 August 1668, *The State of the Defects of ye Cathedral Church as described and enumerated by Christopher Wren* (Cathedral Archive FA/4/1668, 9)

Notes

1 The early history of Old Sarum and of the erection of the current cathedral is well documented by Tim Tatton-Brown and English Heritage. See Tatton-Brown, 2009 and various publications by English Heritage. The research that I undertook on the work which was carried out between the late seventeenth century and the end of the eighteenth was published in *Sarum Chronicle* 19. See Elliott, John, 2019, 'From Wren to Wyatt', in *Sarum Chronicle*, 19, 41-59. Work on the Chapter House and the Bell Tower that originally stood in the Close is also not considered here as both are the subject

of separate publications, See Elliott, John, 2017, *The restoration of the Chapter House of Salisbury Cathedral.* Information on the Bell Tower is published in the Bell Tower Café

2   Tatton-Brown, 2013, 52

3   Ibid, 94 and see Miles et al, 2004, 21

4   Tatton-Brown, 2009, 94

5   Ibid, 95

6   The external flying buttresses are not consistent and not of the same date. Those around the angle of the tower have pinnacles and ballflower and are probably contemporary with the spire. Others are later. (Cocke, 1993, 11)

7   Tatton-Brown, 2009, 95 and information from Gary Price, Clerk of Works

8   Miles et al, 2004, 9

9   Ibid, 10

10 Miles et al 2002 & 2004

11 Miles et al 2004, 20

12 Ibid

13 Ibid, 22

14 Ibid, 20

15 Cocke, 11 and Miles et al, 2004, 22

16 Elliott, 2019, 41-58

17 It was plumbed by Naish in 1681, Price in 1737 and Wyatt in 1787

18 Wren also commented upon the Chapter House and the Cloisters, neither of which are discussed in this chapter

19 See Jardine, 2002, 210 & Little, 1975, 71

20 Little, 1975, 71

21 Cited in Jardine, 2002, 211

22 See Price, Francis, (1753), A Series of particular and useful observations made with great diligence and care, upon that admirable structure, the Cathedral-Church of Salisbury

23 The first step of the original pulpit still exists in the south aisle

24 He had worked on Lichfield cathedral before he came to Salisbury and had gained a reputation for his handling of Gothic and his ability to 'improve' cathedrals and not just to repair them. He later worked on Durham (to which Bishop Shute Barrington was transferred) and Hereford

25 Dodsworth, 1814, 184

26 They also approved alterations to, and enlargement of, the organ loft, the stalls of the Dean and Precentor and erecting a new north porch from the remains of the Hungerford Chapel

27 Salisbury Cathedral Archive: Bundle 3

28 Cocke, 1993, 7

29 Miles et al, 2004, 7, 22 & Table 1, Cocke, 1993, 19

30 Miles et al, 2004, 22

31 Salisbury Cathedral Archive: Bundle 3

32 Scott, 1995, 301

33 The Chapter House was surveyed by Anthony Salvin (1799-1881) in 1843 and again by Henry Clutton (1819-93) from 1855, when it was decided to restore the Chapter House as a memorial to Bishop Denison who had died the previous year. Clutton then worked with William Burges (1827-81) until 1856 when Clutton converted to Roman

Catholicism and was replaced by George Gilbert Scott (1811-78)

34 Scott, 1995, 300

35 Salisbury Cathedral Archive: CH/13/24, 128-141

36 Salisbury Cathedral Archive: CH/13/25, 1

37 Scott, 1995, 301

38 For further details of what happened at Chichester see Elliott (1995)

39 Salisbury Cathedral Archive: Scott Papers Bundle 11. He also advised against listening to any contrary advice from a building contractor

40 Salisbury Cathedral Archive: Scott papers Bundle 13

41 Ibid. Also see Richards, David, 'F W Wentworth Sheilds 1820-1906. The Engineer who saved Salisbury's Spire', in *Sarum Chronicle* 13, (2013)

42 Letters Scott to Dean 9 August 1865, 11 August 1865 and 23 January 1866. Salisbury Cathedral Archive: Scott papers Bundle 11

43 Letter dates 31 August 1865. Salisbury Cathedral Archive: Scott papers Bundle 13 and Scott to Dean 31 March 1866 Salisbury Cathedral Archive: Scott papers Bundle 11

44 Salisbury Cathedral Archive: Scott papers Plans 6

45 See letter 23 January 866 from Scott to the Dean and printed appeal leaflet dated 13 February 1866 in Salisbury Cathedral Archive: Scott papers Bundle 11

46 Salisbury Cathedral Archive: CH/13/25, 42-65. It was for a total of £4,263

47 Ayres, 2000, 94

48 Ibid, 98. The first part was valued at £2,272 and the second at £1,991

49 This was an arrangement with Christ in Majesty at the top then angels and archangels, old and new testament prophets, the four gospel writers, Peter and Paul and finally with an arrangement of local worthies at the base

50 A very comprehensive account of the detailed work Scott suggested, including work on the statues, is provided by Ayres

51 Brown, 1991, 51

52 Salisbury Cathedral Archive: CH/13/25, 92-8. The work was contracted at £1,986

53 See chapter by Jane Howells elsewhere in this volume

54 Salisbury Cathedral Archive: CH/13/25, 244. Farmer & Brindley were given a contract for £1,700 on 5 April 1875 to create a new reredos

55 Salisbury Cathedral Archive: CH/13/25, 172. Clayton & Bell were given a contract on 15 September 1871 for £970 to restore and repaint the roof and spandrels of the choir

56 Scott, 1995, 301

57 Salisbury Cathedral Archive: CH/13/25, 196. The contract was for £3,296 and the specification runs to 28 pages

58 Salisbury Cathedral Archive: CH/13/25, 270. The contract was for £3,595 with a specification of 14 pages

59 Salisbury Cathedral Archive: CH/13/25, 318. For £5,940 and the specification was of 13 pages

60 Street, George Edmund, *Brick and Marble in the Middle Ages: Notes of a tour in the north of Italy*, 1855

61 For £1,250

62 Salisbury Cathedral archive: CH/13/26, 7

63 Salisbury Cathedral Archive: CH/13/26, 69. Also the *Builder* 1 May 1880

64 The hinges etc were purchased from James Lever, King Street, Maidenhead on 5 August

1880 at a cost of £58 and a pair of wrought iron gates cost a further £85

65   Salisbury Cathedral Archive CH/13/26, 120. Also the *Builder* 1 Feb 1879 and 7 July 1883. The contract was dated 12 August 1882 and work was to be completed by 12 May 1883 at a cost of £930

66   The fourth son of Charles Blomfield, the Bishop of London

67   Salisbury Cathedral Archive: Letter 20 June 1895 Thompson to Blomfield in Scott Papers Bundle 22/4

68   Salisbury Cathedral Archive: Scott Papers Bundle 22/4

69   Ibid. The cost of repairs had now escalated to £15,000

70   Ibid

71   Letter from Ponting dated 3 August 1912 recorded in Dean & Chapter Minutes on 6 August 1912

72   Dean & Chapter minutes 30 July 1912

73   Letter of 16 September from Ponting recorded in Dean & Chapter minutes

74   Dean & Chapter minutes 18 October 1921

75   Dean & Chapter minutes 30 January and 3 April 1922

76   Dean & Chapter minutes 3 April, 5 June and 7 November 1935

77   Dean & Chapter minutes 3 June 1936

78   The topic was discussed numerous times, the main occasions being recorded in the Dean & Chapter minutes of 15 December 1936, 5 January, 11 February, 3 March, 8 April, 3 May, 7 July and 1 December 1937, 27 April, 2 June and 3 November 1938

79   Dean & Chapter minutes 5 January, 26 May and 7 September 1938

80   Dean & Chapter minutes 3 January, 24 April, 13 June and 2 July 1946

81   Dean & Chapter minutes 6 August 1947, 7 April and 5 May 1948

82   Dean & Chapter minutes 4 & 4 October, 2 & 4 November 1949 and 9 February 1950. However also see 7 July and 3 November 1948

83   Dean & Chapter minutes 9 February 1950

84   Dean & Chapter minutes of 4 November 1949

85   Dean & Chapter minutes 4 January 1950

86   Dean & Chapter minutes 7 September 1949

87   Dean & Chapter minutes 9 February and 14 March 1950

88   Dean & Chapter minutes 3 August 1950

89   Dean & Chapter minutes 6 September, 2 October and 7 November 1950

90   Dean & Chapter minutes 5 September & 7 November 1951 and 5 March 1952 but also see 7 March, 17 May, 5 October 1951 and 1 January 1952. The cathedral archive contains a unique photograph album compiled in the 1950s recording the different stages of the restoration programme, plus a film by Pathé news on the restoration that was mostly shot from the top of the Spire

91   The report was compiled by Gifford & Partners, consulting engineers; Alan Rome, cathedral architect; and Roy Spring, clerk of the works. The report is in the Salisbury Cathedral Archive: 5:33

92   Salisbury Cathedral Archive 5:F22

Fig 1: From Truby, J, (1948) *The Glories of Salisbury Cathedral*, 58

Mrs Lear and the Skidmore Screen

Jane Howells

Over the centuries service to the Cathedral and its community has taken many forms, from discreet and unassuming personal contributions, to professional activities, generous donations and grand gestures. One of the most visually dramatic was the new choir screen made by Skidmore & Co of Coventry and opened to the public along with other restorations by Sir George Gilbert Scott in 1876.[1] (Fig 1) It was described thus in the *Salisbury and Wiltshire Journal*:

> This screen will be of brass and iron. The design consists of an open arcading corresponding to the spacing of the western stalls. The central opening forms the entrance. This has an arch enriched with cusping and scrollwork enclosed within a gable. Above the gable, on steps, supported by an additional base of arcaded work, is a cross of considerable size, inlaid with filigree and other ornaments. [2]

The newspaper stated clearly that the screen would be 'the gift of Mrs Sidney Lear in memory of her late husband'. Why, therefore, is the benefaction of the Skidmore screen surprisingly frequently attributed to Dean Francis Lear's widow, (Isabel Majendie) even in otherwise authoritative accounts of the history of the cathedral?[3]

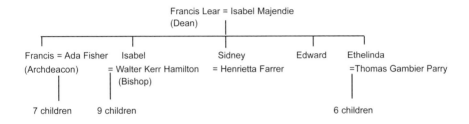

Fig 2: Photograph described as 'Mrs Lear', assumed to be Mrs Isabel Lear, early 1860s. Courtesy of Anthony Hamber Collection

This short chapter will outline briefly the Lear family in the Close of Salisbury, examine the role of Henrietta as a philanthropist, including her donation of the screen to the cathedral, and attempt to explain how the erroneous link to Mrs Francis Lear (senior) might have arisen.

Francis Lear (1797–1850) was Dean of Salisbury from 1846 to 1850. He was born in Downton, and held the livings of Chilmark and Bishopstone, and the prebends of Stratford and Netheravon, and was Archdeacon of Sarum for a decade before becoming Dean.[4] In 1822 he had married Isabel(la) Majende, (Fig 2) and they had five children, Francis, Isabel, Sidney, Edward and Ethelinda. The first Mrs Lear in this account died in 1862, over ten years before Scott's work in the cathedral and any question of a new choir screen arose. Her eldest son the second Francis Lear (1823-1914) held a number of posts in the diocese; he was Chancellor, Precentor, and then Archdeacon of Sarum from 1875 to 1914. His wife, the second Mrs Lear, was Ada Fisher but as she died in 1892 she was never 'Rev Lear's widow'.

The third Mrs Lear was Henrietta Louisa Farrer who married Dean Lear's second son Sidney in 1859. (Fig 3) Her family came from Yorkshire, and her father was a lawyer in London. Henrietta's first book, *Tales of Kirkbeck*, was published when she was 18. This was followed by the 'Aunt Atta' series for her nieces' and

Fig 3: Henrietta Lear, from *The Sunday Magazine*, reproduced with kind permission of Berkshire Record Office D/EX73/4/2/3

nephews' religious education. A further dozen titles were completed during the 1850s, some co-authored with Rev W J E Bennet, with whom she had shared her brothers' lessons.

Rev Sidney Lear was domestic chaplain (and brother-in-law) to the Bishop of Salisbury Walter Kerr Hamilton, but he was never strong. Henrietta nursed her mother at the end of her life, and her father at times in his later years, and then proceeded to do the same for her husband. They lived in Torquay and in the south of France for his health; he died in Mentone (*sic*) on the French Riviera in 1867.

Henrietta settled at No 17 the Close and took up her writing again.[5] She had the means to undertake philanthropic work and was closely involved with the foundation of the House of Mercy at Horbury in Yorkshire, and with the Sisterhood of St John the Baptist at Clewer. In Salisbury she contributed to the new chapel at the Theological College designed by William Butterfield. Later in her life she organised the Lear Rooms in Gigant Street to provide a place for labourers to turn as an alternative to a pub in the evenings.[6]

As regards the choir screen in the cathedral it seems that Henrietta was keen to support a new screen in memory of her husband. *The Pall Mall Gazette* reported in May 1867 that she had written to the Dean of Salisbury to propose erecting an open screen of metal in the cathedral between the nave and the choir in memory of her late husband the Rev Sidney H Lear.[7] But she was determined that it should be to her liking, and that she would contribute £1000. Her discussions with the Dean & Chapter and with Sir George Gilbert Scott were carried out

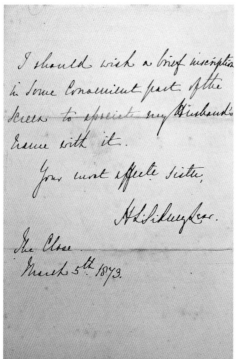

Fig 4: Detail from letter from Henrietta Lear to Rev Francis Lear regarding the screen, courtesy of Salisbury Cathedral Archives:
I should wish a brief inscription in some convenient part of the screen to associate my Husband's name with it.
Your most affec[iona]te sister H L Sidney Lear, The Close March 5th 1873

at one remove, via her brother-in-law Archdeacon Francis Lear.[8] In March 1873 she wrote of 'disliking the proposed design ... I return to my original wish ie to put a <u>light metal</u> screen ...which shall be dignified ... distinctly marks off the choir [but] in no way obstruct[s] the full view of the Choir and Altar from the nave. ... Designing in metal is not in Sir G Scott's line ...".[9] (Fig 4)

The following summer Rev Francis Lear told her he had returned the slightly altered design criticised by Henrietta to 'Sir GS (*sic*)' who had replied that he would make the effort to meet her views.[10] Henrietta liked the screen made by Skidmore at Lichfield[11] and considered a similar one would be appropriate for Salisbury. Scott did not like the result, and disapproved of Henrietta's interference and financial constraints, which, he felt 'was the means of depriving the church of a far nobler screen'.[12] There are commentators who agreed with him – 'an appalling lacquered iron erection' (Smethurst, 1958 and later editions, *Pictorial History of Salisbury Cathedral*); 'one wonders just why it is there at all' (Fairbairns, 1928, *Salisbury Cathedral*). Gleeson White thought it 'a good example of its class', but stated it was a memorial to Sidney Lear in the 1896 first edition of *The Cathedral Church of Salisbury* and Dean Francis Lear in another, undated. *The Cathedrals of Old England* (no author and no date) described it as 'a very beautiful screen', but continued '... was given in memory of Mr Sidney Lace, son of Dean Lace, by his widow in 1876'!

Not only was Henrietta the sole widowed 'Mrs Lear' at the time of the creation of the Skidmore screen, but as has been demonstrated, there is ample evidence to confirm her links with its design and with its funding. There was, of course, no contemporary doubt. Over the years in both the numerous guide books to the cathedral and other publications, some authors make the correct attribution and others do not. It is not a simple linear case of one person making the error and later ones following suit. More likely it will depend on the sources used by the author, and guide books do not generally cite references. Using local and national newspapers of the time should provide the correct information. Consulting Scott's autobiography reveals 'Mrs Lear' as the donor, and, as demonstrated above, taking into account the dates readers should reach the right conclusion.

Notes

1   See above chapter on Restorations, and for the subsequent fate of the Skidmore screen after it was taken down in 1959 see Babb P, and West T, 2019, 'Salisbury Cathedral Choir Screen' in *Salisbury Civic Society Magazine* December 2019, 4

2   *Salisbury & Winchester Journal* 4 November 1876, 6

3   For example Spring, Roy, 1991, *Salisbury Cathedral: A landmark in England's Heritage,* 87; Brown, Sarah, 1999, *Sumptuous and Richly Adorn'd: the Decoration of Salisbury Cathedral,* 49

4   Ross C, 2000, *The Canons of Salisbury,* 6

5   Howells J, and Newman R, 2018 reprint, *Women in Salisbury Cathedral Close,* 56-58

6   *Salisbury Journal* 14 November 1896, 5; *St Martins Parish Magazine* December 1896, 5

7   *Pall Mall Gazette* 22 May 1867

8   Chapter Minutes 1878-79 4 July 1878 'The Chapter unanimously resolved to record upon their minutes their grateful thanks to Mrs Sidney Lear for her liberal gift of £1000 towards the Choir Screen'.

9   Letter Henrietta Lear to Francis Lear, 5 March 1873 Salisbury Cathedral Archives, Scott Papers Press 3 Bundle 6

10   Letter Francis Lear to Henrietta Lear, 20 June 1874

11   The collaborative work between Scott and Skidmore, and more details of Skidmore's career and business may be found in Alicia Robinson's beautifully illustrated articles https://www.britishartstudies.ac.uk/issues/issue-index/issue-5/scott-skidmore accessed 7 December 2019

12   Stamp G, (ed), 1995 *Personal and Professional Recollections. The Autobiography of the Victorian Architect Sir George Gilbert Scott 1879,* 487

Repairing the Spire: Two Cathedral Masons' Experiences Aloft

Richard Deane & Rod Baillie-Grohman

The construction of Salisbury Cathedral's extraordinary crowning feature, almost certainly in the first quarter of the 14th century, gave rise to concerns right from the outset. The addition, both externally and internally, of 46 flying buttresses, some contemporaneous with the building of the tower and spire and some later, attests to this. Controversy continues over whether the spire's internal timberwork dates from the original construction, or is a later insertion, but there is no gainsaying the occurrence of a great storm in 1362. The later insertion theory cites this storm as the reason for the timbers, to allow access to the spire top for the repair of damage. The original spire of Norwich Cathedral came down in the same storm, and there is a contemporary record of Salisbury Cathedral being 'riven', the exact location of damage unspecified.[1]

Further records state that in 1363 'the walls and tower are threatened with ruin'[2], that in 1387 the steeple 'threatened ruin'[3], and that in 1423 'the stone tower in the centre of Salisbury Cathedral is ruinous'.[4] The succeeding centuries yield further references to a structure which was a continual source of worry. 'Ruin' may be a deliberately emotive word, designed to encourage the direction of funds towards repairs, but it is no surprise that the addition of five thousand tons of stonework, on piers designed to take only a low lantern tower weighing no more than one and a half thousand, generated a maintenance problem which would never go away. No modern engineer would ever countenance such a

Opposite: Fig 1: Plumbers' labourer Brian McGiveron working on the spire (*Richard Deane*)

project, which must make us very grateful that medieval builders operated by different principles.

The Save Our Spire appeal for £6.5 million, launched in 1985 and aimed primarily at tower and spire repairs (the West Front was also included, but with less emphasis on it) therefore takes its place in a long continuing story. It was however responsible for what was almost certainly the greatest single repair exercise in the spire's history, and one recorded at a level of detail absent for any of the earlier parts of the story. Here two former Cathedral stonemasons describe their own experiences of working on the spire at this time. Later, Rod Baillie-Grohman gives an account of being at the heart of the enterprise to repair the structure's stonework. To begin with, Richard Deane describes his own more intermittent involvement, starting with a preliminary project, eight years before the launch of the appeal.

Richard Deane

In May 1977, a piece appeared in the *Salisbury Journal,* stating that the Cathedral Clerk of the Works, Roy Spring, was about to lead a team of his masons in first-aid repairs to the spire, from bosun's chairs. The work was a holding operation, ahead of a planned major campaign, and was anticipated to take six weeks.

The reality turned out to be rather different. On being asked if they'd like to participate, the fully trained masons either said 'no I don't think so' on the spot, or went up to where the two chairs had been rigged, contemplated stepping out into one of them through the weather door, 30ft below the top, and then said 'no I don't think so'.

Roy Spring, never a man lacking in confidence when it came to executing his plans, was unabashed by this setback. He cast his net rather wider, and gathered a small team comprising a plumbers' labourer, a glaziers' labourer (the current co-author, in a rather younger guise), and a first-year apprentice stonemason. Luckily for him, both of the labourers were competent and adaptable people, happy to turn their hand to something new. The actual stepping out of the weather door, once the decision has been taken to do it, is a short process. Either you're comfortable sitting on a plank of wood, 370ft above ground level, or you're not.

This improvised team were all happy enough, adjusting rapidly to a very novel environment, where a 500ft length of 1in diameter sisal rope, passed through a steel pulley at the base of the capstone, enabled access to most of the spire. Both upwards and downwards movement of the chairs was possible, the former rendered astonishingly easy and rapid, at the higher levels, by the counterweight effect of some 300ft of rope dropping down to the main roofs below. Lower down the sensation of near weightlessness disappeared and moving upwards became much more laborious.

Anywhere near the top, however, sitting in a bosun's chair was a remarkable and exhilarating feeling. In fact it's hard to beat the sensation of hanging around on the upper reaches of the spire on a nice sunny day, without too much wind, with Salisbury laid out all around, and its countryside beyond. River valleys to north, west and south, glimpses of Salisbury Plain in the far north, and the woods of Clarendon to the east, with the undulating lands towards Winchester behind them. It's a rare privilege to be able to take all this in, quite apart from being paid to do it.

Obviously we were there to do some work rather than just to enjoy the view, and the chief focus of the campaign was to counter damage to the stonework from rusting cramps. To avoid adding any more weight than was necessary, the 14th century masons built a spire whose walls were about 2ft thick for the first twenty feet or so, and then slimmed down drastically above that. The standard thickness was established in 1977 as being $8^5/_8$ins. To reinforce this relatively slender structure, each stone was connected to its neighbour horizontally, using an iron cramp about 8ins long, turned down at each end. The stones were recessed to take the cramps, which were sealed in by having molten lead poured around them. Vertical connections, from course to course, were not used.

The lead had some rust-proofing properties but could never keep the threat of rust away permanently. In many cases, the expansion of the metal, generated by its rusting, was enough to burst off the corners of the stones being connected. We were there to cut rectangular holes where this had happened, back to the centre line of the stones, remove the cramps, and fit new pieces of Chilmark stone. If one of the two connected stones had so far been undamaged, it still had to be cut back, to enable the cramp to be removed. Finding a way to insert replacement cramps, in a non-rusting metal, was not part of the project, in other words the original reinforcing system was not regarded as an essential one.

Buckets tied to the chairs held tools, mortar and replacement stones, and provided receptacles for debris. Iron lump hammers, rather than mallets, were used for striking chisels, and had holes bored through their handles so that they too could be tied to the chairs. In the upper regions, everything had to be taken up the nine ladders which give access to the weather door from Eight Doors, the top of the tower level. In practice most of the work took place lower down, simply because there is much more stonework in the lower half of the spire than in the upper half. Down here, buckets could be lowered for emptying, or hauled up if more mortar was needed. There was also a need for the ropes falling away down to the main roofs to be looked after, given an occasional tendency for them to wrap themselves round projections.

With the Cathedral's small stock of labourers involved in the chair work, reinforcements were required to do the jobs at ground level, which meant that some of the trained masons did get involved in the project – labouring for the labourers. They had no complaints about this, but because there was generally not a great amount for them to do, additional work was found. It was decided to remove all the original surface cramps connecting stones in the south western squinch arch, one of the four features at Eight Doors level which connect the octagonal spire to the square tower. There was little sign of the cramps doing any damage, but their removal, without any non-ferrous replacements going back in, was harmless enough. What the foreman mason thought about the idea was unclear – he had no great belief in the premise behind the entire repair project, and hardly got involved at all.

All things considered, with an awkward working environment, and largely untrained operatives, the external repairs were carried out to a reasonable standard. As well as repointing any open joints, the other main focus of work was fixing new stone ornaments to the corners of the spire. These are short cylindrical objects, with rounded ends, probably describable as an uncarved form of crocket, but generally referred to at the time as 'balls'. They are simplified forms of the tower and spire's most numerous motif, the ballflower, an ornament which exploded into Gothic architecture in huge numbers in the early 14th century, and then vanished again just as quickly. On the spire, it vanishes at the bottom of the lowest of the three decorative bands, with the uncarved balls taking over at the corners. The new ones had copper pins attached to them, let into holes in the stonework laboriously cut by hammering – no cordless drills back then. The standard stonemason's glue, polyester resin, did the fixing. It's suspected now of having a finite lifespan, but no rapidly descending lumps of stone have been reported. Had they just have been glued on, without the pins, it would probably be a different story.

Roy Spring spent the first of the notional six weeks working from the chairs, and appeared a couple of times the next week, after which other duties claimed him and he was seldom seen up there again. The others carried on, largely unsupervised. The six weeks expanded inexorably, and in August the plumbers' labourer, Brian McGiveron (Fig 1), departed, for a pre-organised European trip of three or four weeks, assuming that was the end of his spire work. Returning in September, he found the project still in progress, and re-joined us. Early autumn weather included two or three days of rain and strong wind, necessitating the finding of work on the internal spire walls. These had seen far less in the way of stone corners breaking off, which was just as well, because gaining access to the inside can be a lot more difficult than to the outside. Whatever the reason for the insertion of the spire timberwork, it certainly is not in its present form a functioning internal scaffold. It may perhaps be the remaining bare bones of such a scaffold, though why all the other members would have disappeared is unclear.

They could hardly have been dispensable bits of three by two softwood, given that the medieval masons were working with stones of up to half a ton weight.

The period of wind and rain is one illustration in hindsight, and not the only one, of how ignorant the untrained crew was in operating in an environment more often the province of steeplejacks. While we worked inside, the chairs were down inside at Eight Doors, with their ropes secured as tightly as possible. Given the 180ft from there to spire top, this was never going to be all that tight, and they could be heard slapping against the spire in the wind. Returning to the outside when the weather relented, I was pulling myself up from the bottom level, and had reached around the midway point before becoming aware that the rope coming down on the other side of the pulley was seriously frayed. The slapping had clearly included repeated contact with one or more of the ten square-edged copper reinforcing bands which circle the spire at intervals. Quite apart from the fact that it might be worse higher up, the visible condition of the rope dictated a rapid descent back to Eight Doors, followed by replacement of the ropes.

As much by luck as by judgement, we all survived intact, and our employers never had to invoke a 'disclaimer' we were required to sign. 'I hereby acknowledge...that the Dean and Chapter of Salisbury Cathedral accept no responsibility whatsoever for my safety'. Luckily for both parties, this highly dubious document never had to be put to the test in a court of law.

The project was finally deemed complete after a period of more than sixteen weeks, rather than six, and we went back to our normal jobs. It was a wonderful time, despite occasional hazards and discomforts, and a remarkable memory to have in the bank.

In the years after the first aid campaign of 1977, plans were developed for the repairs proper, leading up to the Save Our Spire Appeal launch in 1985. The next year Rod Baillie-Grohman joined the workforce, and he now describes his two years of intensive involvement in the project.[5]

Rod Baillie-Grohman

S.O.S. Save Our Spire. The start of a big change for the Cathedral workshops, the masonry department in particular. A transformation from a somewhat sleepy workshop to a setup fit for a multi-million-pound restoration project, that 30 years on still continues. With a workshop extension, masons were imported from, amongst other projects, Hereford Cathedral, the Houses of Parliament and myself from Wells Cathedral. With new apprentices, new saws and operators and new pneumatic chisels (well, new to the Cathedral at any rate, and the subject of much grumbling amongst some of the old guard), the project was ready to go.

The spire stonework was in a dire state. The three ornamental carved bands were exceedingly thin and decayed in many places. Some stonework was down

to 2ins thick, and the strength of the spire was compromised. But how do you safely remove and replace tons of stone from a slender, 180ft high cone, perched on top of a tower which already reaches 220ft above ground? The answer was to fix steel bands inside the spire above and below each carved band and connect these bands with vertical steel props. This would transfer the weight of the spire above past the area being worked on to the remaining structure below. All the masons would have to worry about was the stonework of the band itself. This was, however, to prove no small problem.

In October 1986 the steel work arrived amongst great excitement, and the structure for the central band was erected on the grass. This was partly publicity, and partly so us masons who were going to fix it in place could see how it all went together. Work then started on fixing the lower band steelwork. A hoist fixed at Eight Doors level was used to hang a rope through the height of the tower and through the central crossing to the floor of the Cathedral. The pieces were then lifted up through the crossing and stored above the central crossing ready for the journey into the spire. This all required a six man team, with communication by walkie-talkie.

Thoughtfully the central crossing area on the Cathedral floor was roped off against stray visitors during this hoisting operation, though I'm not sure it would have stopped a 7m long steel beam ricocheting around the Cathedral should it have fallen from any height.

The team then spent the next couple of months up inside the spire clambering amongst scaffolding built amongst the medieval oak framework in the spire. From the base of the spire all the pieces were hauled up manually using a block and tackle and fixed in place. Working in the spire, with only electric lighting, was akin to working in a mine. The sense of place and time was entirely absent in the enclosed and ancient world and coming down (although we almost felt we should be making our way upwards) at the end of each day into a bright and modern existence was, I found, rather discombobulating.

A joyful end to the day's work was the 'Mason Train'. Three or four of us would pile noisily down the spiral stone staircases at a good running pace, only one synchronised step behind the mason in front, to emerge boisterous and reeling into the murmuring hush of the North Transept.

And then there was the stonework. As opposed to the tower, which weighs 6000 tons, the spire weighs 500 tons. It is a skin of stone, and the medieval woodwork inside the spire is important for its stability. It 'hangs' from the cross, giving downward tension to the stonework, and so strength to the spire. The individual stones that make up the spire are, however, individually very big. Too

Opposite: Fig 2: Rod Baillie-Grohman at the weather door (*Rod Baillie-Grohman*)

big as we were to discover. A two deck 'crow's nest' scaffolding had been built around the top carved band by a team of three steeplejacks, with a railway track up the side of the spire to carry materials up to the scaffold from Eight Doors. The first stone was measured, templates made, and the stone carved in Chilmark limestone. It weighed over 300kg and instantly posed a problem. The spire hoist was unable to carry that weight. It was decided to cut the stone sizes down and create a new jointing pattern for the top band. (Fig 4) This would have the additional advantage of making more stone sizes available from the quarry, as supply of good stone from the mine at RAF Chilmark was always going to be a problem. Despite the new sizes, the spire hoist still needed a good pull on a rope from the top to help it grind its way up with the new stonework. I would love to have beeen able to see the medieval masons manhandling their huge, half ton stones up to the top of the spire.

The usual way for the masons to reach the scaffolding was up inside and out through the weather door at the top. There was also a fixed ladder up the outside. A diary entry in 1987 recalls:

'One day this summer Brian [Moors] the steeplejack wanted to show me how the spire hoist worked & I went up the outside ladder with him – quite tremendous. I put on a safety belt – (he doesn't) and hooked myself onto the safety rope. Only when I got to the top I discovered I had it on the wrong hook on my belt. It wouldn't have taken my weight at all – All in the mind!!' [It turned out later that Brian knew all along I was using the wrong hook].

There were going to be 112 stones needed for the top band. With a new source of stone from a recently re-opened quarry at Chicksgrove, the masonry workshop kicked into an effective production routine and many of the stones would take upwards of 30 hours to carve. It was a labour intensive process getting them aloft. Up a hoist into the window of the south transept, lifting off from where the toilets now are. Along inside the transept roof to above the central crossing and up the height of the tower into the base of the spire and from here out onto the tower parapet. A chain block up 30ft to where the spire hoist started from and then out onto the little railway truck and a dash up the spire ladders to help pull on the rope for the heavier stones to bring the truck up and unload it. Repeat in reverse to bring all the old stonework down. The little railway truck was simply a metal box with a back, two sides which could open sideways and a base. It was completely open to the front, and the slight slope of the spire and a secure knot or three kept the contents in place as it trundled up the outside. When sending up, or down, a mixed load of smaller items, buckets, tools, cables etc it often resembled an overloaded and bulging shopping trolley trundling down the spire.

The weather wasn't always great, and a diary entry from 29th January 1988 describes an aborted fixing attempt:

> 'Up top with Simon [Cartwright] and Gordon [Tucker]. It was still, but raining a bit, so we put a sheet over our side of the scaffolding, great clambering over the top set of bars. Then Simon and myself put three course 6 stones on the hoist, & Gordon rolled them off at the top. We then went up to join him, having sent up the muck [mortar]. By the time we got up it was starting to blow. Simon & I tried to grout yesterday's stones, but the wind blew the grout out of the jug, and wet hands resulted whilst sponging it off the stonework. It was really getting raw, & we tried to put wind break up, but my hands were dead, & I suddenly felt sick – Gordon came up & we had to take down sheeting and netting as we decided to pack up. Felt awful & could hardly concentrate on wrapping the sheet & netting over the spire hole. A really quite incredible transformation in "body well–being". A vicious squall. Very relieved to get all ship shape & head on down. Back on the ground it all seemed so calm that we half wondered what all the fuss had been about. However it took an hour or two in the workshop to feel really OK again.'

An entry for Friday 12th February 1988 reads:

> 'Up top all day with Simon – Bedded, pinned and grouted the three stones we dry fixed yesterday. Windy but sunny most of the day. OK with my two pairs of gloves on. Yesterday Gordon used socks for gloves.'

The stones were cut to templates made by Gordon Tucker, who had to allow for the rake of the spire, the differing sizes due to historic asymmetry and the new stone plan necessitated by the size problem. The diagonal ribs of the carved band all intersected with its neighbouring stone at 90 degrees, meaning the stones also had a zig zag in their top and bottom beds. With Gary Price [who became Cathedral Clerk of the Works in 2012] on the saw taking out much of the 'rough', twelve masons have their workmanship aloft in the top band. The stones were all fitted to their neighbours in the workshop before going aloft, and stainless steel cramps bent to fit the various shapes prepared ready to be buried in pre-cut slots after fixing. Each course of stones around the spire would therefore become a locked ring of material. However, making room in the wall in order to fix the next stone often meant taking out an alarming quantity of the old stone first. At one point we had made a hole in the top band that stretched 180 degrees around the spire. The steel bracing was certainly doing its stuff, and small steel Acrow props held up the stonework within the carved band.

Looking back, it's incredible how much more safety conscious we have all become. No bad thing. I have photographs of masons casually leaning out of openings 100ft high with no harness or barrier of any sort. Hard hats were not routinely worn (or never worn might be more accurate in some cases). No protective clothing was provided and Hi Viz hadn't been invented. Though we had put netting on the sides of the scaffolding, there was only one rail at waist height. Nothing particularly strong at 'crouching level' to prevent an object (or person) going through, and much of the work was done at the crouch! I once watched, heart in mouth, as my hammer dropped through space onto the lead roofs below, before arcing out in slow motion to fall harmlessly into the grass by the North Transept.

A diary entry for Wednesday 2nd March 1988 is an example of a more relaxed approach to safety considerations:

> 'Went up top fixing with Gordon. Fitted my 7 BT [stone number] on the south face. Had to move some scaffolding around – Gordon was itching to do it. "It's only Brian put it up" he says. The stone fitted quite nicely.'

By October 1988 the work was complete, and the scaffolding was being moved down to the undecorated ashlar band below, and the tower was also being scaffolded, with the weight being taken on the aisle walls with huge steels inserted through the roofs.

I think all of us who had the amazing experience of taking part in this early phase of the restoration project will never forget the work and the people we worked with. Personally, one of my strongest memories is of walking back through the roofs at the end of a day aloft in the winter. There is a timeless atmosphere and dusty woody smell in the dim twilight, and if you hop off the wooden walkway to lie on the mounds of the vaulting, you can look through the bosses at the centres of the vaults to the Cathedral beneath, and maybe catch a choir practice way down below in their twinkling light, with the sound of the singing drifting up to a watching mason as it has done for 800 years.

★

Richard Deane, by now graduated from glaziers' labourer to fully fledged stonemason, had one principal involvement in the work described by Rod. He gives his account of it here.

The temporary erection of the spire steel framework in autumn 1986, near the North Porch (Fig 3), brought home to the public the complex (and expensive) nature of the project now getting under way. It did not however convey any information about an added complication in the whole enterprise, which had already been resolved, two or three months earlier. The three separate sections of framework, for the spire's three decorative bands, had been designed by the Cathedral's consultant engineers so as to have optimum positioning on stretches of internal spire wall.

At top and bottom of the three frameworks were steel bands, which were to run above and below the decorative ones, with connections between them to take the load while stones were replaced, as already described by Rod. In the case of four out of the six bands, their locations coincided with areas in which external copper bands, already mentioned for their rope-damaging properties, had been fixed, very early in the 20th century. Only in the case of the lowest decorative band were there no copper ones nearby. When it came to the middle and upper bands, the earlier metalwork had been fixed through the stonework with bolts, their heads outside and their nuts inside. And these nuts protruded from the inner

Fig 3: Internal framework after assembly on the ground (*Rod Baillie-Grohman*)

walls, exactly in positions in which they prevented the 1986 metalwork lying flat. In other words, there was no way, as things stood, in which this could be fixed. The only thing for it was to flip the bolts round, so that the nuts were on the outside. On the inside, the stonework could be cut out slightly so that the bolts no longer protruded. To achieve all this, external access was essential.

For the Cathedral's now established bosun's chair operator, this complication was welcome news. A couple of minor post 1977 repair exercises had seen a chair set up at low levels on the building, but the chance to return to the spire was greeted with glee. The gear from 1977 had all been stored, with the two long ropes in good condition, having been replaced relatively late in the earlier project, after the fraying incident. One of them was now sufficient, as this task just required two people. One on the inside, initially to undo the nuts, and one, myself, on the outside to withdraw the bolts. These were then transferred inside and put back in their holes, the other way around before. A bit of tightening up with spanners, and the inside walls were ready to take the metalwork.

The problem of accessing the internal walls had already been overcome with the insertion of temporary platforms, to meet the needs of the subsequent steel framework operation. The bolt reversal project was a straightforward one, fairly brief and blessed with good summer weather. A photo shows me returning to the weather door, with a haul of extracted bolts, strung out like fish on a hooked line. (Fig 5) I look happy to be back up there, in that unique environment, floating 370ft above ground level, and suspended from the top of one of mankind's most remarkable architectural achievements.

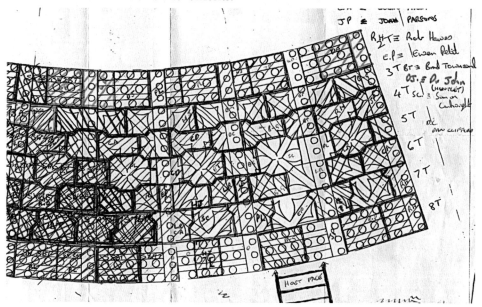

Fig 4: Rod Baillie-Grohman diary drawing of the decorative band (*Rod Baillie-Grohman*)

Fig 5: Richard Deane returning to the weather door (*Jonathan Prestidge*)

After that unexpected task was complete, and the steelwork all fixed, scaffolding went up round the top decorative band, below the weather door, and the masonry team, with Rod among them, began their momentous stone replacement exercise. (Figs 6 & 7) Bosun's chairs never went back up on the spire, with different rope access techniques used these days when there's a need for any work on the structure. The two 500ft long ropes had no further function, and were discarded. Mostly I was working away from the cathedral, on commercial stonework projects undertaken by the works department on other buildings, for instance in 1987 the Palladian Bridge at Wilton House, and then subsequently the house itself. There were occasional returns to the spire, most notably in July 1992, when a concert to mark the end of the appeal culminated in the launching of a firework from the spire top. There was a publicity exercise

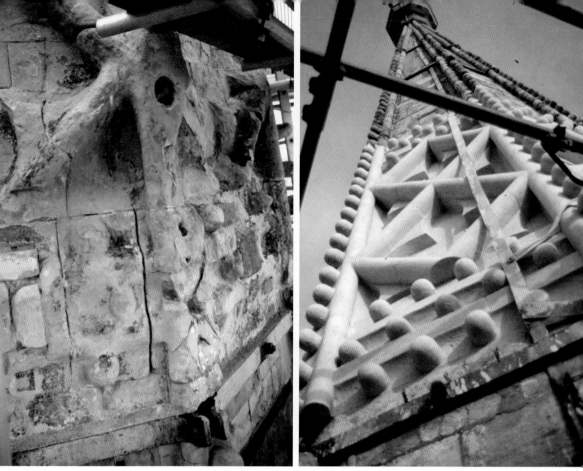

Figs 6 & 7: The decorative band before and after restoration (*Rod Baillie-Grohman*)

involved with the 'fixing' of the firework, but in fact this just meant someone dropping it into a holder, set up beforehand. Getting this in place and wiring it up, and then removing the holder and spent firework after the concert, were other opportunities to get back up there.

In the next few years I found the odd excuse to return – checking the very unmedieval anemometer at the spire top, for instance. But in fact each trip was just as much to enable someone else from the workforce to go along as well, and have the chance to experience, if only briefly, the sensation of being right at the top of a unique structure, otherwise never seen from much above ground level. Being restricted to those views nowadays can hardly be described as a hardship, having had the privilege, purely by chance, of so much close contact with the spire in earlier years. I've never stopped marvelling at the perfection of its design, and at the achievement of those who built it.

Notes

1 English Heritage Centre for Archaeology Report 44/2004 *The Tree-Ring Dating of the Tower and Spire at Salisbury Cathedral, Wiltshire,* 31 (Cal. Papal Registers: Petitions I [1342–1419], 462)

2 English Heritage Centre for Archaeology, 31 (Papal Letters IV [1362-1404], 89)

3 Dodsworth, William, *An Historical Account of the Episcopal See and Cathedral Church of Sarum,* 1814, 157

4 The Victoria History of Wiltshire Vol III, 178 which refers to Salisbury Cathedral Archives, CH/1/8, ff50-52)

5 The diary that Rod Baillie-Grohman kept while working on the spire has been deposited in the Cathedral Archive together with a collection of 35mm slides, Salisbury Cathedral Archive DC/RB/1 and DC/RB/2/IM/001-155

Save Our Spire

SALISBURY APPEAL

Save Our Spire: A £6.5m Fundraising Appeal, 1985-1993

Pam Wall

Throughout the many centuries of its existence, Salisbury Cathedral has faced the onslaught of wind, weather and war, all of which have taken their toll, requiring many phases of repair and re-strengthening. In the last couple of centuries the additional menace of industrial pollution has aggravated the damage to the building considerably.

During the twentieth century many remedial works were undertaken but by the late 1970s the Cathedral's governing committee, Chapter, started to recognise that on-going work on the tower and spire was in effect tinkering at the edges, and in 1979 the first mention of this is made in the Chapter minutes by the Canon Treasurer:

> 'He reported that the Dean and Chapter are engaged in a far-reaching reappraisal of the programme of repair and maintenance work needed on the Cathedral, the Chancels and other properties for which they have responsibilities. It is likely that there will be an expansion of the Works Department to cope with the work ... major repairs are likely to be needed over the course of the next 10 years ...'[1]

A quinquennial report was undertaken to plan repair work over the years 1980 to 2000 and at this point discussions were held regarding the launch of a major appeal to raise the funds, locally, nationally and internationally.[2]

The estimated costs were phenomenal. In 1984 the cost of repairs to the Spire were estimated at £518,000 (£1.6m) and to the Tower at £930,000 (£2.9m).[3]

Opposite: Fig 1: Save our Spire poster original watercolour by Brenda Jones, Piddle Valley, winner of the Mid-Dorset Women's Institute poster competition 1986 held to raise money for the Spire appeal. (*Roy Bexon*)

Eventually the Cathedral Dean and Chapter along with their technical advisors came to the conclusion that an even greater sum of money needed to be raised in order to carry out the necessary repairs to the spire, tower *and* west front. A target figure was set for the 1980s appeal to raise £6.5m, with the first £1m being raised within the Diocese of Salisbury. In today's terms those figures equate to £20.5m and £3.2m respectively.

It is appropriate at this stage to include a word about source material for this chapter. All material was drawn from Salisbury Cathedral Archives, particularly the Chapter minute books. The archives also contain files kept by the Clerk of Works, which were tapped into for this chapter but need further sorting and cataloguing, as well as photographs, printed leaflets and some event programmes. All the information about the fund-raising events was taken from local press reports which have been saved in the Cathedral archive in a series of albums of press cuttings: they can also be found in the archives of local and national newspapers.[4]

What Did the Appeal Involve?

The nature of the 1980s appeal touched the imagination and sympathy of many, and huge numbers of people became involved in the fund-raising effort, from local schoolchildren right up to royalty in the person of HRH The Prince of Wales, who took a keen and active interest in the whole process. The initial requirement was to establish an Spire Appeal Trust which would manage the fund-raising, and this was set up in 1984, with Prince Charles as its President. Lord Tryon became the Chairman, Mr Christopher Benson the Deputy Chairman, and Mr Nicholas Tate the Director General. Mrs Jo Benson chaired the Diocesan Appeal Committee. The Cathedral was represented by Dean Sydney Evans, who deferred his retirement by a year in order to throw his assistance into the appeal.

A launch date was set for April 1985, but before that date a frenzy of activity resulted in contacts with the Surveyor of Fabric at Westminster Abbey, a 'Basic Appeal Paper' sent to the Cathedrals' Advisory Committee; and an appeal office being set up at Wren Hall in the Cathedral Close.[5] The appeal was announced in the *Salisbury Journal* on 17 January 1985, with release to national press the following day. Dean Sydney Evans told the Salisbury Journal: 'There is no danger in the sense of "Danger, Keep out" … but these things can only get worse, and as they get worse the danger does increase.' Roy Spring, Clerk of Works at that time added: 'It is easy to leave it for someone else. Some time, someone has got to take that decision. Sydney Evans and the Chapter have taken it.'[6]

Three exhibitions about the work required and the need for an appeal were planned for the early days: one at Wren Hall, one in the north transept of Salisbury Cathedral, and one in Church House in Westminster. On 10 April 1985, the appeal was officially launched by Prince Charles in Salisbury. On that day, at the service to inaugurate the appeal, Dean Sydney Evans made the following comments in his address:

> 'The Appeal will be organised in three phases. Phase I will be addressed to residents, institutions and industries in the two counties (Wiltshire and Dorset) and the one diocese. The Trustees are convinced that charitable giving should begin at home! When we who live in these parts have demonstrated our commitment to the saving of Salisbury's Tower and Spire, we shall with greater assurance be able to approach national sources in Phase II, and international sources in Phase III. What better beginning could we make than a thanksgiving Celebration of the Builders whose faith, audacity and skill achieved this marvel of engineering and art nearly 700 years ago? We ask God's blessing on their successors, the builders of today, who during the next ten years will secure its future. But always in the immediate years ahead we shall need to keep in mind these words of Sir Francis Drake:
>
> "There must be a begynning of any great matter, but the continuing unto the end until it be thoroughly finished yieldes the true glory".[7]

Because the Cathedral and the Spire Appeal Trust wanted the first million pounds to be raised within the diocese, a series of 'road-shows' were staged throughout Wiltshire and Dorset to explain the need for urgent and extensive work, and the cost. (Fig 2) Newly retired Chief Superintendent of Police, Frank Lockyer, took on the role of Diocesan Director of the appeal. Frank, together with Roy Spring, the cathedral's clerk of works, travelled to every parish in the diocese with a presentation that combined technical information about the urgent restoration of the spire with the vital importance of the necessary fundraising. It was made clear that a ten pence piece in a retiring collecting box would not be adequate. In this way many organisations and individuals were encouraged to help raise money, which they did with great gusto. By October of 1985 the Dean was able to report that £250,000 (£744,000) had already been banked in the fund, with promises for much more.[8]

It was hoped that all parish councils would hold at least one fund-raising event during 1986, but in fact many other people came forward during that year to raise money for the appeal. The Chairman of Salisbury District Council, Jim Burden, ran the London Marathon and raised £2000 (£5900). In similar sporting endeavour, the Rural Dean Michael Christian-Edwards took part in the Great Cycle Ride organised by Wiltshire Historic Churches Trust. The ride was 100 miles long, and the Rural Dean planned to split any money he raised between the Spire Appeal and the Historic Churches Fund.

The stately homes of Wiltshire and Dorset were asked to donate items of artistic merit: the auction, sponsored by Woolley & Wallis, was run by the Chairman of

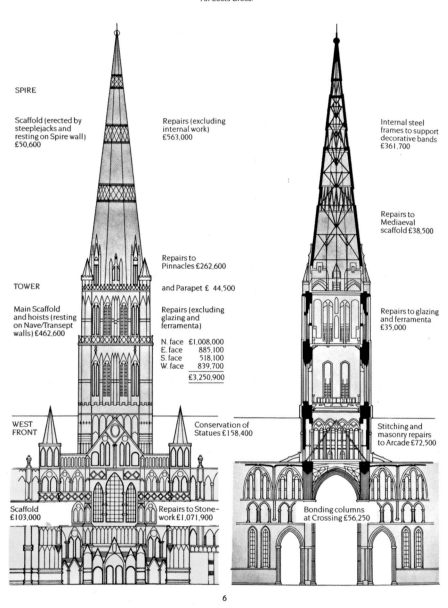

SALISBURY CATHEDRAL SPIRE TRUST

HOW THE MONEY WILL BE SPENT

All Costs Gross.

SPIRE

Scaffold (erected by steeplejacks and resting on Spire wall) £50,600

Repairs (excluding internal work) £563,000

Internal steel frames to support decorative bands £361,700

Repairs to Mediaeval scaffold £38,500

Repairs to Pinnacles £262,600

TOWER

and Parapet £ 44,500

Main Scaffold and hoists (resting on Nave/Transept walls) £462,600

Repairs (excluding glazing and ferramenta)

Repairs to glazing and ferramenta £35,000

N. face	£1,008,000
E. face	885,100
S. face	518,100
W. face	839,700
	£3,250,900

WEST FRONT

Conservation of Statues £158,400

Stitching and masonry repairs to Arcade £72,500

Scaffold £103,000

Repairs to Stonework £1,071,900

Bonding columns at Crossing £56,250

6

Fig 2: How the money will be spent – Spire Appeal 1987 issued by the Salisbury Cathedral Spire Trust (*Roy Bexon*)

Christie's International at Wilton House, and raised £800,000 (£2.3m) twice the amount that had been anticipated. Sailors from HMS Osprey did a one-week charity event in Guernsey, washing cars: they split the proceeds between the Spire Appeal and the Save the Children Fund. A flower festival was arranged at Compton Chamberlain; a Shakespeare production at Wilton House; a pageant at Fonthill. Mr Stancomb, a farmer who confessed to 'nearly pranging the Spire' while in the RAF during the Second World War, gave a Farm Open Day at his farm in Donhead St Mary. Former MP John Cordle gave a garden party at Malmesbury House. Later that year former Prime Minister Edward Heath conducted a concert by Sarum Chamber Orchestra; and the Christmas Carol Service was recorded and broadcast by the BBC in support of the Spire Appeal, with readings by actors Michael Hordern and Dorothy Tutin.

Donations were also made in kind, sometimes in order to raise cash, for example several artists painted pictures of the spire for later auction. Aerial photographs were donated for a similar purpose. A cookbook of soup recipes – including one from Prince Charles - was published, with all the proceeds of sale going to the appeal. However sometimes an 'in-kind' donation was given just to help the project along, notably the donation by a company called MicroAge of an early type of personal computer worth £7000 (£19,500 today) - an indication of just how expensive computing equipment was in the 1980s, and what a generous donation it was. This practical gift meant that most of the administration and accounting could be done in-house at the appeal office instead of having to buy-in these services.

Prince Charles was not just a President in name. In May 1985 he persuaded Heathrow Airport to donate £2500 (£7500) to the appeal when he opened the new Terminal 4, and in June he revisited Salisbury for a 'Save Our Spire' event. He also convinced contacts in Chicago to throw a lavish ball on behalf of the appeal, for which attendees would pay handsomely.

Councils gave donations: Bournemouth Council donated £1000 (£3000), and Wiltshire County Council donated £100,000 (£287,000) as the Cathedral was deemed to be an important part of the local economy. This decision was not made without a considerable amount of dissent within the Council. And many, many 'ordinary' people throughout the diocese staged events, too many to list, in order to do their bit, such as garden parties, shows, an auction of unwanted trinkets. One example of interest is an 11-year old girl who did a sponsored silence for 10 hours and raised £5 for the appeal. This equates to £14.39 now: a noble effort. One can only assume her family promised to pay £5 for a day's silence from a chatterbox! As a result of all the fund-raising within the diocese, a cheque for the first million pounds was presented by Mrs Jo Benson, the Diocesan Appeal

Figs 3 & 4: Signatures from an autograph book commemorating the Symphony for the Spire concert on 6th September 1991 (*Roy Bexon*)

Committee Chairman, to Lord Tryon, the Appeal Trust Chairman, in September 1986, nineteen months after the official launch. In the November the new Dean, Hugh Geoffrey Dickinson, reported that the appeal had raised £1.25m (3.7m) and Phase 1 was complete.[9] But the money was still pouring in, and a further quarter million pounds was in the coffers by mid-February 1987.

Phases Two and Three of the Appeal

In 1987 the appeal expanded to become both a national and an international one, and was supported by the publication of books, the production of films and the giving of concerts. A national committee, with its head office in London, was led by Sir Austin Bide and Sir Maurice Laing to secure donations from across the UK and overseas. Visitors to the Cathedral were encouraged to feel a part of the movement by etching their names on panes of glass or buying a piece of the original stone that had been removed, each of these for a £5 (£14) donation. The appeal was promoted in America as it was felt that many Americans who had visited Salisbury might feel inclined to donate to the cause. However, it was not all plain sailing. A plan to encourage rich Americans to contribute by offering luxury stays in stately homes in Wiltshire did not deliver its promise, as many were deterred from flying by the terrorism threat arising from the Libyan crisis at that time. And the Clerk of Works was driven to hit back at critics of the appeal, stating that Salisbury would be nothing without the Cathedral.

By May 1989 the appeal reached its halfway target, and by February 1991 had reached £5m (£15m). Appeals tend to have a habit of losing momentum and it seemed an extra effort was needed to achieve the full amount of £6.5m (£20.5m). The final push came as a suggestion by Prince Charles to stage an event that many local people will recall: the Symphony for the Spire concert in September 1991. Using his own contacts, the Prince of Wales approached several well-known celebrities to perform in the concert; not only did they all agree to perform but by good fortune they were all available on the date set. The result, on 6 September 1991, was an evening of eclectic entertainment including pop music, opera, Shakespearean readings, classical music and more. Contributors included well-known personalities such as Phil Collins, Charlton Heston, Kenneth Branagh and Placido Domingo. (Figs 3 & 4) The stage was constructed before the west front, and the audience of 10,500 people were seated on the west lawn. Kenneth Branagh, before the event, confessed to feeling terrified:

> 'After the first phone call, I misunderstood. I thought it was an evening of poetry inside the Cathedral . . . I have never played to an audience of anything like that number . . . and to be doing Shakespeare in the midst of everything else that's going on, it will be quite challenging to get people's attention'.[10]

It seems, however, that all the performers overcame their stage fright to give sterling performances, aided no doubt by the special effects for the evening: the coloured searchlights that swept the sky, and last but not least two tons of fireworks. (Fig 5)

A Successful Outcome

In May 1993 the work on the spire was complete, within budget, and the scaffolding removed. Hopefully it will be a very long time before this medieval masterpiece will be obscured by scaffolding again. Tributes should be paid to all the people who worked so hard to realise the herculean tasks of raising the sums of money required and seeing the job completed, not least the two Deans, the Clerk of Works and all of the Appeals Trust. There were people who questioned why so much effort was put into raising funds to preserve a building when there

Fig 5: Fireworks at the end of the Symphony for the Spire concert 6 September 1991 (*Roy Bexon*)

were many other urgent calls upon our money and our humanity. Dean Hugh Dickinson gave this explanation:

> 'The Cathedral says something about the human spirit . . . that's why it's so important. If you believe, as I do, that human beings have huge spiritual potential, it is important to have works of art and architecture in our landscape which stretch the self-understanding of the human race, and to keep the pinnacles of human achievement in our vision'.[11]

Roy Spring, Clerk of Works from 1968 to 1996, had a slightly different take on it. He describes climbing up to the pinnacle of the Spire, as he did on many occasions, and his feelings when he got there:

> 'So delicate is the balance of the Spire that every tremor can be felt, whether it be from one's own movements, or that caused by the wind blowing. It is like standing on a living being, like feeling the heartbeat of another person'.[12]

Save our Spire Appeal

A work of art, a house of God, a living being, however people view Salisbury Cathedral, the efforts of so many to raise the necessary funds to restore this beautiful building says a lot for the importance they give to it and the affection that it inspires. Should another huge appeal be needed at some time years from now let us hope that future citizens will feel just as motivated to take on the task.

Notes

1   Salisbury Cathedral Archives (SCA), Chapter minutes 15 October 1979 CH/1/43
2   SCA, Chapter minutes 21 November 1980 CH/1/43
3   Figures quoted in brackets throughout the article are values in 2018 taking into account inflation. These have been calculated using the Bank of England Historic Inflation Calculator: www.bankofengland.co.uk/monetary-policy/inflation-calculator accessed Dec 2019
4   SCA, press cutting albums: microfilm copies of *The Salisbury Journal* are available for consultation at Salisbury public library.
5   SCA, Chapter Executive minutes 15 November 1984 CH/1/45
6   Salisbury Journal, 17 January 1985
7   SCA, DA/1/1/15/1/34
8   SCA, Chapter minutes 14 October 1985 CH/1/45
9   SCA, Chapter minutes 17 November 1986 CH//1/45
10   SCA, *Symphony for the Spire* commemorative booklet, 1991
11   SCA, *Symphony for the Spire* commemorative booklet, 1991
12   Spring, Roy, 1991, *Salisbury Cathedral A Landmark in England's Heritage*, Dean & Chapter Salisbury Cathedral, 107

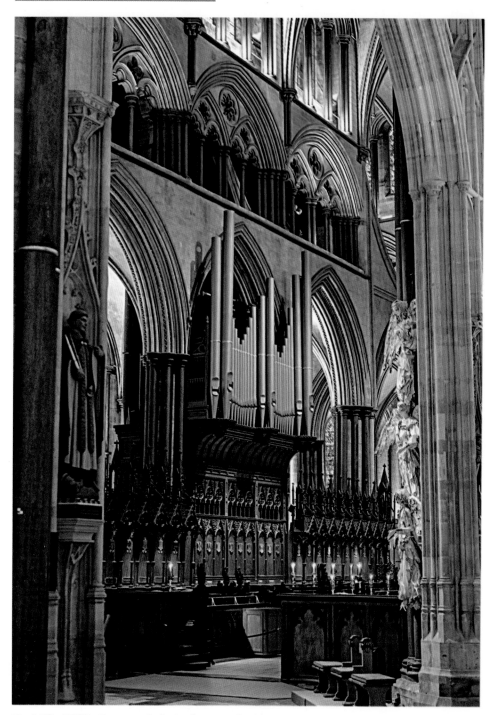

Fig 1: The Willis Organ and choir photographed in January 2016 and viewed from the south transept. (*Ash Mills*)

Water or Gas? The Struggle to Power the Father Willis Organ

Alan Willis

This chapter is the result of a project to transcribe a collection of documents, primarily letters, written by various participants in the building of Salisbury Cathedral's "Father" Willis Organ in the 1870s. The project was one of a number of activities linked to a major restoration of the organ 2019-2020. (Fig 1) The story of the birth of the organ and the characters involved described in this chapter comes not only from the transcription of the archive letters (mostly in a variety of hard to read 19th century hands) but also by determining how the disordered letters related to each other.[1] Unless otherwise stated, the quotations are from those letters. For reasons of space, they have mostly been significantly edited, with some words inserted to preserve their sense. All underlinings and abbreviations are in the originals.

The main participants in the story of the Willis organ were:

- *Archdeacon Francis Lear.* (Fig 2) Born in Downton in 1825 Francis was Rector of Bishopstone from 1850 until his death in 1914. He became rural dean in 1851, chancellor of the Cathedral 1861-64, precentor 1864-75 and Archdeacon of Sarum 1875-1913. Francis was the recipient of most of the correspondence since the Dean as head of the Chapter was described as 'aged and infirm'.

- *Sir George Gilbert Scott.* Scott (1811-1878) was a prolific English Gothic revival architect, chiefly associated with the design, building and renovation of churches and cathedrals. He designed or restored over 800 buildings, including the Midland Grand Hotel at St Pancras Station and the Albert Memorial. It was Scott's report to the Dean and Chapter on the state of the

Left: Fig 2: Archdeacon Francis Lear (*Roy Bexon*)

Below: Fig 3: Henry Willis

Fig 4: Julia Chafyn
Grove
(Mere Museum)

Cathedral in 1869 that led to its drastic reordering including the installation of the Father Willis organ.

- *Henry "Father" Willis*. Henry (1821–1901) (Fig 3) was an English organ player and builder, regarded as the foremost organ builder of the Victorian era. He built the organs at the Alexandra Palace, the Royal Albert Hall and St Paul's Cathedral, as well as some 1000 other organs in the UK and abroad.

- *Julia Chafyn Grove*. (Fig 4) Born in 1825, Julia inherited Zeals Estate, Mere,

Wiltshire in 1865, where she lived until her death in 1891. She was a lady of considerable wealth and charitable frame of mind, endowing many charities in and around Mere as well as the school in Salisbury that bears her name. Her significance in this story is that she paid for the organ and its case, to the tune of some £4,500, well over £500,000 in today's values.

- *Francis Webb Wentworth Sheilds.* Sheilds (1820-1906) was resident engineer to the Crystal Palace between 1852 and 1858. He submitted the successful plans for the Victoria Embankment in London and designed a tunnel under the Thames from Millwall, not built only for lack of funds. Sheilds worked with Scott on the repair and restoration of the Cathedral.

★

By the middle of the 19th century, Salisbury Cathedral was not in a good way. In *Reminiscences of 80 Years* by Francis Lear, published in 1910, he refers to the 'cold and desolate condition of the Cathedral.'[2] It was doubtless this state of affairs that led the Cathedral to commission Scott to undertake a full survey of the building, which he submitted in 1869. Scott's report was thorough and wide ranging. It set out proposals for substantial changes to the works undertaken by architect James Wyatt in the previous century including detailed suggestions for the re-siting of the organ. At the time of his report, the instrument in the Cathedral was that built by Samuel Green in 1792. It had originally been placed over the entrance to the Choir (Fig 5), although it was taken down and placed somewhere in the Nave in the 1870s during Scott's reordering works.[3] (Fig 6)

The original siting of the Samuel Green attracted differing views. One was that 'The organ, elegantly constructed to correspond with the architecture of the Cathedral is placed over the entrance of the Choir and as seen from the altar, produces a grand effect.'[4] Another was that '... as to the organ case, which is the most conspicuous object in the whole church, and forms a screen that dissects the Nave of the Church in the middle of it, it is difficult to assign the style of Gothic to which it belongs. Certainly, nothing can be more despicable in the design, or more flat and incorrect in the execution than the said screen.'[5]

Scott was in sympathy with the former view. His 1869 report stated:

> 'I believe it is universally admitted by those who have considered the subject from a musical point of view that, though many positions will do, that there is none so good as the customary place on the Choir Screen … I am aware that the modern 'Vista' theory is dead against it, but, to my own apprehension, it is only the inordinate growth of organs which (viewing the question as one of taste alone) has any weight against this customary position.'

His recommendation was that:

Above: Fig 5: Samuel Green organ placed above the pulpitum (*Roy Bexon*)

Right: Fig 6: Scott's screen across the entrance to the choir (*Roy Bexon*)

> I would construct double open screen supported by light marble columns …
> and carrying a narrow loft. On this I would place such portions of the Organ
> as may be limited to moderate and slight dimensions. I would draft off all the
> cumbersome parts to the back of the stalls in the first arches (right and left) in
> the Choir aisle where they would be very much concealed or possibly, if found
> practicable, into the triforium. I would place the organist in his usual place on
> the loft …'[6]

There is nothing in the archive about the arguments that obviously ensued regarding these recommendations, but Scott lost the day. There was a measure of compromise in the form of the metal screen designed by Francis Skidmore that remained in place at the entrance to the Choir until 1959 when, it may be felt, happily, it was taken away and the full "vista" so disliked by Scott fully restored, as it appears today. Scott himself was not involved in the design of the new organ.

This rest of this chapter will deal with the often verbally vicious dispute that arose about the means by which the organ would be provided with wind to its bellows. Traditionally, bellows were fed by the labour of human organ blowers, using hand pumps. That, although rather tiring, worked adequately for modest instruments requiring relatively low wind pressure. However, as the size of organs increased, manual blowing became insufficient. Electricity was in its infancy and no electric blowers existed in the 1870s. The principal means of securing wind pressure was to use water to create pressure to power hydraulics to do the job.

Put very shortly, Henry Willis was an enthusiastic water supporter. The paymistress, Julia (and there is no evidence in the archive that they ever met) supported Henry. Both, as we shall see, rarely held back in supporting their cause. Against them was Sheilds. As we shall see, he feared for the structural safety of the Cathedral resulting from the digging of water tanks under or near the walls and from the siting of large water tanks on some of the Cathedral walls. Fortunately for the well-being of all concerned, Sheilds seems to have been a far milder tempered man than his professional counterpart.

The first extant relevant letter from Julia is to Francis. It is dated 17 February 1872:

> '... I was much interested in the works going on for the renovation of the Choir in the Cathedral when I was in Salisbury. I do not know whether you are the person to write to on the business but my slight acquaintance with the Dean, and his age and infirmities make me unwilling to trouble him.'[7]

In view of what Francis had later to endure in letters from Julia and Henry, it is tempting to wonder whether he might have wished that he had disclaimed any knowledge of or responsibility for the whole scheme!

The archive contains nothing from October 1872 until 8 February 1875 when Julia wrote to Francis in rather moralistic tones:

> '... I imagined that the Chapter would have known what help I proposed to myself for the Cathedral Organ. I now write to say that altho' I cannot make it carte blanche, yet I wish to include the whole work of the organ, comprising the case ......, wch I perceive in the last Sarum Journal a record of the meeting at the Deanery, is excluded. What do you imagine would be the cost of that in a style consonant with the Architecture of the Cathedral? All this work is for futurity, therefore we ought to bear that in mind, as did the grand old Monks, Bishops and Barons who gave their substance to raise these Houses of God and not skimp the work as we do in these days, everything that does not make us a profitable return? in this world, at once!'[8]

By June 1875, at least, Henry was plainly being considered as a suitable person to build the new organ. The Rev Sir Frederick Arthur Gore Ouseley, Bt, Warden of St Michael's Tenbury, a man much respected for his views on organ matters wrote to Francis on 9 June 1875:

> '… I shall be very glad to be of any use in any way. Willis has restored New College Organ so magnificently and has also rebuilt mine here so uncommonly well, that I am strongly in favour of employing him'.[9]

And in the same month Canon H T Armfield, principal of Salisbury Theological College wrote, also to Francis:

> '… The most important point is to get the right [organ] builder; & for an organ of our size, I should advise you not to think of any Engl: builder but either Hill or Willis. Pray don't choose Gray & Davison. Most of their recent work that I have played on is dreadful. There are some good builders abroad [ie in existence]; but you never can tell when you will get your organ from some of them'.[10]

On 2 August 1875, we find the first evidence of Henry's concerns. Cathedral Canon Gordon wrote to Francis a letter that tells us a little of Henry's character.

> '… I had a long visit from Mr. Willis the Organ Builder, late on Saturday night. He is distressed about the proposed position of the new organ & would prefer the 2nd bay from the Tower – or better still – two large chambers in the middle of each great Transept! He thinks they might be made to look like Tombs or Chapels … He seems a determined man & inclined to have his own way. He had to leave early on Sunday morning & I began to fear it would arrive before he left me, so prolonged was our interview.[11]

On 20 December 1875, there is the first letter from Henry (to Francis):

> 'I have this day been very carefully considering the organ for this Church with the view of submitting my plans & specifications but I am somewhat hindered by not knowing what you intend to do behind the stalls. Nor can I quite see where we shall put the bellows for at an interview I had with the Dean this morning I was told that the North East Transept is usually a Morning Chapel … It appears to me that if the Southern half of that North East Transept were fitted up as a chapel he might very well appropriate the northern half to the Bellows & mechanism for Blowing and in the most remote locality that we can find in the church'.[12]

Those familiar with the Cathedral might imagine the impact of 'Bellows & mechanism for Blowing' on the Morning Chapel.

By 1876, Henry had produced his specification for the organ. Gore Ouseley (writing on 7 February 1876) evidently liked it, but note his wary comment about Henry:

> '… I like Willis' specification very much – with one or two little exceptions – nor do I think the price exorbitant, considering what he gives you. It is evident that he wishes to do you justice and to erect for himself in your magnificent Cathedral "Monumentum aere perennius" [a monument more lasting than bronze]…it is well to reflect whether a man like Mr Willis wd not do better if his honour be implicitly trusted'.[13]

On 15 March 1876, Julia had also seen and evidently approved the specification. She wrote to Francis:

> '… I am very thankful to be able so materially to assist in the work of the cathedral, in the town with which my family has been connected for nearly a century, & which place I remember from my early childhood through frequent visits … Music has always been my favourite art and the only one I am at all conversant with, and it is very pleasant to me to feel that the praises of God when sung will be supported in a manner worthy of the grand Temple where they will be heard, and that the thrilling tones may fill the hearts and raise heavenward the thoughts of those who worship therein, as mine have been by the notes of many a fine organ, and when hearts are so softened, the donor, long passed away may be kindly remembered and her memory blessed'.[14]

The correspondence is not clear why, but by August 1876, the question of how the organ should be blown was being raised. On 1 August, E Hoskin (seemingly a clergyman in Westminster) wrote to Canon Gordon:

> 'I send you … a prospectus of a hot air engine which I think it may be worthwhile to suggest to Willis as a possible means of blowing the organ in Salisbury Cathedral. We have thought very much about the question of getting rid of manual labour in blowing organs & these difficulties presented themselves to us in one case with regard to water. When we were collecting facts with regard to employing water I learnt that to blow the Westminster Abbey organ it would require 1,000 gallons of water per hour the organ going the whole time: the price of water being at Westminster 1/– per 1000 gallons … [Although] these hot air engines are as yet wholly untried in England, they are known in America, should Willis think them satisfactory, the combustion of gas with atmospheric air might be found more useful in some cases than coke for the fire. It is allowed that Hydraulic engines easily get out of order; a piece of cotton waste will stop them. Your conversation with me at Sarum has led me to put down these odds & ends of experience thinking they may be of use to the Dean and Chapter. I hope these hot air engines will solve what is now a difficulty - and I am anxious that Willis should look into the matter'.[15]

Henry had other ideas. On 10 October 1876 he wrote:

'The organ must be blown by water I think and in order to secure this beyond the possibility of failure it may be necessary to have a small steam engine (anywhere) and pump the water into a tank for yourselves …'[16]

On 14 November 1876, Julia wrote to Francis:

'I have heard with <u>painful</u> surprise that the Chapter of Salisbury have abandoned the absolutely necessary plan, of blowing the new organ by water. This will render the use of the <u>whole organ</u> only possible on rare occasions. If you have so resolved, I must consider what course I shall adopt, to diminish the size and expense <u>very greatly</u> of the organ & reduce it to an <u>ordinary instrument</u>. You remember that at the meetings, [of a committee formed in connection with the building of the new organ] this question of blowing was early brought to the front … & I considered it solved, & proceeded to build a large and expensive organ upon the assurance that it would be appreciated. If its power be thus crippled I shall feel that my efforts have <u>not</u> been appreciated by the Chapter & shall proceed with pain and mortification to retrace, in some measure, my steps before it be too late. I hope soon to hear from you that there is no question of such an extraordinary omission, which in fact would entirely reduce the instrument to an ordinary level'.[17]

It may be that Henry was by now slightly wavering. On 24 November 1887 he writes to Francis:

'… A pressure of at least 40lbs must be secured and if it cannot be done direct from the Water Company main it must be derived from other means …'[18]

If he was, Julia was not. On 25 November 1887 she writes, also to Francis:

'Your letter of 16th has caused me anxiety. I see in it nothing but <u>hopes</u> that the difficulty may be overcome regarding the blowing of the organ by water – which was <u>clearly assumed</u> to be no difficulty at all at the Committee Meetings. This is the opinion of one of the members imparted straight to me; for naturally since I received yr letter, I have not been silent on the subject, & have directly & indirectly gathered up more than one counsel on this point, from persons qualified to judge, & three competent and interested, have said that there can be no lack of pressure. I confess, & shall not disguise from any member of the Chapter concurring in raising a difficulty, that I have been <u>deeply mortified</u> at my efforts to do my best for the solemnity of worship in the Cathedral, having been met in such a manner. I think it best to be quite plain spoken in declaring my intention to stop the work, if I do not receive the <u>surest promise</u> on the part of the Dean and Chapter that water power shall be <u>always</u> available, and the power and beauty of the organ not reserved only for a rare High Festival. Until I am re-assured on that point I shall hold from making payment to Willis – and if the Chapter decides not to use water power, they shall not find me fail in my agreement to provide an Organ, but it will [be] done as a fulfilment of a duty, & I shall of course provide a totally different instrument. The failure of power to use a large instrument, entirely exonerates me from the necessity of providing one. I must request you to convey my decision to the Dean – did his health permit, I should address myself to him, as the Head of the Chapter'.[19]

On 9 December 1887 the Dean of Winchester quite forcefully expressed his reservations about water blowing, based on Winchester Cathedral's experience:

'When the water fails we are obliged I believe to have 4 men (old men) to take turn two & two in blowing. I am told the pipe which conveys water to work our organ is frequently diverted into other pipes before it comes to us & hence the failure of supply ….'[20]

Fig 7: Some of the documents from the Cathedral Archive used in compiling this chapter (*Roy Bexon*)

Henry remained unmoved and writes to Francis on 12 December 1887:

'Organ blowing by water power is most extensively adopted all over the north of England. The organs at St Pauls London & Durham Cathedral Manchester Cathedral (I think.) Heaps of churches large & small [sic] and so perfect is the system that no one ever regrets going into the final outlay'.[21]

The Salisbury Cathedral Chapter was clearly unable to decide how to proceed so, in a draft letter, the only one in the collection, dated 18 December 1887, Francis wrote to Scott:

'I write respecting the Blowing of the new Organ by Water Power. The pressure from the Water Works of this Town is not sufficient to meet Mr Willis' requirements … [The Chapter] therefore propose to call in Mr Sheilds, who assisted us before, to seek his sanction providing for the storage of water. The Chapter remembering the confidence you placed in Mr Sheilds …'[22]

That decision, although eventually proven to be wise, led to some memorable insults from Henry (see later).

In February 1877, the Chapter resolved to consider entering into a contract with United Sanitary Authorities, the local water suppliers, for the provision of a main water pipe 'from the reservoir to the Cathedral' for the organ, with a pressure 'equal to 140 feet' at a cost of 'sixpence per 1000 gallons'.[23] That contract was never concluded.

On 11 July 1877, Sheilds submitted a very lengthy report to the Chapter about his inspection of the Cathedral and the works initiated by Henry that he found. It makes startling reading:

'In accordance with your instructions that I examine and report as to whether the proposed Scheme for supplying water to the Organ Blowing Machinery of Salisbury Cathedral would be suitable to the Building, I proceeded to Salisbury to examine the locality; and having now considered the matter I beg to report as follows. The proposed Scheme consists of sinking a Brick Water Tank in the ground to contain about 6,000 gallons to which a water supply would be provided. – Also to construct a timber framework upon the walls of the North East Transept a little above the level of the springing of the Roof, upon which would be placed Iron Tanks containing rather more than 5,000 gallons of Water. The water would be pumped from the lower to the upper Tanks, where it would have a sufficient elevation to work the Organ Blowing Machinery; after which it would be again returned to the lower Tank. On my arrival at Salisbury, I found the excavation of the lower Tank nearly completed. – Its position was on the Northern side of the Cathedral between the Great Transept and the North East Transept, and close to the Walls – It was about six feet deep, and, (as I was informed,) was below the adjacent foundations of the Cathedral … As the position was a most improper one, I recommended that the work should be discontinued at once; that the lower part of the excavation should be filled in again with concrete and the upper part with the excavated material … I consider that a Tank of this description should be kept at a distance, (say 25 yards at least,) from the Walls of the Main Building. I now beg to report on the projected Tanks in the roof of the North East Transept. These tanks are in the form of three sides of a square; one side resting on the North Wall of the North East Transept, and the weight of the two others being conveyed by the timber framework above referred to, to the East and West sides of that Transept. The weight of tanks of proper construction with water and accessories, may be taken at about 40 tons; and the greater part of this weight would be imposed on the comparatively slender columns under the Eastern side of the Transept Roof, on the slight shafts of the North window, and on the North West angle of the Transept which is perforated by a staircase well – I should mention that the inside wall of this Staircase upon which the weight must necessarily come, is merely a shell; and is the more likely to fail under additional pressure from the circumstance, that the external buttresses connected with it are of comparatively massive construction, but cannot assist in sustaining the weight of the Tanks. - Although I did not discover any indications of failure in the masonry at the points above referred to, yet on full and careful consideration I beg to recommend, that no such additional weight be imposed upon them, as it is impossible to tell with certainty the effect that such loading may have upon the parts of the building referred to, which have never been intended to carry extraneous weight'.[24]

Sheilds had also written at the same time to Crossley Bros of Manchester (who were makers of gas engines) and by ill (or good) luck, Henry was in their offices when that letter arrived. Henry was not pleased, and wrote to Francis on 11 July 1877:

'I was in the north making my arrangement for the rapid execution of this work when my people in London informed me of Mr Sheilds' obstruction and singularly enough I was in Crossleys office on Saturday morning when Mr Sheilds' letter to them arrived. It began. "I have a work on hand" – and then proceeded to ask questions as to the merits of the gas engine and as to whether it would or could be depended upon to move water to a considerable height (It did not state what height). I had been over that ground several months ago & had made myself sure of its capabilities before I recommended it to you. My feeling when I read that letter was an inclination to throw up the whole matter. This morning I have your letter which still leaves me in doubt how to act. I quite understand the policy and propriety of getting an official sanction of some ancient authority to permit my plan to be carried out but from two interviews I have had with Mr Sheilds I find myself in contact with a man for whose abilities I have no respect. To me his attitude appeared to be obstructive from the first … I fear that Sheilds will recommend an elaborate expensive very heavy and cumbersome system of iron girders that will be worse than useless save that they will of course carry the water. He no doubt wishes to have more than one finger in the pie and will cost you large sums quite unnecessarily if you let him … I hope to be able to shew frivolity of Mr Sheilds objection and that it arises from timidity and not from scientific reasons'.[25]

On 25 July 1877 Henry wrote again to Francis:

'I think that you will find my advice the soundest … You know my opinion of [Sheilds] … & his prejudices. I think his advice absurd. He uses his influence to frighten you. I am thinking of something else for you & you may be sure that the blowing of that organ I have very much at heart. Gas direct is impossible … without noise. My next plan will be something that will not require an appeal to Mr Sheilds. Wait for it.[26]

After a period of silence, Julia wrote to Francis on 27 August 1877:

'I was on the point of writing to you to know what progress was being made towards making a satisfactory use of the organ. At present it is almost useless, being only fully available on Sundays … I have only heard it once, & then by special arrangement, and such a result is to me, at least, & to most others, very disappointing. I hoped there would have been an opening of it on a fitting scale this year, but that seems as far off as ever. I thought you had long since given up the idea of water being supplied from the reservoir but intended to have yr own supply, & that I am credibly informed would have been a matter of no difficulty, as you are surrounded by water in Salisbury; storing it is another affair. I have heard the water power was mismanaged at York but that proved nothing against it, very many organs are blown by it. However it does not matter how the necessary power is obtained, so long as it is forthcoming, for human machinery cannot do it, & when you have the gas engine at work I shall certainly like to see it'.[27]

Henry persisted with his objection to a gas engine other than to raise water from the ground tanks to others on the walls possibly by a gas engine inside the building. Disagreement between Henry and Crossleys about the use of a gas engine continued throughout that autumn, with one or two revealing comments by Crossleys about the eminent organ builder. On 18 October 1877 Crossleys wrote to Canon Sanctuary:

'We think it [Henry's plan for a gas engine inside the building] would do perfectly well, but if it turned out otherwise it would doubtless be unpleasant for the Chapter to have to say so to Mr Willis, & on this ground we advise Mr Willis excellent alternative. (We wd also much rather have Mr. Willis as an ally than an opponent!).'[28]

So, as 1877 drew towards its end, no resolution seemed probable. However, Henry held his high reputation for good reason. On 11 December 1877 he wrote (we hope to Francis as he deserved to be the first to know):

> 'I think that you will be pleased to hear that I have discovered means to blow the Salisbury Organ most satisfactorily by Gas and air pumps that can now be governed to the greater nicety. This apparatus is of the most durable kind so that once done its primary parts will last for ever almost. The means are novel & extraordinary and I have thought it wise to protect the invention & within a week from this time I shall have all the details for your consideration. Its cost will I think be below what we had calculated for the water engines, pipes, &c &c. Supposing that we can rely upon the Gas engine (there will be but one) doing its work I shall be willing to take all responsibility as I did before and as I shall be Patentee I must be also the contractor and deal with Crossleys firm on your behalf. Please let me know if I may act in this way for you and I will lose not one moment in carrying it out to the end'.[29]

So, all of a sudden, the apparently insoluble was resolved. The organ was completed and Julia appeared placated as well. Its first official outing was on All Saints Day 1878, evidently to a rapturous reception. However, joy at such a satisfactory resolution may not have been fully shared by George Kellow as on 27 September 1878, the Chapter resolved that:

> 'The Cathedral Organ being now blown by means of a Gas Engine and consequently the services of George Kellow the Organ Blower being no longer required It was resolved to make him a gratuity of £20 in consideration of his long and faithful service, and the Chapter Clerk was directed to inform him thereof and that his services were no longer required'.[30]

There is no gain without pain.

Notes

1 The transcriptions were undertaken by six volunteers: Caroline Burrows, Donna McBride, Moura MacDonagh, Penny Peat, Susan Turner, and Alan Willis.
2 Lear, Francis, Mar 1914, obituary, Salisbury Diocesan Gazette, 56-57
3 This organ was given in 1877 to St Thomas' Church Salisbury where, subject to current restoration, it is still in use.
4 Cooke, W A, 1810, *Topographical and statistical description of the county of Wilts,* London
5 Milner, Rev John, 1811, *A dissertation on the modern style of altering antient cathedrals as exemplified in the Cathedral of Salisbury*, London
6 Salisbury Cathedral Archive Scott papers bundle 2
7 Ibid, item 19
8 Ibid, item 21
9 Ibid, item 20

10   Ibid, item 22
11   Ibid, 2 item 24
12   Ibid, item 28
13   Ibid, item 18
14   Ibid, item 5
15   Ibid, items 2 & 37
16   Ibid, item 0/2
17   Ibid, item 46 & 47
18   Ibid, item 27
19   Ibid, item 48 & 4
20   Ibid, item 44
21   Ibid, item 26
22   Ibid, item 43
23   Salisbury Cathedral Archive CH/1/26 Chapter minutes 26 Feb 1877
24   Salisbury Cathedral Archive Scott papers bundle 2 item 42
25   Ibid, item 43
26   Ibid, item 57 & 58
27   Ibid, item 56
28   Ibid, item 74 & 75
29   Ibid, item 0/1
30   Salisbury Cathedral Archive CH/1/27 Chapter minutes 27 Sep 1878

Summary of various depositories of Cathedral property
from 1 Sept. 39 to July 20. 42.   42

Glass
Rose Window   Wiveliscombe
3 lights XIII cent. glass from S.E. Transept   "
2   "   "   "   "   "from W. end of Nave aisle   Bishop's Palace
2   "   "   "   "   "   "   "   "   Wiveliscombe
Heraldic panels from great W. window   Lloyds Bank, Sarum
3 lights from N.E. end of Choir aisle   Brit. Museum Repository
2½ "   "   "   S.E "   "   "   "   "   "   "

Charters
MAGNA CARTA   "   "   "

King Stephen, 1137   Registry Strong Room

MSS
renumbered vols
in Libr. Catalogue
1880.
1. 38. 103. 132. 148. 149. 150. 157. 158. 175. 180 ⎫
23. 27. 37. 52. 53. 80. 96. 101. 153. 179. 187   ⎬ 32. B. M. Repository
82. 85. 105. 112. 113. 117. 133. 162. 172. 173   ⎭

17. 22. 48. 76. 78. 126. 152. 182. 184   Registry Strong Rm.

All the remaining renumbered MSS vols.   Wiveliscombe

Other MSS
~~Printed Books~~
2 MSS dealing w. Canonis'n of S. Osmund   B. M. Repository
Sir Chr. Wren's autograph MS on work for Cath.!   "
Printed bk T. 2. 48, Browne's Pastorals (3rd Bk in MS)   "
Liber Evidence. C.   Registry Strong Rm
Constitutions & other Kalendars ⎫ Registry   "   "
Bk of 7 Sermons in MS by Gilb Ward / Arch d. of Ayrault 1748–50 ⎫ Wiveliscombe
Sarum Doceway MS by Ja. Walton / Fabric Yc 1529–43 copy/ from r Prince ⎬
                                                    ? Reg 1673?/   Rg 1673?/

Printed Books (1)
Incunabula Caxton, Legenda Aurea 1493 ?   B. M. Repository
Wynkyn de Worde, Horae 149– ?   "   "   "
28 other Incunabula   Wiveliscombe

(2) Other Books: 122 + 38 = 160 . . . .   "
T. Bright Characterie 1588, Map & Descr'n of Virginia by W.S. 1612 ⎫ B M Repository
Js. Walton's copy of Donne's Sermons & Life of Donne ⎭

Muniments
Nearly the whole of the ancient charters etc from   Wiveliscombe
Muniment. Rm., packed in 43 cardboard boxes

Muniments &
Miscellaneous items
1 Tin box, 1 Wooden box   Westminster Bank, Sarum

Seals and
Sealed documents
17 metal seals   Registry Strong Rm.
9 sealed documents 1285–1454   "   "   "
facsimile of K. John's seal.   "   "   "

Effigies
Wm. Longespée The Elder & Bp. Mitford   St Andrews.

Effigies
Plate etc.
2 wooden chests containing Plate, Chapter ⎫ Registry Strong Rm
Act books, Baldwyn chasuble & other objects ⎭

ALSO
property of
5 Tapestries   ● Registry Strong Rm

Saving the Cathedral Treasures in the Second World War

Emily Naish

Throughout the history of mankind where there has been armed conflict and violence, so too has there been the destruction of cultural heritage, either deliberate or accidental. During the Second World War in order to protect the fabric of Salisbury Cathedral volunteer firewatchers nightly patrolled the cathedral floor, roofs and grounds. Meanwhile, the Cathedral contents, the treasures accumulated over many centuries, particularly the Cathedral's ancient books and documents but also silverware, tombs and many other precious articles were, from the very outset of war, sent away to places of safety and secrecy. In the end Salisbury Cathedral escaped very lightly from enemy damage. Salisbury was not targeted in the Nazi's Baedeker raids from late April to early June 1942 as Exeter Cathedral, Lincoln Cathedral and Bath Abbey were. Of course, this could not have been foreseen by the Cathedral authorities when news reached them of Hitler's invasion of Poland on 1st September 1939 and two days later, on 3rd September, Britain's declaration of war on Germany.

On 6th September 1939 the Cathedral chapter met. The impending war must have been foremost in their minds. At this meeting it was reported that steps had already been taken to safeguard some of the Cathedral's treasures from possible enemy action. They had been removed, presumably from the cathedral library, muniment room and vestry, and deposited in the Diocesan Registrar's strong room for safe custody.[1] A list of the items, signed by the Canon Treasurer Robert Quirk, was pasted into the chapter minute book and dated 1st September 1939.[2] (Fig 1) This list included: three sets of silver candlesticks, Magna Carta, sixteen chapter minute books dating from 1329 to 1599, two 15th century volumes concerning the canonisation of Bishop Osmund, twelve of the library's

Opposite: Fig 1: A sample of Canon Quirk's meticulous notes recorded in the Chapter Minutes. (*Roy Bexon*)

Fig 2: Wiveliscombe Church: entrance to the catacombs (*Emily Naish*)

manuscript books (including a 15th century text in Middle English known as *Jacob's Well* and the 10th century *Salisbury Psalter*), *Liber C* (a 13th century cartulary containing a contemporary copy of Magna Carta), Sir Christopher Wren's 1688 report upon the state of the fabric of the building, and the Baldwyn Chasuble. Further deposits quickly followed over the coming days: the head section of the silver processional cross, an 1136 charter of King Stephen, chalices, five tapestries on loan to the Cathedral from Sir William Burrell, and a short piece of a wire noose purportedly used to execute Lord Stourton in 1557.

Before their removal from the Cathedral they were packed in 'plain rough wooden boxes (locked) made by our workmen.'[3] Full details of the items were meticulously recorded in the Chapter minute books by Canon Quirk who as well as Canon Treasurer would also shortly be appointed Canon Librarian and thus coordinate the evacuation and storage of all the Cathedral treasures throughout 1939-1944.[4] Canon Quirk made two further copies of these lists: one copy he kept for himself, the other was deposited at the Salisbury branch of the Westminster Bank. Several months passed with no further reference to the safeguarding of 'treasures' in the Chapter minutes until a meeting on 5th June 1940 when it was recorded (and another list by Canon Quirk pasted in) that a further nine library manuscript books were deposited in the Registrar's strong room and 20 deposited in the Chapter Clerk's strong room.

The Chapter Clerk's and the Diocesan Registrar's strong rooms were not permanent solutions. The Cathedral authorities must have been aware that although moving books and documents out of the Cathedral itself would protect them from a direct hit on the Cathedral they were not far enough away to guarantee their safety. What was needed was offsite storage. Thus at the Chapter meeting on 5th June 1940 Canon Quirk reported that he was making enquiries to deposit books at Oxford or Aberystwyth.[5] These particular enquires must have come to nothing as at the next Chapter meeting on the 3rd July 1940 he reported that 'he was forwarding two cases of manuscripts and printed books to Dr Eeles at Wiveliscombe for safe custody'[6] and attached to the minutes is, as usual, Canon Quirk's detailed list (five pages) of 223 manuscript and printed books which on 3rd July 1940 had been deposited at St Andrew's Church, Wiveliscombe, Somerset. (Figs 2 & 3) A note accompanies the list:

> 'The above, packed in 2 strong wooden boxes (one screwed down, one locked, both secured with strong wire binding secured by staples) both sealed by me were deposited by me on 3 July 1940 at the house of Willoughby Hancock Esq, Wiveliscombe, Somerset, for transfer to the vaults of the parish church, as suggested by Dr Eeles of the Central Committee [later Council] for the Care of Churches and sanctioned by the Chapter at the meeting of July 3 1940.'[7]

Canon Quirk describes the vaults, or catacombs as they are also called, as 'excellent' and 'admirable in every way.'[8]

The Council for the Care of Churches was formed in 1927 to co-ordinate and assist the work of Diocesan Advisory Committees (DACs) which advise chancellors and bishops on artistic and archaeological matters and proposed works on church buildings. At the outbreak of war Dr Francis Carolus Eeles, the Council's secretary, was looking for safe places to store valuables belonging to churches and cathedrals. Several suitable venues were eventually identified but having moved to Somerset in 1938, Dr Eeles already knew about the Wiveliscombe catacombs and quickly decided that, with a little alteration, they would be ideal for his

Fig 3: Wiveliscombe Church: the catacombs where many of the cathedral's treasures were stored (*Emily Naish*)

purpose. These catacombs would prove to be by far the most heavily used of all the Council's storage locations. An advertisement in *The Times* encouraged clergy and churchwardens to take advantage of the Council's arrangements, although secrecy of the actual locations was understandably paramount:

> 'The Central Council for the Care of Churches has at its disposal for this purpose some excellent accommodation, not all in one place, in as safe an area as exists at present time. It would not be in the public interest to disclose the actual whereabouts of the storage places.'[9]

The present church of St Andrews, Wiveliscombe is relatively recent, having been built between 1827 and 1829 on the site of an earlier church dating back to at least the late 12th century. This earlier church was demolished when it was discovered that the pillars were out of the perpendicular and the tower was seriously cracked and oscillated when the bells were rung. The parish decided not only to rebuild the church but also to construct extensive catacombs beneath the church to accommodate 36 vaults. Families could apply for the use of a vault and initially 18 were allocated on payment of a minimum fee of £20. These 18 vaults have, since 1827, been used to a greater or lesser degree but only two today are full and bricked up.[10] No internments have taken place since 1926 and the vaults are now mainly used for storage with two of the front vaults acting as a meeting room, children's play area, kitchen and toilet.

F Hancock in his history of Wiveliscombe published in 1911 describes his memories of the catacombs:

> '[I] well remember as a child, and once indeed in later years, entombments in
> these dreary resting places – the descent from the sunlight into the damp vaults
> where the darkness was but just made visible by a few flickering lights and the
> placing of the coffin on the committal, on the shelf awaiting it.'[11]

Having visited the church and catacombs myself in recent years I can confirm that they are still very much used for storage and are still dark, damp and a little dreary.[12] If you visit the tea rooms in Wiveliscombe today you can, I am told, buy a t-shirt bearing the words 'Where in the World is Wiveliscombe?' This was supposedly Winston Churchill's response when told about the role that this small town had played in safeguarding the nation's treasures.

The Cathedral's deposit in the catacombs on 3 July 1940 was only the first of several: so how much from Salisbury eventually came here? Throughout the remainder of 1940 and 1941 further books from the library and archive documents usually kept in the muniment room were deposited. In July 1940 Canon Quirk asked Dr Eeles whether there was room for two large wardrobes and two large book cases followed by a request for space for four further large wardrobes in December 1941.[13] In total the Wiveliscombe catacombs held: the Jesse Window (first stored temporarily in the Bishop's Palace at Salisbury), three packing cases of 13th century grisaille glass from the South East transept,[14] nearly all the library manuscript books (around 180 volumes), all 30 incunabula books published before 1501, 24 books originally belonging to Izaak Walton, author of *The Compleat Angler*, nearly 100 other printed books, and about 80% of the charters and documents from the muniment room together with all the seal matrices.

The catacombs therefore were rapidly filling up, but they were not only used by Salisbury Cathedral although Salisbury does seem to have deposited the largest quantity of material (around 20 packing cases); the next highest deposit was three cases from Exeter Cathedral. Deposits made by other organisations included: the great 15th century east window of St Peter Mancroft in Norwich, records and documents from the City of London Guildhall, the 8th century Gospel of St Chad from Lichfield Cathedral, the entire library of the French Protestant Church in London, and the Tangier plate and model of the Mary Rose from Portsmouth Cathedral.[15]

Despite extensive records about the use of the catacombs in the archives of the Council for the Care of Churches and in Salisbury Cathedral archives the Wiveliscombe Church's own records, now held at the Dorset History Centre, are nearly completely silent. There is one reference at the beginning of the war:

'It was agreed that Mr Willoughly Hancock together with the vicar and churchwardens be empowered to dispose of the junk accumulated in the catacombs.'[16]

Presumably this was in preparation for the new arrivals. There is only one further reference which comes at the end of the war:

'A letter of thanks and appreciation was read by The Vicar for the safe custody

Fig 4: One of the library MS books – the 10th century *Salisbury Psalter (Ash Mills)*

of valuable church glass and properties which had been stored in the catacombs during the period of the war.'[17]

Fears that the parish records could have fallen into enemy hands is undoubtedly the reason for this lack of written information.

Although by far the largest, Wiveliscombe was not the only storage location for the Salisbury treasures. Alongside the books, archives and glass[18] there was also considerable concern for the tombs and monuments. Advice was sought from The Society for the Protection of Ancient Buildings (SPAB). The Dean visited Winchester Cathedral to ascertain what steps they were taking. After discussion at a Chapter meeting on 5th November 1941 'it was decided not to carry out the elaborate scheme suggested by the secretary of the Society for the Protection of Ancient Monuments but to endeavor to make arrangements for the temporary removal to a place of safety of the tombs of [William] Longespée and Bishop Mitford and for the 'building in' of the tombs of Bishops Jocelyn and Roger and the Earl of Salisbury at the West End.'[19] What the SPAB's scheme was is not recorded. So, the tombs of William Longespée the elder and Bishop Mitford were sent to, and stored at, St Audries' School (West Quantoxhead, Somerset) in January 1942.[20] The tombs of Bishop Roger, Bishop Jocelin, the boy bishop and William Longespée the younger (previously referred to as the Earl of Salisbury) were protected by 'walls of breeze blocks and covered with sand'.[21]

The 'crown jewels' of the library and archive treasures were destined, not for Wiveliscombe, but for the British Museum. An entry in the Chapter minutes on 6th May 1942 reads 'Authority was given to the treasurer to take Magna Carta from the strong room in the Chapter Clerk's office in order to deposit it with the Keeper of Manuscripts of the British Museum for safe custody during the present emergency.' Following this meeting Canon Quirk duly delivered Magna Carta to the British Museum on 21st May 1942, and its receipt survives.[22] A further receipt dated 11th July 1942 confirms deposit of all the items eventually given into the care of the British Museum namely: four cases (not opened) containing stained glass, Magna Carta, 36 manuscript books, five printed books (three in a sealed packet), and a report and plan with drawings. Canon Quirk's summary on the opposite pages gives further details as to what these items were. The stained glass was five and a half windows from the choir aisles. The 36 manuscript books included: MS 150 the 10th century psalter, (Fig 4) two manuscripts concerning the canonisation of Saint Osmund, and Sir Christopher Wren's report. A second receipt records a subsequent deposit on 25 August 1942 which included the 13th century Liber C and 29 printed books.[23] Essentially these were the items which had been deposited in the Diocesan Registrar's strong room for safe custody at the very beginning of the War.

Bradford on Avon Museum

Fig 5: Westwood Quarry, Bradford on Avon where Magna Carta was stored (*Bradford on Avon Museum*)

But where was this British Museum repository? It was actually part of Westwood Quarry in Bradford upon Avon, Wiltshire. (Fig 5) The quarry had been worked from at least the 15th century, if not earlier, with small scale quarrying continuing through the nineteenth and twentieth centuries. In the 1930s areas were used for growing mushrooms. In the 1940s Royal Enfield motorcycles used one part of the quarry as an underground factory for war work making anti-aircraft predictors. At the same time the quarry was also used for storage of items from national museums in an area separate to the rest of the quarry extending perhaps to some 20,000 square foot. Air conditioning was installed to create a consistent temperature and humidity, as well as one of the first ever smoke detectors, and two large safe doors were requisitioned from a London bank.[24]

So, in the Wiveliscombe catacombs, Westwood Quarry and St Audries' School the Cathedral treasures waited undisturbed and in safety until the end of the war when the task of reclaiming and returning them began.

As the departure of the treasures was coordinated by Canon Quirk so was their return. The effigies of William Lonespée the elder and Bishop Mitford at St Audries' School were the first to be reinstated on 6th June 1945 closely followed by the return of Magna Carta on 25th July 1945. Canon Quirk recorded the moment he collected Magna Carta:

> 'Magna Carta Returns: An official led us into a rock hewn tunnel floored with cement and lit by electric light. "Above our heads," he said, "is a rock 80 feet thick." We followed him 250 paces into the heart of the hill. At last we came to doors opening into a great chamber. It was cool, clean and dry in there: the rushing sound in our ears was air poured in to keep a constant temperature of 63 degrees Fahr. "What are those blue lights?" asked my friend. "Ah!" he replied, "we are taking no chances with what we have here. In the event of fire, smoke would rise and interrupt the beam between those two lights, causing a bell to ring in the control room." We looked around us. As far as the eye could see were shelves arranged in bays left and right, and on the shelves innumerable cases. "We may take ours?" I said. In reply he took us aside into a small room and used as an office, and sat down to write. My eye caught some Greek words cut in the rock, which in English might run: – "Fearing a sudden stroke from heaven above, I hastened hither to the gods below." Scarcely had I taken this in when he handed me a form to sign. I signed the form he gave me and took my deposit. It was Magna Carta.'[25]

The storage conditions in the Wiveliscombe catacombs did not prove to be quite so ideal as those experienced by Magna Carta in Westwood Quarry. Canon Quirk made meticulous notes of each document, manuscript, and printed book as they were unpacked in the Cathedral plummery from the crates newly arrived from Wiveliscombe.[26] Unfortunately, some manuscripts were, on their return, discovered to be suffering from damp. This was a considerable blow to Canon Quirk who had taken such pains with their well-being. On 31st August 1945 he wrote to Dr Eeles at the Council for the Care of Churches:

> 'I unpacked S2 *[the reference number of one of the crates]* this morning. Most of the manuscript vols appear to be all right but the bottom layer has suffered from damp. This is grievous, but I don't see that it could be helped. The cases were drilled with many ventilation holes, and this seems to have saved the upper strata. We have Hitler to thank for the damage.'[27]

In retrospect the manuscripts condition could have been a lot worse as in 1947 a sewer adjacent to Wiveliscombe church burst and flooded the catacombs to a depth of up to eight inches.[28]

Steps were quickly taken to dry out the manuscripts and to repair any damage:

> 'Fortunately, the end of August and the beginning of September 1945 it was warm and sunny. Trestle tables and planks were set out in the open, the manuscripts and books stood on these. It meant someone must watch all the time, and the whole day we took it in turns, gradually turning each folio or

page until it was dry. This went on for a week until the books were ready to carry into the Library. Here they were placed open on tables and on the presses. Canon Quirk consulted the [Public] Record Office as to the best means of treating the manuscripts. Some were sent there for expert repairs. When we knew how to clean the vellum volunteers from the students of the Training College met in the Choir Vestry in the afternoon of the Autumn Term and cleaned the manuscripts so that by Christmas they were back once more in their original home."[29]

So happily all the books, documents, stained glass and tombs which had been sent away for safe keeping returned safely with Dean Henry Robins declaring in 1946 'We have rescued our treasures from incarceration in places of safety.'[30] To a large extent the treasures owe their survival to the dedication of Canon Quirk. Today, alongside the ongoing repair and maintenance on the fabric of its 800 year old building, Salisbury Cathedral continues to preserve the books, documents and objects in its care, endeavouring to ensure their survival for generations to use and enjoy for another 800 years.

Notes

1   Salisbury Cathedral Archives (SCA), CH/1/34, 285. The offices of the administration of the diocese (separate to the administrative offices of the Cathedral itself) were, in 1939, located at 6 The Close – now known as the Chapter Office.
2   SCA, CH/1/34, 288
3   SCA, CH/1/34, 290
4   Canon Fletcher the previous canon librarian died on 23 February 1940. Canon Quirk was appointed librarian in his place at a chapter meeting on 6 March 1940. Canon Quirk also became captain of the Cathedral Close firefighting service: 'Many a long "Alert" period did he spend night after night in either patrolling the Close and his beloved Cathedral or at the Post.' SCA ,LA/5/2/1, 84. He also deputised for the Cathedral organist.
5   SCA, CH/1/34, 330
6   SCA, CH/1/34, 335
7   SCA, CH/1/34, 336 insert
8   Church of England Record Centre (CERC), CARE/WARSV/3 Letter from Canon Quirk to Dr Eeles 3 July 1940
9   Council for the Care of Churches form: 'Emergency Storage of Valuables from Churches', SCA, CH/1/34, 339-340 insert
10 Farrington, Susan Maria 2001, *Sancti Stones Parish Memorials of Wiveliscombe Somerset*, Colden Publications, 41
11 Hancock, F, 1911, *Wifela's Combe: a History of the Parish of Wiveliscombe*, The Wessex Press
12 My thanks to the Wiveliscombe churchwardens for facilitating my visit to the catacombs and particularly to Susan Farrington for her assistance with my research.

13 CERC, CARE/WARSV/ 3 Letters from Canon Quirk to Dr Eeles 11 July 1940 and 16 December 1941

14 CERC, CARE/WARSV/3 Letter from Canon Quirk to Dr Eeles 17 August 1940

15 Commemorative plaque at one time displayed in Wiveliscombe Church and reproduced in Farrington, Susan Maria 2001, *Sancti Stones Parish Memorials of Wiveliscombe Somerset*, Colden Publications, 25.

16 Somerset Record Office.

17 Somerset Record Office.

18 In addition to the glass already mentioned other glass removed was from the West Window (3 December 1941) and the north and south choir aisles (3 June 1942), SCA, CH/1/34, 403 and 419

19 SCA, CH/1/34, 400

20 SCA, LA/5/2/7. See also Stafford, Duncan, 2006, *The Book of St Audries & West Quantoxhead*, 50-51.

21 SCA, LA/5/2/1, 6

22 SCA, CH/1/34, 416

23 SCA, CH/1/34, 424 and 427

24 https://history.wiltshire.gov.uk/community/getfaq.php?id=163, accessed Jan 2019

25 Friends of Salisbury Cathedral, 1946, Annual Report, 6-7

26 SCA, LA/5/2/1, 6-60

27 CARE/WARSV/3 Letter from Canon Quirk to Dr Eeles 31 August 1945

28 CARE/WARSV/12 Letter to R Granville Harris 17 July 1947

29 SCA, LA/5/2/1, Dr Elsie Smith's tribute to Canon Quirk, March 1949

30 Friends of Salisbury Cathedral, 1946, Annual Report, 3

Writers Inspired: Salisbury Cathedral's Literary Heritage

'They tell us here long stories of the great art us'd in laying the first foundations of this church' (Defoe)[1]

Linda B Jones

While the connections between authors and the city of Salisbury have been well-documented, this chapter seeks to explore those links which draw together writers and specifically Salisbury Cathedral in this, its 800th anniversary year. Cathedrals have shared a relationship with prose writers and poets alike for centuries, sometimes as background for a novelistic setting; a central motif in poetry; or as the main influence on works of fiction. Salisbury Cathedral with its magnificent towering spire is no exception and has long served as both a source of inspiration and a symbol of the pinnacle of literary achievement. It is not possible to cover here the extensive range of writers associated with such an ancient cathedral, so this article is necessarily selective.

Novelists

Salisbury Cathedral has provided an impressively atmospheric setting for a number of novels. The earliest of these is Charles Dickens' *Martin Chuzzlewit*, in which architecture plays a prominent role. Dickens' novel is a satirical attack on greed and selfishness, featuring the villainous Seth Pecksniff as an architect who had 'never designed or built anything.'[2] Rather, it is his exploited pupils who are engaged in drawing 'elevations of Salisbury Cathedral from every possible point

Fig 1: Tom Pinch playing the organ, *Martin Chuzzlewit* (1844), illustration by Hablot Knight Browne ('Phiz')

of sight'. Dickens makes use of the pathetic fallacy in setting the scene here as his narrator describes:

> The vane upon the tapering spire of the old church glistened from its lofty station in sympathy with the general gladness; and from the ivy-shaded windows such gleams of light shone back upon the glowing sky.

However, autumn suddenly turns to winter as the sun sets and 'the shining church turned cold and dark'. In this shifting depiction, Dickens effectively conflates mood and cathedral. Later in this novel, Dickens highlights the emotional impact of both the Cathedral's architecture and its music. Mr Pecksniff suggests to Jonas that he show his disreputable friend, Mr Montague, around:

> Salisbury Cathedral . . . is an edifice replete with venerable associations, and strikingly suggestive of the loftiest emotions. It is here we contemplate the work of bygone ages. It is here we listen to the swelling organ, as we stroll through the reverberating aisles.[3]

It is not known whether Dickens actually visited the Cathedral, but he travelled extensively around the West Country and must surely have been inspired in writing *Martin Chuzzlewit* by a view of the city. (Fig 1) However, there is a record of Dickens staying in Salisbury later in 1848, lodging at the White Hart from where he wrote to his wife as follows:

> My Dearest Kate,
> I have just time to say that we have been out on the Plain on horseback, all day – the greater part of it at full gallop . . .[4]

Another writer influenced by Salisbury Cathedral is Anthony Trollope, whose 1855 novel The *Warden* is the trajectory for the whole series entitled the *Chronicles of Barsetshire*. In this, Salisbury is re-configured as Barchester. Trollope's inspiration arose from a visit he made to Salisbury in 1852, as he records in his Autobiography: 'whilst wandering there one mid-summer evening round the purlieus of the cathedral I conceived the story of *The Warden* – from whence came that series of novels of which Barchester, with its bishops, deans, and archdeacon, was the central site.'[5] A copy of *Barchester Towers* was notably sent by Thomas Hardy to his sister, Mary, in October 1865, with the recommendation that it was 'considered the best of Trollope's [novels].'[6]

Thomas Hardy also re-creates Salisbury when he uses it as the background for several of his novels, renaming it 'Melchester' in his fictional Wessex. A detailed account of Hardy's connections with the city of Salisbury as a whole has been provided by Hugh Thomas in an earlier edition of *Sarum Chronicle*.[7] More specifically, the Cathedral itself features in at least two of Hardy's novels, *Jude the Obscure* and *The Hand of Ethelberta*. In *Jude,* the eponymous hero manages to find work on the restoration of the Cathedral which, as Hugh Thomas points out, would have been that carried out in the 19th century under George Gilbert Scott. As the son and grandson of stone-masons and having trained as an architect, Thomas Hardy had himself made a study of the Cathedral when aged 20. (Fig 2)

Like Dickens, Hardy also makes use of the Cathedral's organ as a novelistic device. In *The Hand of Ethelberta*, Lord Mountclere invites the heroine to 'a morning instrumental concert at Melchester'.[8] On arrival there, he points out the Cathedral and tells Ethelberta that 'it boasts of a very fine organ', although it is not clear which organ Hardy had in mind (if any). As this novel was first published in 1875 in the *Cornhill Magazine* as monthly instalments, this just predates the Henry Willis instrument which has graced the organ loft in the cathedral since 1877. Hardy describes Ethelberta's entry to the cathedral's nave in terms which meld the sound of the organ with her feelings for the organist, Christopher Julian:

> peals broke forth from the organ on the black oaken mass at the junction of nave and choir, shaking every cobweb in the dusky vaults, and Ethelberta's heart no less . . . before quite leaving the building Ethelberta cast one other glance towards the organ and thought of him behind it.

Following this, the head blower presents a humorous picture of Julian's performance on the stops:

Fig 2: Thomas Hardy's drawing of the nave, *Wessex Poems* 1898

When 'tis hot summer weather there's nothing will do for him but Choir, Great, and Swell altogether, till yer face is in a vapour; and on a frosty winter night he'll keep me there while he tweedles upon the Twelfth and Sixteenth.[9]

In *Jude,* Hardy alludes to a composer encountered by the eponymous hero, who 'once tried to get the Cathedral organ when the post was vacant'.[10] At the time of Hardy writing this text, the Henry Willis organ was installed, which would have been most prestigious to play.

In a lesser known work of Hardy's, *On the Western Circuit*, the protagonist sees Salisbury Cathedral as 'the most homogeneous pile of mediaeval architecture in England, which towered and tapered from the damp and level sward in front of him.'[11] Presumably, he is referring to the integrity of its Early English Gothic style of architecture. The portrayal by Jude Fawley is rather more favourable when he describes his arrival in the Close at 'Melchester':

> The day was foggy, and standing under the walls of the most graceful architectural pile in England he paused and looked up. The lofty building was visible as far as the roof-ridge; above, the dwindling spire rose more and more remotely, till its apex was quite lost in the mist drifting across it.[12]

This atmospheric description by a fictional narrator closely mirrors Hardy's own personal view when visiting Salisbury, in which he refers to 'its graceful cathedral pile'.[13]

It is the soaring spire above all which has attracted novelists and poets as it symbolically reaches up to the heavens. As that prolific 18th century writer Daniel Defoe admiringly writes in one of his letters, 'The cathedral is famous for the height of its spire, which is without exception the highest, and the handsomest in England, being from the ground 410 foot'.[14] Defoe goes on to refer to the survey conducted by Sir Christopher Wren following which 'a consultation was had, whether the spire, or at least the upper part of it should be taken down'. Thankfully, Wren decided against such drastic measures. It is not only the spire which attracts Defoe's notice, as he continues by declaring that 'The cloyster (*sic*), and the chapter-house adjoyning (*sic*) to the church, are the finest here of any I have seen in England'. Further praise accorded to the Cathedral's spire stems from another 18th century writer, Henry Fielding. Probably best-known for his picaresque novel *The History of Tom Jones* – some of which was notably written while he was living in the Close – Fielding praised the height of the spire in poetic mode:

> Sarum, thy Candidates be nam'd,
> Sarum, for Beauties ever fam'd,
> Whose Nymphs excel all beauty's flowers,
> As thy high Steeple doth all Towers[15]

Fig 3: Portrait of William Lisle Bowles, Salisbury Cathedral library, artist unknown. (*Roy Bexon*)

These lines were created in an attempt to woo Charlotte Craddock, whom Fielding went on to marry and reside within the Close.

The spire is itself the subject of, and inspiration for, William Golding's novel of the same name, published in 1964. Interestingly the original title for this was *Barchester Spire,* a tribute to Anthony Trollope's work. *The Spire* is a rather disturbing tale, the plot of which centres on the building of this feature as an addition to a medieval cathedral. Notably, Golding was teaching at Bishop Wordsworth's School (founded by the great-nephew of the Romantic poet) between 1945 and 1961, during which period the top of the spire was being restored. Golding himself called Salisbury's spire 'a perpetual delight, a perpetual wonder, with the whole of our little body politic shrugged into shape about it'.[16]

Although as critics have pointed out Salisbury Cathedral is not named as such in this novel, there are clear indications that it is the basis for this story. For example, the fictional Dean Jocelin's model is said to be 'a construction of wood and stone and metal . . . Four hundred feet high'.[17] This is close enough to Salisbury's 404 foot towering spire to endorse this idea. Moreover, the reference to the 'great bell in the detached belltower' may be an allusion to Salisbury's separate campanile which was demolished under Sir James Wyatt in the 18th century. Finally, the Cathedral bears several 'corkscrew stairs' which recur frequently in Golding's text. Notably, both 'spire' and 'spiral' are rendered by the Latin 'spira'.

Golding's novel functions on (at least) two levels. Firstly, it recounts in fictional form the *literal* building of the Spire in the thirteenth century. The tale is also *metaphorical* since the 'spire' signifies many aspects. For instance, it operates as a symbol of the human condition whereby 'Life itself is a rickety building'[18] as well as representing a 'stone ship'.[19] *The Spire* is both a testimony to, and warning against, man's hubris: as the protagonist Dean Jocelin claims, his project is 'a monstrous pride'.[20] Icarus-like, Golding's dean aims too high, and his ultimate fall is not only psychological – a *descent* into madness ('you have to be crazy to build as high as this')[21] – but literal as he ultimately falls onto the floor stones. The Cathedral, in contrast, is denoted as 'sane'.

The central tropes which play out the tragedy in this text are the binary oppositions of joy (Jocelin) and pain (Pangall); while oxymorons such as 'painful happiness' abound. The building of the spire is referred to as 'Jocelin's Folly', the ambiguity in this phrase underscoring both its ornamental function and the perceived foolishness of the dean's aspiration. Appropriately, one of Golding's several metaphors illustrates the connections between literature and the Cathedral: 'inside it was a richly written book to instruct [praying] man'.[22]

In 2012, Golding's novel was given dramatic representation when it was spectacularly performed on stage at the Salisbury Playhouse, adapted by Roger Spottiswoode in a production by the Artistic Director, Gareth Machin. One reviewer commented that the design of this adaptation 'not only evokes the monumentality of the cathedral, but also, through ropes, pulleys and capstones, shows it as a vertical building site'.[23]

Poets

Poets too have voiced their admiration for the building of Salisbury Cathedral. Almost certainly the earliest poet to do so is Henry d'Avranches (died 1260). In his 13th century Latin poem *De Translatione Veteris Ecclesie Saresberiensis et Constructione Nove*, d'Avranches identifies several reasons for the population leaving Old Sarum and for its move to the new location.[24] He depicts this place on the one hand as resembling a Garden of Paradise, using such Biblical phrases as 'the hind was not afraid of the bear, nor did the stag fear the lion.' On the other hand, he suggests that Adam would have preferred this new site to Eden. D'Avranches heralds the erection of the new Cathedral, and concludes in upbeat vein with: 'Happy the man who lives to see this Cathedral finished! It will be glorious after such pleasant labour'. That the work was 'pleasant', however, is surely debatable.

Another poet who wrote about the first Cathedral, albeit 600 years later, is William Lisle Bowles, an interesting figure whose poems about the Cathedral seem to have been largely overlooked. (Fig 3) Bowles was a residentiary Canon at Salisbury Cathedral in 1828 and elected Master of the Choristers four years later. His significance as a poet lies mainly in his influence on the Romantic movement. Samuel Taylor Coleridge in particular initially thought highly of his sonnets, praising these in his *Biographia Literaria* with reference to 'the genial influence of a style of poetry ... so dignified and harmonious.'[25] Bowles' *Fourteen Sonnets, Elegiac and Descriptive* published in 1789 were extolled not only by Coleridge, but also William Wordsworth and Robert Southey. In these, Bowles revived the sonnet form much favoured by Shakespeare.

Less commendable perhaps is Bowles' involvement in what is now referred to as the 'Alexander Pope controversy', concerning the merits of Pope's work. This debate essentially surrounded the question of the very nature of poetry, of its proper subject and form. The dispute began when Bowles published an edition of Pope's writings in 1806, setting out what he considered to be the right treatment for poetic images, which he claimed should be drawn from nature, rather than art. Several poets of the time disagreed, most notably Lord Byron who met Bowles in 1812. In response, Byron produced a pamphlet attacking Bowles for his diatribe on Pope. Bowles retorted that Byron 'has hardly, I think, done justice to my estimation of Pope's poetry'.[26]

Two of Bowles' poems are of particular relevance here. *Salisbury Cathedral* refers to the first cathedral at Old Sarum and its pagan roots.[27] Its form as an irregular sonnet, with 13 lines, perhaps plays out the nonconformity of the Druids and bards prior to the adoption of 'her latest seat Religion'. The longer final line significantly draws out in Alexandrine hexameter Bowles' plea for posterity:

Salisbury Cathedral
Here stood the city of the dead; look round –
Dost thou not mark a visionary band,
Druids and bards upon the summit stand,
Of the majestic and time-hallowed mound?
Hark! heard ye not at times the acclaiming word
Of harps, as when those bards, in white array,
Hailed the ascending lord of light and day!
Here, o'er the clouds, the first cathedral rose,
Whose prelates now in yonder fane repose,
Among the mighty of years passed away;
For there her latest seat Religion chose,
There still to heaven ascends the holy lay,
And never may those shrines in dust and silence close!

Another of Bowles' poems *The Blind Man of Salisbury Cathedral* provides a moral lesson to 'the rich, the vain, the proud.'[28] In this, despite his adversity, the blind man is spiritually exalted since 'Faith and Hope uphold / His heart'. Bowles is allegedly the last person to be buried in the Cathedral where he was laid in 1850, alongside his wife. His monument proclaims him to have been 'A Poet, Critic and Divine'. This was erected 'by their kindred as a tribute of respect to departed worth, of which the writings of the Poet afford a more enduring and unimpeachable memorial'.[29]

Thomas Hardy always considered himself to be more a poet than a novelist, writing in total about a thousand poems, a few of which refer to the Cathedral. 'The Impercipient' subtitled 'At a Cathedral Service' expresses Hardy's lack of faith.[30] His concern over this 'mystery' is evident in the first stanza:

THAT with this bright believing band
I have no claim to be,
That faiths by which my comrades stand
Seem fantasies to me,
And mirage-mists their Shining Land,
Is a strange destiny.

The alliterative 'faiths / fantasies' inextricably bind together the concept of agnosticism and Hardy's strong sense that belief is a chimera. Moreover, the antithesis of 'blind / see' in the subsequent stanza re-enacts Hardy's frustration at the unerring gap between those who are able to have faith, and those who cannot.

Another of Hardy's poems relating to Salisbury is *A Cathedral Façade at Midnight* which explores his experience of seeing by moonlight the 'pious figures' on the West front.[31] Hardy's Diary entry dated 10th August 1897 records the occasion that inspired this poem: 'Went into the Close late at night . . . the Close of Salisbury, under the full summer moon on a windless midnight is as beautiful a scene as any I know in England – or for the matter of that elsewhere.'[32] Like the poem cited above, this also has resonances of agnosticism, lamenting the loss of faith in an age of Reason.

However, Hardy's views would seem to be called into question by one poem in particular. The Cathedral's place in faith and prayer is explored in a very moving sonnet, composed by a soldier from the First World War, Alec de Candole. Born Alexander Corry Vully de Candole, Alec was a lieutenant in the 4th Wiltshire regiment and was tragically killed on 3 September 1918 at the age of 21 just two months before the end of the conflict. He is buried at Aubigny-en-Artois. Alec had intended to be ordained into the Church of England before enlisting in the army when he was posted to France in April 1917. It was while he was on leave and stationed on Salisbury Plain that he wrote the following poem, which adopts the form of a Shakespearean sonnet:

1. *Salisbury Cathedral*

I PRAYED here when I faced the future first
Of war and death, that GOD would grant me power
To serve Him truly, and through best and worst
He would protect and guide me every hour.
And He has heard my prayer, and led me still
Through purging war's grim wondrous revelation
Of fear and courage, death and life, until
I kneel again in solemn adoration
Before Him here, and still black clouds before
Threat as did those which now passed through are bright;
Therefore, with hope and prayer and praise, once more
I worship Him, and ask that with His might
He still would lead, and I with utter faith
Follow, through life or sharpest pain or death.[33]

The antithetical concepts of fear / courage and death / life mirror the precarious extent to which life hung in the balance during that dark period of our history. De Candole's early war-time death adds a great sense of poignancy to this poem. He also produced a profoundly thoughtful (if controversial) collection of essays entitled *The Faith of a Subaltern* which give an insight into his religious views.[34] His headmaster St J.B. Wynne Willson wrote a pensive tribute to him in which he stated that these *Essays* reveal 'one who had the power of envisaging truth, and truth whole'.[35]

Modern poets have also risen to the challenge of representing the Cathedral in verse form. One of the Cathedral's *Friends' Reports* contains a short but picturesque poem by Ruth Marden, entitled *The Spire Restored.*[36] This portrays the unveiled beauty of the Cathedral's spire following its restoration:

> The steeplejacks are gone. A wintry sun
> Throws fitful streaks of paleness, shifting the greys
> Of tracery mossed over, danker now,
> And slated roofs in the foreground, tinged with mauve.
> The cloudscape moves, closes in, engulfs the light;
> Then thins, reveals cold sky. The spire regains
> Authority, soars splendid, confident.

The final sibilant line invites a comparison between the spire and the flight of birds. This soaring image recalls the many birds which have inhabited the spire for centuries, prefiguring and culminating in the recent nesting of peregrine falcons at the top of the tower. Indeed, in the year in which Marden's poem was published, kestrels were reported as nesting in the SE corner of the tower in the quatrefoil opening. The uplifting sense here provides a modern contrast with d'Avranches' medieval allusion to Old Sarum as a place where 'no nightingales ever sang'. The correlation between birds and the Cathedral was taken further by the poet Maurice Hewlett in 1920 who likened the spire to a mother hen protecting the neighbouring houses from the elements.[37] The opening phrase from Handel's opera lends authority to Hewlett's imagery in this extract:

> WHE'ER YOU WALK about the shire,
>   If you may trust our people,
> You'll not escape the arrowy spire
>   That beacons Sarum steeple.
>   . . .
>
> But best of all, from Harnham meads,
>   I see the homes of men
> Beneath her shadow hide their heads
>   Like chicks below a hen
>
> She spreads her wings and calls them there
>   Safely beneath her height;
> They cluster, while in upper air
>   The great winds scream and fight . . .

Another contemporary female poet is Eleanore Zuercher whose soul-searching verses focus on the Cathedral's modern font installed in the centre nave in 2008. Ms Zuercher resides in Northamptonshire, but visits the Cathedral periodically and was inspired to write this poem by the font's ambivalence - the simultaneous stillness of its surface and the contrasting flowing water.

The Font at Salisbury Cathedral
In the black obsidian surface
I see defined and reflected the hidden
Facets of my character, starkly etched
Into the accusatory glass,
Accurate to a sin's breadth, shining
Darkly and immovably leaden,

Set in stone,

So seeming-indissoluble except,
In humility, betrayed, Christ's human
Hand, pierced the resistant vulcan glass
Like Maundy water, loosing ripples
Across its surface to disrupt my guilt,
Restoring the truth of God reflected

In my soul.[38]

A newspaper cutting in the cathedral archive includes an interesting article by David Horlock (1942-90), lately Artistic Director of the Salisbury Playhouse. This piece entitled *Point of view*, considers the meaning of the spire.[39] Horlock quotes from a poem whose author it has not been possible to trace:

One sees the spire from the London train,
And knows that one is home again.

This ends with the lines:

And God on the spire looks kindly down
on this snug little, smug little market town.

Horlock notes other descriptions of the spire such as John Aubrey's 'fine Spanish needle' and William Golding's 'Juggling act of stone thrown up to poise and peer over our shoulder – the heart of some huge question'. Horlock himself alludes to the Spire in this way: 'above us all soars one of the world's most triumphant symbols of faith and freedom of spirit'.

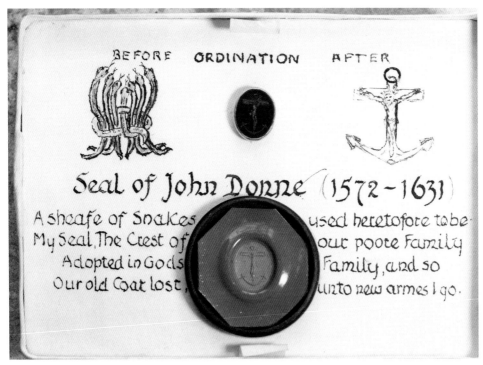

Fig 4: John Donne's seal, Salisbury Cathedral library. (*Ash Mills*)

Prose

Besides its spiritual role, the Cathedral has acted as a visual guide to travellers, as Samuel Pepys, diarist *par excellence*, records. Pepys evidently had sight of the Cathedral spire when he visited the area on 10 June 1688 while on his way to Stonehenge at night-time. He noted that he was led 'all over the Plain by the sight of the steeple'.[40] Perhaps Charles Dickens encountered a similar view whilst riding there in 1848. Pepys also makes reference to Old Sarum: 'before I come to the town, I saw a great fortification, and there light, and to it and in it; and find it prodigious, so as to frighten me to be in it all alone at that time of night, it being dark. I understand, since, it to be that, that is called Old Sarum'. Pepys' diary continues the following day to the effect that he had visited the church which had 'a very good organ'. A further connection between Pepys and the Cathedral arises in his capacity as a patient of Dr d'Aubigny Turberville, an oculist whose memorial lies in the Centre Nave.

Through all these works of literature, in both prose and poetry, Salisbury Cathedral has been at once metaphorically and literally praised to the skies.

And all shall be well and
All manner of thing shall be well
When the tongues of flame are in-folded

Into the crowned knot of fire
And the fire and the rose are one

TSE

We die with the dying
See, they depart and we go with them
We are born with the dead
See, they return and bring us with them

The moment of the rose and the moment of the yew tr
Are of equal duration

TSE

Figs 5 & 6: Glass plaques engraved by Laurence Whistler, Salisbury Cathedral. (*Roy Bexon*)

Memorials to Writers

Such adulation is duly returned by the Cathedral in its commemoration of a number of writers within the vast fabric of its building: as Defoe has pointed out, 'there are . . . some very fine monuments in this church'.[41] One of these is the George Herbert window in the North Aisle, designed by Christopher Webb in 1953, a tribute to one of Herbert's poems entitled *Love-joy*.[42] This metaphysical poem is beautifully imaged in the stained-glass motifs of grapevine and the initials J and C.:

> AS on a window late I cast mine eye,
> I saw a vine drop grapes with *J* and *C*
> Anneal'd on every bunch. One standing by
> Ask'd what it meant. I (who am never loth
> To spend my judgement) said, It seem'd to me
> To be the bodie and the letters both
> Of *Joy* and *Charitie*. Sir, you have not miss'd,
> The man reply'd; It figures *JESUS CHRIST*.

Herbert was Rector of nearby Bemerton from 1630-33, and from there the spire was visible from the bottom of his rectory garden, as his biographer Amy M. Charles has noted.[43] As a lutenist, music lay at the heart of Herbert's love of the Cathedral and he would regularly visit it for services and to enjoy the music. John Aubrey records in *Brief Lives* that George Herbert 'was buried (according to his own desire) with the singing service for the burial of dead, by the singing men of Salisbury'.[44] He is further commemorated by a statue placed on the West Front in 2003.

An impressive artefact related to George Herbert is held in Salisbury Cathedral library. Herbert was sent a seal by his fellow metaphysical poet John Donne, one of many made and given to various close friends by which to remember him.(Fig 4) The Library houses one of these seals which was sent by Donne to Isaak Walton, well-known for writing *The Compleat Angler,* but also author of *The Life of Dr John Donne* and *The Life of Mr George Herbert.* Quite how the cathedral acquired this seal is not known, although Walton's son (also called Isaac) was Canon of the Cathedral from 1678-1719. Made of blood-stone, this seal is engraved with a representation of Christ crucified on an anchor, Christian symbol of the cross.

Two commemorative plaques, to be found in the North Quire Aisle and exquisitely engraved by Laurence Whistler, bear inscriptions from T S Eliot's Dantesque poem *Little Gidding*.[45] These plaques are profoundly touching memorials to two sisters, both of whom died tragically at a young age towards the end of the 20th century: Joanne Winnifrith and Serena Booker. The final lines of these quotations from Eliot read respectively as follows (Figs 5 & 6):

> The moment of the rose and the moment of the yew-tree
> Are of equal duration

and

> Into the crowned knot of fire
> And the fire and the rose are one.

Through these images, Eliot seems to suggest, life and death are united on an even plain.

Thus all is timeless, as are the associations linking writers and the Cathedral and so, it would seem, is the building itself. Still standing after 800 years, Salisbury Cathedral harks back across the centuries to its long and variable past, echoing the voices of poets and authors now long gone. But it also looks forward to those who will be inspired to write about its sublime beauty (both architecturally and spiritually) in the future. It seems fitting to conclude by quoting from a particularly descriptive article held in the Cathedral library.[46] This account entitled *Salisbury Cathedral Spire* is partly by Elsie Smith, erstwhile Librarian. In this, she notes that 'the Spire adds a touch of poetry to the lovely Cathedral'. Poetry and Salisbury Cathedral seemingly go hand-in-hand.

Acknowledgements

Grateful thanks are due to The Dickens Fellowship for their helpful advice regarding Dickens' visit to Salisbury and to Eleanor Zuercher for her kind permission to publish her poem.

Notes

1   Defoe, Daniel, *A Tour Thro' the Whole Island of Great Britain* 1724-27, Vol 1 'Letter 3, Part 2: Salisbury and Dorset'

2   Dickens, Charles, [1844] 1999, *Martin Chuzzlewit*, Penguin, ch. 2

3   Ibid, ch 44

4   Letter to Mrs Charles Dickens [27] March 1848. MS British Museum, extract kindly provided by The Dickens Fellowship.

5   Trollope, Anthony, cited in 'Trollope and the Close', lecture by Pamela Neville-Sington, available on www.salisburyclosepreservation.org accessed November 2019

6   Hardy, Florence Emily, 1928, *The Early Life of Thomas Hardy 1840-1891*, MacMillan and Co, 67

7   *Sarum Chronicle* 8 (2008), 3-10

8   Hardy, Thomas, [1876] 1978, *The Hand of Ethelberta,* Penguin, ch XLI

9   Ibid, ch XLII

10   Hardy, Thomas, [1895] 1978, *Jude the Obscure* Penguin, Part Third ch X

11   Hardy, Thomas, [1912] 2008, *On the Western Circuit* in *Life's Little Ironies*, Oxford University Press, 93-118

12   *Jude the Obscure*, Part Third ch I

13   Cited by Hugh Thomas in *Sarum Chronicle* 8 (2008), 3

14   Defoe, Daniel, *A Tour Thro' the Whole Island of Great Britain* 1724-27, Vol 1 'Letter 3, Part 2: Salisbury and Dorset'

15   From *Advice to the Nymphs of New Sarum*, 1727.   www.thewordtravels.com accessed November 2019

16   Golding, William, 1982, *A Moving Target.* https://books.google.co.uk accessed December 2019

17   Golding, William, 1964, *The Spire*, Faber and Faber, 7

18   Ibid, 190

19   Ibid, 10

20   Ibid, 191

21   Ibid, 146

22   Ibid, 192

23   Billington, Michael, 12 November 2012, *The Guardian.* The set design was by Tom Rogers.

24 Translation by W J Torrance, 1960, in *The Wiltshire Archaeological and Natural History Magazine*, Vol.57

25 Cited in https://en.wikipedia.org>wiki>William_Lisle_Bowles. See also article on Bowles by Ken Smith in his blog in www.salisburycathedral.org.uk>news>poetic-canon-salisbury accessed October 2019

26 Greever, Garland, ed 1926, *A Wiltshire Parson and his Friends: The Correspondence of William Lisle Bowles*, London Constable & Co Ltd

27 *W.L. Bowles Poetical Works*, Vol. II, 1855, James Nichol, Edinburgh. The poem is dated 1834.

28 Ibid

29 Moody, Robert, 2009, *The Life and Letters of William Lisle Bowles: Poet and Parson*, Hobnob Press, 356

30 *The Collected Poems of Thomas Hardy*, 2006, Wordsworth Editions Limited, 59. Hugh Thomas has convincingly argued that this poem relates to Salisbury Cathedral.

31 Ibid, 652-3

32 Hardy, Thomas, ed Michael Millgate, 1984, *The Life and Works of Thomas Hardy*, MacMillan, 296

33 *Poems*, 1920, Cambridge University Press, no XXXI. Underneath the poem is inscribed 'December 27th, 1917. In the train near Salisbury'.

34 de Candole, Alec, 1918, *The Faith of a Subaltern*, Hard Press Publishing

35 Ibid., Preface

36 Friends f Salisbury Cathedral (FSC), 1979, 49th Annual Report 1979, 5

37 From *Flowers in the Grass* cited in *A Salisbury Assortment* by John Chandler, 1996, Ex Libris Press

38 https://www.poemhunter.com accessed November 2019

39 Salisbury Cathedral Archive (SCA), 1989, 6 July 1989, Newspaper cuttings Book 9,

40 https://www.pepysdiary.com accessed October 2019

41 Defoe, Daniel, *A Tour Thro' the Whole Island of Great Britain* 1724-27, Vol 1 'Letter 3, Part 2: Salisbury and Dorset'

42 From *The Temple*, 1633, available on www.cambridge.org>core>books accessed November 2019

43 Charles, Amy M., 1977, *A Life of George Herbert*, Cornell University Press, 156

44 Aubrey, John, [c17th century] 1993, *Brief Lives*, The Boydell Press, 138

45 From Eliot, Thomas Stearns, 1943, *Four Quartets*. Makes the point that Little Gidding is where George Herbert had sent one of his manuscripts of poems not long before he died.

46 *Friends' Report*, June 1958

Fig 1: A wedding arrangement October 2016 (*Ash Mills*)

Cathedral Flowers: Festivals and the Liturgical Year

Michael Bowyer and Susan Branch

Flowers have been used to beautify and enhance religious and spiritual buildings from the very earliest times. They not only bring pleasure through the senses of sight and smell but are integral to, and complement, faith and religious customs. The use of flowers is ubiquitous across religions and across the centuries. Here at Salisbury Cathedral, as with many Christian churches, a dedicated and talented group of volunteer flower arrangers work throughout the year to create arrangements which are not only visually attractive, but are designed, often using specific flowers and foliage, to link with the Cathedral's annual cycle of services. This annual cycle is complemented by ambitious and stunning flower festivals.

In many societies it was felt that offering to God something that was pleasing to the senses was the right thing to do. Throughout the centuries gardens have been considered places of rest from battle and labour and places of shelter from the sun and wind; maybe it is not surprising therefore that gardens in the form of flowers and foliage are brought into religious buildings which are themselves places of rest and sanctuary.

While the Reformation of the western Christian Church in the 16th century swept away many of the decorative elements associated with church adornment and worship there was a move, after the accession of Queen Elizabeth I, to fill the emptiness that this created with flowers. It seems likely that these arrangements would have been relatively simple displays involving plants such as rosemary, bay, holly and ivy. Holly, ivy and mistletoe are strong life symbols, evergreen and fruiting in winter. Holly represents Christ's crown of thorns and the divided leaves of ivy represent the Holy Trinity. Mistletoe is not normally allowed in churches, but paradoxically has long been used in domestic houses as a protection against evil. It is in the nineteenth century, with the great explosion of plant collecting and interest in the classification of flora and fauna by Victorian naturalists and

Fig 2: A large foliage pedestal design from 1984 (*Ash Mills*)

Fig 3: An interpretation of hell fire and damnation from 1984 (*Ash Mills*)

collectors with access to the foreign lands in the British Empire, that flowers and foliage were used in churches in greater numbers than ever before.

Today ornate and intricate floral displays are commonplace showcasing the skill and imagination of the arranger. At Salisbury Cathedral a special cut flowers garden is maintained, hidden away behind the medieval Chapter House where during the summer months over 150 stems of dahlias, iris, Michaelmas daisies, hydrangeas and shrubs are cut and supplementary foliage is often gathered in the private gardens of individual arrangers. Additional flowers are acquired from a specialist supplier.

In this chapter Michael Bowyer, floral artist and Creative Director of Cathedral Flowers, describes the numerous flower festivals held at Salisbury over the last 50 years. Head flower arranger, Susan Branch, then describes how the tradition of flowers to enhance worship and document the liturgical year continues in the work of the Cathedral's team of flower arrangers ensuring that the floral arrangements complement the liturgy rather being stand–alone exhibition pieces.

In 1966 the first major flower festival was held in Westminster Abbey to mark its 900th anniversary. Staged by the National Association of Flower Arrangement Societies (NAFAS) it was entitled *One People*. Arrangers came from all over the country and flowers were sent from all four corners of the world. The success of this event led to flower festivals spreading across the land, some in large imposing cathedrals, others in small country churches. The earliest in Wiltshire was at Malmesbury Abbey in 1968 in the diocese of Bristol where local industries were depicted in flowers. On display were the priceless silver treasures of the Abbey guarded by Hussars in full dress uniform!

Here in Salisbury the enterprising Dean Haworth invited Mary Pope, from Dorchester, founder President of NAFAS, to stage a festival in Salisbury Cathedral in 1969. With the title *Flowers In Glory* it depicted the colours and interest of its surroundings. The nave was filled with soaring pillars of flowers in colours from ruby red through scarlet to peach and finally cream.

Fig 4: A popular style in early festivals was to decorate tombs and memorials

The Wessex and Jersey Area of NAFAS (one of the 21 Areas of the Association) was responsible for flower festivals in 1984 and 1990. In 1984, from 5 to 7 July a constant stream of visitors arrived to view over 250 arrangements designed by Joan Rose and Lilian Holdman in aid of the preservation fund. Arrangers included guest designers from Zimbabwe and Australia. (Figs 2 - 4) As this coincided with the Silver Jubilee of NAFAS the west end of the nave depicted various aspects of the Association. Trumpets incorporated into the designs in the nave heralded the beauty of the flowers arranged to the glory of God.

By 1990 the great Spire Appeal for the preservation of the spire, tower and west front had been underway for five years under the chairmanship of Lord Tryon. With the financial success of the 1986 festival at Winchester Cathedral, entitled *The Cathedral and the Crown,* a similar spectacle was planned for Salisbury. With the title *Spirit of Salisbury* it ran from 5 to 8 July 1990. An executive committee of eleven was chaired by Dreda, Lady Tryon assisted by a task committee of 20 more. The Marchioness of Salisbury kindly agreed to be the festival's patron which was supported by an impressive list of sponsors. The design team was led by Janet Smith assisted by Michael Bowyer, Wendy Howden, Barbara Hudson and Rosemary Stott.

On staging day Janet Smith's husband was assigned two young apprentice stone masons to help hang the 32 banners. Observing their long hair, tattoos and ear rings, her husband Ted remarked 'I can't work with them!' 'You'll have to' she replied. By the end of the day they were a great working partnership and firm friends. The apprentices were fascinated in all that was being done during staging and loved the Cathedral with a passion.

Over 200 exhibits depicted the history of the Cathedral and well-known people and places associated with it. Clerk of Works Roy Spring inserted hooks into the nave pillars between the stones to hang impressive banners made from dried materials and backed with blue fabric. These hooks are still in use today, especially at Christmas. Towering wrought iron replicas of the spire to be filled with blue flowers were made by the rehabilitation workshops at St Leonards Hospital, Ringwood and strategically placed pairs of urns led the visitor from one area to another; called the Chalice and the Thorns they took their inspiration from the colours and swirling movement of the High Altar 'Energy' frontal. Over 1,000 schoolchildren were involved in creating a flower carpet 'woven' in aluminium foil trays which were displayed in St Edmund's Chapel (then separate from St Thomas' Chapel). Worked on in their own schools the completed trays were delivered to the Cathedral and pieced together like a jigsaw. (Figs 5 to 7)

A craft fair in the cloisters, tours of the Cathedral workshops, including a closer look at the west front restoration using the stonemasons' lift, an evening entertainment by national demonstrator Susie Edwards and poetry and prose with

Fig 5: The author working on his design: St Michael, sponsored by Marks and Spencer in 1990

Fig 6: The nave looking west in 1990

Fig 7: A flower carpet created by school children from across the diocese in 1990

husband and wife team Ludovic Kennedy and Moira Shearer gave added interest. After this highly successful event the then unprecedented sum of £72,000 was donated to the Spire Appeal.

In 2008 the Cathedral was celebrating the 750th anniversary of its completion. I was approached by the Cathedral at the start of 2006 to see if I was interested in creating a 'spectacular and celebratory' flower festival. Six months later the idea had been agreed by the Dean and Chapter and I had recruited two outstanding colleagues – Angela Turner and Pam Lewis – to be my co-designers for what would clearly become an event of great magnitude. It was decided to recruit arrangers from every parish in the diocese along with all the churches in Salisbury and all the flower clubs within the diocese. The Salisbury Diocese covers three of the 21 NAFAS areas. Pam, from Devizes in the north, represents the South West Area, I represent the central Wessex and Jersey Area, and Angela lives in the Dorset and Guernsey Area in the south. An invitation was extended to every flower club within these three areas resulting in a total of over 500 arrangers. This pattern has been followed for successive festivals, each time resulting in a splendid workforce of over 500.

For the 2008 festival representative churches from each of the 19 deaneries designed interpretations of their own deanery. In addition, hanging curtains of green carnations graced the spire crossing arches with vibrantly colourful designs running through the nave. The north transept contained hammocks of flowers each held in a sisal covered tube – a nightmare for the waterers. The south transept contained an installation of 21 obelisks topped with spheres of gypsophila, hung with gerberas and capiz shells.[1]

The success of the 2008 festival led to another in June 2011, held at the request of the Dean, the Very Reverend June Osborne. Above the nave the designers staged a huge hemisphere constructed from wild clematis vine, the interior was decorated with hanging tillandsia (Spanish moss) and orchids. It hovered over a nave full of over 60 pedestals filled with flowers of high summer in all shades of blue, lilac and white. This spectacle greeted visitors, just as it greeted *Songs of Praise* presenter Pam Rhodes who remarked, while filming a segment for the BBC programme, 'this is a festival on a truly grand scale.' The blue theme was carried into the crossing with a floral chandelier of blue perspex, hung with bright yellow gerberas and callas. In the south quire aisle a series of tiered stands held carnations in every shade of red, contrasting with the ivy leaves which covered each stand. Each group of arrangers glued 3,000 ivy leaves to each stand – a labour of love. Troughs of white flowers ran through the quire and green blooms and berries complemented Anthony Gormley's *Flare 11* in the south transept and clashing colours of pink, mauve and orange were arranged in rings in the quire aisle.

Two innovations for this festival which proved highly popular were firstly the daily music recitals accompanied by live flower demonstrations, musicians organised by David Halls, Director of Music, and flowers arranged to the music by the designers. On most occasions it was standing room only. Secondly, the brochure contained many photographs of the actual festival, taken at the end of staging and printed overnight.

In 2011 it was also the 400th anniversary of the completion of the King James Bible, which the flower festival brochure described as a labour of love produced by 50 individuals working in committees. The north nave aisle contained interpretative designs depicting texts from the Bible and the south aisle depicted famous people linked to Salisbury, such as artist John Constable, author Leslie Thomas and the protestant martyrs burned at the stake at the city's Gallows Gate.

Whilst 2008 marked a special anniversary so too did 2015: the 800th anniversary of Magna Carta. This festival had the title *Magna Flora* and concluded the programme of events staged at the Cathedral that year. Giant flowers fashioned from aspidistra leaves greeted visitors and hung high above the altar. The font acted as a bridge between two differing styles in the nave, chaos before Magna Carta on one side and order after on the other. Floristry students from Kingston Maurward depicted the Magna Carta clauses directly concerned with women; all 25 barons present at Runnymede were interpreted on two-metre high panels in the north nave; members of the Mothers' Union included the names of pioneering women in their work; and in the cloisters four panels resembled the four surviving original copies, all slightly different in shape and size. A huge installation in the south transept depicted the legacy of Magna Carta, that the exercise of political power must follow the law.

Above the performance area in the north transept, where flowers with music were again incredibly popular, hung a series of designs dubbed the 'lampshades.' Here Cathedral arrangers strung over 10,000 individual heads of physalis (Chinese lanterns) from fabric and rope wrapped frames.

A tribute to Queen Elizabeth II as the longest serving British monarch stood before the quire pulpit, and in the quire aisle innovative contemporary designs each using just one type of flower proved influential, as did a 10 metre long run resembling a still life painting depicting the clause 'there shall be equal measures throughout our kingdom.' At the express wish of the Canon Chancellor clause 33, concerning the removal of fish weirs, was included. Outside in the cloisters the richness of the autumn season was celebrated with a series of harvest tableaux. On the final day one visitor remarked 'I have accompanied my wife to many flower festivals through the years; this is the first one which shows intellectual depth.' Magna Carta - Great Charter. Magna Flora – Great Flowers!

And so to 2020: at the time of writing, with eight months to go, all designs are on paper, volunteer arrangers have been given a time to visit the Cathedral in March to discuss their design in situ, order flowers and sort logistics. Tickets are already on sale and several coaches have been booked in by the visitors' department.

With the title *Confluence* the festival takes its themes from the Salisbury 2020 celebrations. *City On The Move* is a year of events and activities that celebrate the 800th anniversary of the Cathedral's move from Old Sarum and the development of the new city as well as the movement of the surrounding five rivers and of time. Also included are the movement and change in ideas and attitudes, the movement of construction materials on land and water (illustrated by flower arrangements incorporating wood, stone, lead and glass), and the shifting population who arrive at and depart from the Cathedral and city. There will be a restlessness about the displays, echoing the striving of our forebears. Natural growth and the shift in colour across the seasons will also be reflected and the theme of recycling will be explored with materials being reused in unusual ways.

What does it take to stage a festival of this magnitude? Over 530 flower arrangers, 30,000 stems of flowers with countless stems of foliage from hundreds of folk who have had their gardens stripped, 1,000 test tubes, a few hundred blocks of foam, wood and metal mechanics in all shapes and sizes produced by those behind the scenes who have responded to the call to just 'knock up a stand.' Add an administrator with superb computer skills, a Clerk of Works and staff willing to haul up the suspended designs, a traffic team who keep the city moving, guides to interpret the building and a catering team ready with an endless supply of tea, coffee and cake.

So how have festivals changed since their inception? Early ones tended to decorate every pillar and tomb. Since the groundbreaking 1997 festival to mark the 900th anniversary of Canterbury Cathedral the design work stands alone, to enhance the building, never to swamp it, where repetition echoes the work of the modern artist, but never forgetting the best of our traditional design.

★

Advent, the four weeks before Christmas, is the beginning of the church year, and for the Cathedral flower arrangers is one of the busiest times. Beginning on the fourth Sunday before Christmas the start of Advent is marked by the Darkness to Light service. Due to the vast numbers of people wanting to experience this beautiful service it is repeated on three nights: Friday, Saturday and Advent Sunday. The preparation for these evenings is an immense task for the 20 strong flower arranger team who provide one candle arrangement in each transept and six pairs down the length of the nave. Prior to the main team coming in on the

Friday morning, all the bowls are prepared with soaked oasis. Forty-eight candles (ordered in September) are prepared with sticks taped to the base so that they will stand firm in the centre of each arrangement. Pillars and stands are collected and put into position. The final design is of a large crescent of foliage (cut from the arrangers' own gardens) with three tall candles which is set on a plinth against the nave columns. The font becomes the Advent crown, with a crescent arrangement on a metal stand and board bearing a single red candle in each of its four curves. Foliage, not flowers, is used in the Advent arrangements. The use of foliage rather than flowers represents Advent as a time of preparation for, and expectation of, the birth of Jesus. The candles represent the light of God in his son Jesus Christ coming into the darkness of the world.

The Darkness to Light service begins with the Cathedral in complete darkness. Gradually 3000 candles are lit all the way through the building as the processions move around the Cathedral. The font is slightly different as each of the four candles in the font Advent crown marks a Sunday in Advent. On the first two nights, Friday and Saturday, the font Advent crown candles are not lit, but on the Sunday (the first Sunday in Advent) the first of the four is lit. In each week leading up to Christmas a new element is added to the advent candle arrangements, the first week, as mentioned above, is foliage and three candles. For week two fir cones are added, week three, poinsettias, and week four, gold trimmings. During all these weeks a team of six add and check the foliage, do candle trimming and water and spray the arrangements. On each following Sunday of Advent a further candle is lit. The overall effect of the gradual build-up of arrangements is the feeling of waiting and anticipation during Advent for the birth of Jesus at Christmas. (Fig 8)

During the final week of Advent there are many carol services with extra visitors coming to the Cathedral. To give a more Christmassy feel, as the full decoration for Christmas is not yet in place, a team of 18 arrangers come in for three hours and create six column hangings each approximately 12 feet long. These are made up of MDF boards linked together with aluminium wire, a block of oasis strapped very tight to the board and then filled with long lasting conifers, holly and evergreens cut from the arrangers' own gardens. Gold baubles, stars and little artificial gold leaves are added to enhance and catch the light. These are put up by the Cathedral caretakers with the aid of a cherry picker.

The Christmas arranging team of 30 arrives with arms full of wonderful foliage a day or so before 25 December. The colour scheme for Christmas is white and gold with beautiful green foliage. White and gold represent purity and joy; colours which are reflected in the clergy's vestments and the altar frontals. In the region of 1000 stems of flowers are ordered from a supplier in Southampton and delivered a day before the arranging day. A team of two then 'condition' the

Fig 8: An Advent
arrangement (*Ash
Mills*)

Fig 9: Christmas arrangement around the font (*Ash Mills*)

flowers, i.e. trim the stems, remove excess leaves, sort and count the flowers for each arrangement and put them into buckets of water to acclimatize ready for use. A new set of candles is also prepared.

Before starting the Christmas arrangements, (Figs 9 and 10) all the Advent arrangements are taken down. The candles are removed on a large flatbed trolley alongside bowls full of water and oasis. They are taken to the cloisters where the oasis is squeezed out, the bowls washed in the flower room and then refilled with fresh oasis and put back into the Cathedral, with the candles renewed. Once this is done the arrangers recreate the large crescent shape with fresh foliage, candles, fir cones, gold trimmings and white flowers of chrysanthemum blooms and spray, amaryllis, carnations, spray carnations and lilies. The Advent crown is also completely renewed with red candles until just before Midnight Mass on Christmas Eve when it is replaced with new white candles. In addition to the advent arrangements in the nave, the high altar, main pulpit, consistory court, and cloisters are now added to the list. Within the Trinity Chapel, by the Madonna, a 'living' Christmas arrangement is made using pieces of bark, moss, silver birch

Fig 10: Christmas arrangement at the high altar (*Ash Mills*)

twigs or twisted hazel along with hyacinths and small white narcissus bulbs, which will grow over Christmastide until Candlemas in February.

During Advent and Christmastide and starting around 5 December, the flower arrangers create a winter prayer garden in the Chapel of St Lawrence in the south transept, using large trays, silver birch twigs, white flowers, foliage and clever lighting surrounding two wooden trees in the centre of the Chapel. Visitors are invited to write the name of a loved one who has died or a prayer on leaves (or stars) which are tied onto the trees. In 2019 over 10,000 leaves were made!

There is then a small lull in the arranging calendar of one week when a team of six go around and check all the arrangements. Actually, all year round, a special group of waterers go in three times a week with cans, buckets and sprayers to care for the arrangements and keep them looking pristine.

After Christmas comes Epiphany on 6 January, marking the arrival of the three wise men to the crib and, for the arrangers, the need to prepare three

Fig 11: An Ephipany arrangement (*Ash Mills*)

arrangements containing crowns to represent them. Each arrangement is kept to one of three colours, gold (yellow), white and red or purple, symbolising the three kings bearing their gifts of gold, frankincense and myrrh. (Fig 11) In the middle of January, the Cathedral holds an Epiphany procession, when three larger versions of the crown arrangements are placed in the centre of the nave. Candlemas, the presentation of Jesus in the Temple, is celebrated on 2nd February and marks the end of Christmastide. For this service four candle arrangements are introduced again, using white flowers (mainly the longiflorum lily) around the font with four other arrangements in the nave. Everybody receives a candle and at the end of the service all the candles are blown out marking the end of Christmas and the anticipation of Easter.

Sometimes there are only one or two weeks of 'normal' arranging after Christmas before going into the season of Lent. Normal arranging is when there is a weekly team of six creating arrangements: one near the chancel steps in the quire, otherwise known as the high altar arrangement, one in the Trinity Chapel, one in the nave, one by the Mothers' Union Chapel and one at the font crossing. These arrangements are usually kept to white and green in colour with evergreen foliage.

Of the many Christian traditions and practices observed during Lent one of the most visible is the complete absence of flowers. The arrangers look forward to the Saturday before Mothering Sunday when they make about 300 little posies of foliage and daffodils tied with natural raffia. All the posies are placed in large baskets around the font where they are blessed at the Eucharist and then handed out at the end of the service by the children of the Cathedral's Sunday School.

Preparations for Easter start on the Thursday before Palm Sunday. Along with the palms the first of the Easter flowers, lilies and carnations, arrive so that they will acclimatize and (hopefully) open in time for Easter Sunday. On Palm Sunday there are only two arrangements, one on each side halfway down the nave on short plinths but using a large urn. Tall dried palms along with phoenix palm and kentia palms are used reflecting Jesus's entry to Jerusalem. The Palm Sunday procession which starts outside on Choristers Green moves with choir, clergy and donkey in through the west door. The clergy and some members of the congregation carry large dried palms, which are then thrown down in front of the altar at the start of the service. The palm arrangements are cleared away by Wednesday in Holy Week and materials collected ready for the next sessions of arranging on Maundy Thursday. Palms are kept and reused at the Altar of Repose and Easter Garden on Easter Eve.

On Maundy Thursday afternoon, two teams work in two areas of the Cathedral. One team is at the spire crossing creating the Easter Garden with the tomb. (Fig 12)

Fig 12: The Easter Garden (*Ash Mills*)

At this stage the garden is rough, brown with very little green foliage, dark and despairing with no flowers. Using pieces of stone from the Cathedral's works yard and wood chips, a little pathway is created so one of the clergy can lay the shroud in the tomb on Good Friday. The second team is in the Trinity Chapel preparing the Garden of Gethsemane. This garden, also known as the 'Altar of Repose,' represents where Jesus prayed with his disciples before being arrested. It is a very simple garden of foliage with eleven candles (representing the disciples, less Judas as he has betrayed Jesus and fled) and white Madonna lilies giving a hint of perfume. In the centre of the altar, simply covered by moss, are two stones upon which the consecrated host (representing Jesus) is placed in a ciborium.[2] Those attending the Maundy Thursday service walk to the garden in the Trinity Chapel for prayer and devotion after the 'last supper' at the spire crossing. It is very still, peaceful and reflective until midnight when the host is removed and everyone departs.

A further consignment of 1100 stems of flowers in white, mauve, yellow, cream and green are delivered on Maundy Thursday afternoon including anemones, tulips, chrysanthemums, spray chrysanthemums, spray carnations, gypsophilia, primroses, fresh moss for the Easter Garden, and Easter calla lilies. The predominant colours of yellow and white represent new life and light. Very early on Good Friday, the Altar of Repose is taken down. The focus is now on the Easter Garden and tomb prepared on Maundy Thursday afternoon. The Easter Garden is still dark and despairing to look at. There are still no flowers, only a very little dull foliage, and spiky old pieces of wood and stone. A three-hour devotion starting at midday concludes with everyone gathered around the tomb. The shroud (a piece of white linen, representing Jesus) is placed within the tomb, the 'stone' door is rolled to close it, the Cathedral lights are turned off and all is dark.

Easter Eve is a day of prayer and meditation in the Cathedral. At 9.00 am all is dark, the Cathedral itself resembling the tomb. A large number of arrangers arrive with garden flowers and foliage. Over 20 arrangements are to be done; two are behind the high altar on tall plinths using large urns and requiring ladders; another is in the Trinity Chapel, two are in the nave on short plinths using large urns, one is in the Mothers' Union Chapel, and further arrangements are around the base of the font to give the impression of flowers growing up around the font itself. More arrangements are in the north porch and the consistory court – where you might find the odd chick and eggs! The Easter Garden, no longer dark and despairing, is now full of beautiful flowers and foliage.

After Low Sunday, the first Sunday after Easter, the Easter Garden is reduced and re-sited near the pulpit at the spire crossing where it will be cared for week by week by a team of six for the 50 days of Eastertide. The Easter colour scheme of white, yellow, cream, green and mauve is kept until Pentecost and the coming of the Holy Spirit with flames of fire – represented by flowers of vivid colours of bright reds, cerise, orange and purple such as: gerberas, anthurium, allium, and liatris spicata. These colours are so strikingly different from those used at Easter, and the design so much more contemporary, that you may take by surprise.

Settling back into ordinary time a team of six arrangers every Friday create beautiful arrangements for spring, and then summer, colours and flowers including gladioli, delphiniums, alstroemeria, campanula, antirrhinum and veronica to name but a few. During this time, there are also usually one or two weddings to arrange flowers for. (Fig 1) In years when the Southern Cathedrals Festival of choral concerts is held at Salisbury the flower team has a great opportunity to do something a little different. In 2018 the Festival coincided with the 100th anniversary of the end of World War One and poppies became the central feature of the arrangements. Four column hangings were made using 2000 laurel leaves pinned together with artificial poppies and were lit from below by red lights. In front of the hangings cut out figures of soldiers surrounded by poppies and laurel were mounted on platforms.

During the course of a year there are always one-off and special events: a Bishop's enthronement, the installation of a new Dean, funerals, and thanksgiving services. One particularly memorable occasion was when HM The Queen visited during her Diamond Jubilee year in 2012.

Sunflowers, just lots of sunflowers, will be found for one or two weeks usually in August: they are grown by one of the arrangers. These make a large impact with their huge heads of flower and it can sometimes be quite a challenge to get them to stay put, especially when the sun shines as, although cut, they will still try to follow the light.

Next is Harvest Festival at the beginning of October. A large team of 25 will have been out in the hedgerow gleaning wild clematis, berries, autumnal leaves, wheat, fruits, and nuts. These are merged with ordered flowers chosen for their autumnal colours of orange, red, pink, and yellow. Large displays are created in front of the altar at the spire crossing, and halfway down the nave on both the north and south sides with hanging arrangements of hydrangeas, apples, honesty and autumnal foliage on the columns above. Wooden crates, an old watering can, metal troughs, a hoe, a pitchfork, loaves of bread (donated by a local bakery), large pumpkins and donated gourds complete the scene. The feasts of All Saints and All Souls at the beginning of November mark the start of Remembrance Tide when red flowers dominate. The colours in the arrangement at the foot of the altar in the All Souls service are very deep red and black (dark red roses and Leucadendron) with gold spray dried materials, picking up the colours of the clergy's vestments. Remembrance Day arrangements will also be of dark foliage with artificial poppies and figures of soldiers. After Remembrance there are a couple of weeks to finish the church year before Advent comes around and the cycle of flower arranging begins again.

The Salisbury Cathedral flower arrangers feel very privileged to work as volunteers in such a beautiful building. They are a group of 48 eager and keen arrangers, made up of members of the congregation and people from local churches and flower groups who love to take on the challenge of producing large arrangements week by week for all sorts of services and projects, whether it is helping with the 2018 Les Colombes art installation or creating winter scenes for a play in the Cathedral. The work is very generously supported by the Friends of Salisbury Cathedral. Other sources of income come from arranging for weddings, funerals, thanksgiving services and outside events.

The arrangers can be seen working in the Cathedral on most Friday mornings. They always thoroughly enjoy themselves, love talking with visitors while at work, love to laugh together and always have a coffee and a chat half way through each arranging session. At Christmas and Easter they are joined by the Dean, Canon Precentor, Canon Chancellor and Canon Treasurer over a coffee, mince pie or hot cross bun. In the meantime, they just love arranging flowers in the Cathedral!

Notes

1   Many images from the 2008 festival are reproduced in Blacklock, Judith, 2009 *Church Flowers*, Flower Press

2   A ciborium is a vessel, normally in metal. It was originally a particular shape of drinking cup in Ancient Greece and Rome, but the word later came to refer to a large covered cup designed to hold the host and is thus the counterpart of the chalice.

Art Exhibitions at Salisbury Cathedral

Jacquiline Creswell

Churches have employed the visual arts for centuries, not only to celebrate their faith and communicate its truth and beauty, but also to offer a critique of that faith. Churches have found that art has the power to do these things by attracting and engaging people who are outside the formal structures of believing or belonging. It is this potency that has led Salisbury cathedral to embrace the visual arts as a central part of its life, both in its worship, and in its desire to reach out to people who might feel that the cathedral is beyond them.

Salisbury Cathedral is proud of its permanent art collection, which includes, among others, pieces by Dame Elisabeth Frink, Lynn Chadwick, William Pye, Helaine Blumenfeld, Dame Barbara Hepworth, Emily Young and Laurence Whistler. Some of these pieces were commissioned such as the font by William Pye in 2008. Some have been acquired through gifts or bequests. The engraved glass prism of the cathedral by Lawrence Whistler was given in memory of his brother Rex. *Construction (**Crucifixion**)* by Barbara Hepworth, originally a gift, returned to the Cathedral in July 2017 having been on loan to other organisations for many years. The sculpture is now sited in the burial ground (garth) in the centre of the cloisters but due to its size (3.66m x 4.77m) and weight (2.5 tonnes) was too large to be brought through the cloister doors so was winched into place over the roof. (Fig 1) This location sets it in a place of serenity, where its theme of death and rising to new life is given a particular context in what is also a historic burial ground. It also has the practical benefit of ensuring its safety as a significant artwork; the archives record a number of instances of damage by the public when it was previously sited in the Close.

Opposite: Fig 1: Barbara Hepworth's *Construction (Crucifixion)* being installed by crane into the cloisters. (*Ash Mills*)

Over the last 50 years, alongside the permanent art, the cathedral has sought to organise and host art exhibitions, sometimes in collaboration with other organisations such as the Salisbury Arts Festival. Prior to 2008 such exhibitions were staged on an adhoc basis but following the appointment of myself as Visual Arts Advisor and Curator in 2008 and the establishment of a visual arts policy (revised 2012) there is now in place an established rolling art programme. The visual arts policy recognises that:

> In its creation and presentation art elicits wonder, challenges and probes, opens us to hidden meaning, to deep purpose and witnesses to the creativity and energy that has its source in God.

To be displayed in the cathedral any work of art must meet certain criteria. The subject matter must be appropriate and relevant to the context of the cathedral and close. It must have a spiritual/theological dimension which explores aspects of Christianity and/or promotes understanding of other religious faiths. It should engage people with aspects of the human condition and be work which reflects the scale of the architectural surroundings and advances at least one of the cathedral's objectives – social justice, education, and community engagement. In addition, the artwork must be likely to attract significant visitor numbers both from the local community and further afield, visitors who probably would not otherwise come to a cathedral. The policy also stipulates that any art displayed must be 'accessible to the widest possible audience through appropriate interpretative materials and educational activities which inform and explain.' To achieve this considerable attention is paid to sourcing artists and their work, curating, installing and staging exhibitions, providing written supportive material, delivering presentations to guides and offering guided art tours to patrons, donors and the general public. The art program is an essential tool in progressing the cathedral's mission and liturgy. In addition to the arts policy an Exhibitions Advisor Committee (now the Arts Advisory Committee) was established.

Since 2008 the cathedral has become associated with the staging of nationally significant visual art exhibitions. These exhibitions have received great acclaim from critics and the national press, prompting a very positive response from thousands of members of the public. Exhibitions have been opened by high profile guest speakers including Charles Samaurez Smith, Chief Executive and Secretary of the Royal Academy of Arts; Peter Murray OBE, founder of the Yorkshire Sculpture Park; novelist Dame Marina Warner; and Lemn Sissay, official poet of the 2012 Olympics.

There were three significant exhibitions held prior to 2008: *Ten Sculptors Two Cathedrals* (1970), *Elisabeth Frink: a certain unexpectedness* (1997), and *The Shape of the Century* (1999). *Ten Sculptors Two Cathedrals* was jointly organised and hosted by both Winchester Cathedral (6 July – 9 August 1970) and Salisbury Cathedral (17 August – 27 September 1970). In the exhibition catalogue Heinz Henghes explains that:

> Since the end of the war an extraordinary renaissance of the arts has flourished in England. One of its strongest manifestations has been revealed in the powerful and magnificently courageous and inventive forms which modern sculpture has taken in these brief years.[1]

The choice of sculptures was made by Jeanette Jackson and aimed to present 'a true cross section of sculpture in England today.' Artists included Robert Adams, Heinz Henghes, Barbara Hepworth, Robert Holding, Roger Leigh, Charlotte Mayer, Henry Moore, George Stephenson, Wendy Taylor, and Jesse Watkins.

Elisabeth Frink: a certain unexpectedness, a major retrospective of one of Britain's foremost sculptors was organised by the Salisbury Festival with work displayed at both Salisbury Cathedral and Close and Salisbury Library. Before the exhibition was staged in 1997 Frink's *Walking Madonna* (Fig 2) had already become an established feature in the Close. Jeremy Davies, Canon Precentor, described her work as follows:

> They are composed, perfectly collected, and recollected: their massiveness and energy is counter-poised by an interior quality and the beholder is drawn on an inward journey.[2]

Annette Downing, joint exhibition curator with Richard de Peyer, explained how the exhibition attracted and engaged with a great number of people:

> Thousands of people came to see Elizabeth Frink's sculptures in the setting of the Cathedral and Close: some were deeply moved by the humanist and spiritual associations: some were offended: many enjoyed the experience of seeing and touching works of art. None were obliged to love or admire her work but everyone had the opportunity to decide for themselves – for free.[3]

The Shape of the Century, subtitled *100 Years of Sculpture in Britain,* was organised by Salisbury Festival in conjunction with Salisbury Cathedral and The Edwin Young Trust and curated by Annette Ratusniak. The sculptures were located in Salisbury Cathedral and around the Cathedral Close and Salisbury City centre as well as at Roche Court New Art Centre sculpture park which is located just outside Salisbury in East Winterslow. On display were 86 sculptures by 54 artists. The works were placed:

> Very much in the midst of daily life, making use of the theatrically offered by spaces with their own layers of meaning.[4]

Art Exhibitions

Sophie Ryder's 2.25m high *Lady Hare with Dog* could be found in the city's High Street and Giles Penny's *Man with Arms Open* in the Market Place. Several other sculptures were sited in the city centre park Queen Elizabeth Gardens. However, the majority were located within the Cathedral and the Cathedral Close. In his essay *Some Thoughts on Art In Religious Places,* included in the exhibition catalogue Andrew Lambeth observes that:

> In an age of what the critic Robert Hughes has referred to as 'premature canonizations', when every controversial newcomer is accredited star status, we desperately need time to look long at works of art and assess their individual merits. A cathedral or church is an apt place in which to do this. Good art has the power to evoke contemplation, to develop and encourage a spiritual aspect in the viewer. Bad art in a religious context is soon shown up as tawdry: this is the tragedy of much so-called religious art, and it is the prime argument for works of art of the highest quality to be sited in religious places.[5]

Since my appointment in 2008 as Salisbury Cathedral's Visual Arts Advisor and Curator I have worked with over 60 different artists to stage 38 exhibitions. The cathedral, although an exciting challenge, is also a very complex and daunting prospect for many artists. What follows are just some of the exhibitions and projects held at Salisbury Cathedral over the past 11 years.

Liminality Toward the Unknown Region was a 2010 exhibition. Eight of Britain's finest contemporary sculptors were commissioned to interpret the theme of liminality, or transitional space, using the cathedral as inspiration. The sculptors' varying materials, styles and interpretations made for a unique exhibition. The works were positioned in locations individually selected by each artist. Mark Bonney, then Canon Treasurer, said 'We chose the theme of Liminality with the idea in mind that cathedrals and sacred space are an in-between place, a place of possibility and encounter with that which is greater than ourselves.'

The selected artists all needed to understand the cathedral not only as a place of worship, but also as a place of history, ritual and community. Some of the artists had a long experience of working closely with the fabric of the building; Roger Stephens and Jay Battle were cathedral stonemasons. For others, Sean Henry, James Jones, Jonathan Loxley, Rebecca Newnham, Keith Rand and Benjamin Storch, their relationship with the Cathedral was of a more personal or spiritual nature.

To ensure that the exhibition's theme was explored with real variety, the chosen artists worked in a range of materials including wood, glass, metal and stone. Their techniques included such diverse skills as casting, welding, carving and stonemasonry. The result had a real depth of exploration of the theme and a fascinating range of interpretations.

Opposite: Fig 2: Elizabeth Frink, *Walking Madonna* (*Ash Mills*)

Fig 3: Bruce Munro, *Water Towers*, 2011 (*Ash Mills*)

The cathedral's relationship with innovative lighting installation artist Bruce Munro began in 2008. Bruce said, 'Opportunities to create installations in a place like Salisbury Cathedral are not an everyday occurrence; so when I received an invitation from Jacquiline Creswell, I was filled with a curious mixture of enthusiasm and apprehension. The latter feeling caused by concern that I could not 'cut the mustard.'' Since then, Bruce Munro and the cathedral have collaborated on five projects, which have all brought great insight, energy and enjoyment to thousands of visitors. Three of these projects are **Light Shower** (November 2010-February 2011), **Water Towers** (January 2011-February 2011) and **Star of Bethlehem** (2014).

Light Shower was created to complement the cathedral's Advent celebrations. Suspended in the nave crossing 2000 droplets of light created a gentle ethereal quality. Made from fibre optics ending in clear tear-drop shaped diffusers, the lights were turned on at the end of the 'Darkness to Light' service thus integrating them with the liturgy. Bruce said, 'I hope the cascading shower of light acts as a conduit and encourages both visitors and worshippers to see this wonderful building in a new light and really appreciate where they are.'

Alongside *Light Shower* a second work **Water Towers** was installed in the

Opposite: Fig 4: Sean Henry, *Man with a Cup* from the 2011 exhibition *Conflux* (*Ash Mills*)

cathedral cloisters in January 2011. (Fig 3) This consisted of 69 towers each created from 220 used two litre plastic water bottles, illuminated by pitch activated optic fibres. The colours created by the optic fibres throbbed and changed to sound vibrations. The cathedral choristers were encouraged to walk through the maze and as they sang the towers pulsed with different colours of light. The installation was an exercise in creating something magical from simple recyclable materials. Using waste creatively, Bruce Munro created a living 3D abstraction of illuminated stained glass which was particularly effective when viewed through the stone arches of the cloister.

Star of Bethlehem was a literal and visual abstraction of the text from the New Testament, Matthew 2:1-12, telling the story of the wise men following a star to find the baby Jesus. Munro translated the biblical text into Morse code, communicating the story through a series of dots and dashes, or short and long pulses of light. The resulting animation of radiating lines of light was projected onto the still water of the central font, spilling over the ancient stone in the shape of a huge star.

Sean Henry is well known for his polychrome painted figures; they are exhibited all over the world and his seated 'Man on a Bench' can be seen on the platform at Woking railway station; a sculpture which was originally positioned at Salisbury Cathedral in the cloister garth in 2011 as part of *Conflux,* an exhibition which brought together 20 of his sculptures. (Fig 4) Each was dramatically different in scale, the figures occupied vacant plinths, tombs and open spaces both inside the

Fig 5: Squidsoup, *Power of Words*, 2015 (*Ash Mills*)

cathedral and in the Close. The exhibition celebrated the fragile and anonymous; challenging the viewer to contrast the timelessness and indestructibility of the cathedral with the fragility of human life.

In 2012 the cathedral hosted an exhibition called **Avenue of Champions** by Ben Dearnley. Bronze body casts of nine Olympians were exhibited in the cloister, including Steve Williams, Louis Smith, Mark Foster and Ade Adeptain. This afforded us the opportunity for Salisbury to participate in celebrating the UK's hosting of the Olympic Games that year. The Cathedral close also witnessed part of the Olympic flame global relay.

2015 was the 800th anniversary of Magna Carta. To celebrate this historic date, two separate visual art projects were commissioned. Firstly, new works by Squidsoup, an international group of artists, researchers and designers working with digital and interactive media experiences. **Enlightenment** filled the north porch with thousands of beacons of individually controllable lights, creating a virtual world, enveloping and stimulating the viewer who was able to become completely physically immersed in it. **Enlightenment** aimed to represent the ripple effect of the legacy of Magna Carta; how the principles in Magna Carta of justice and freedom have evolved and spread over time to encompass much of the globe. **Power of Words**, the second of Squidsoup's light projects, was a projection on the wall of the morning chapel. (Fig 5)) Here the text of Magna Carta, in light, could be manipulated by visitors to create their own version. This allowed visitors to reflect on the consequences of their actions and how their actions, intentionally or unintentionally, might affected society. It demonstrated the power of words.

Dispersing the Night by Ana Maria Pacheco in 2017 was inspired by hope and a firm belief in the positive side of human nature. It sought to make visitors aware of their vulnerability as well as their own ability to harness their own inner strength in challenging circumstance: there were particular resonances within the exhibition of the plight of modern-day refugees. The exhibition consisted of a series of figures and objects illustrating the journey of life with its contradictions and individual's differing perceptions of reality. One piece, *Shadow of the Wanderer,* was sited in the Cathedral's south transept. Ten larger than life figures, carved from wood and painted, stood on a raised platform. These figures were cloaked resembling shadows, their faces portraying anguish, disbelief, horror and confusion. Pacheco's inspiration was a passage in Virgil's Aeneid in which the ancient city of Troy having fallen to the Greeks the Trojan prince Aeneas flees the burning city with his family carrying his father Anchises on his back. (Fig 6)

As **Dispensing the Night** linked with the current global refugee crisis another exhibition, **Ladders of Light** (2019), was a response to another topical issue: the UK's withdrawal from the European Union. The exhibition was by Mary Branson in collaboration with poet and author Lemn Sissay and SkyArt50. Lemn Sisay's poem *Magniloquent Cartilage*, inspired by Magna Carta, focused on the individual and our responsibilities to one another, particularly our duty of care to the most vulnerable in society. Mary Branson's work was more direct and visual: illuminated ladders spanned up and across the Cathedral's roof space, a metaphor for a socially mobile pathway to a more just and equal society. The ladders encouraged the observer to look up towards a higher plane, to cross divides and overcome barriers. This was a powerful blend of poetry and visual art, the works both mirrored the grandeur and aspiration inherent in the cathedral's gothic architecture and conveyed the fragility of our community.

Community Art Projects

As well as high profile public exhibitions, over the past 11 years, the cathedral has worked on many outreach and community projects some of which are connected

with individual public exhibitions and others which follow a particular theme or mark a significant occasion. One such project was a collaboration with H M Prison Erlestoke in Wiltshire to celebrate the 800th anniversary of Magna Carta in 2015. Over the course of several months around 26 prison inmates took part in workshops to fashion terracotta tiles reflecting the themes of justice, law, human rights and power. (Fig 7) The tiles, decorated with a black and white slip, were made in the style of the cathedral's own surviving medieval tiles. I assembled the finished tiles into montages hung in the cathedral cloisters to create the exhibition *Alternative Perspective*. Alongside the tiles were displayed sketchbooks created by the inmates when developing their designs. Although the prison inmates were not able to visit the exhibition themselves the montages, along with sketchbooks and the exhibition's visitors comments book, were subsequently displayed at the prison itself. This project, although challenging, was extremely rewarding and had a lasting impact on both the cathedral and prison communities. It produced thoughtful and exciting work with a fresh perspective. Ongoing work with the group of inmates at Erlestoke attests to the capacity of this kind of arts project to create sustained engagement with a marginalised community. One participant commented that:

> It's helpful to do these things in prison I think because it is refreshing to know that even though you are in prison you can still be a functional part of society in some small way.

Elizabeth Williams, Learning & Skills Manager, HMP Erlestoke remarked that:

> This isn't just an art project; its implications are far broader. The art sessions function as a forum in which we managed to get the prisoners to really think about issues such as human rights and wrongs, and the justice system. The feedback we have got has been powerful ... It has been a learning experience for them and for us.

Other community projects have included: work with local schools to create banners, also on the themes within Magna Carta; **Do you know**? a film by Susan Francis inspired by conversations with rough sleepers in Salisbury and created in partnership with Alabaré, a Salisbury based charity that supports vulnerable, homeless and marginalised people; and projects such as **Binding the Past to the Present Through Remembrance** and **Shrouds of the Somme** to commemorate the First World War.

One major exhibition in 2018 proved to have a considerably greater element of community involvement than had originally been envisaged. This was *Les*

Opposite: Fig 6: Ana Maria Pacheco, *Shadows of the Wanderer* from the 2016 *Dispersing the Night* exhibition. (*Ash Mills*)

Colombes by Michael Pendry. (Fig 8) **Les Colombes** opened just over two months after the nerve agent attack in Salisbury. It was originally commissioned as part of the themed events marking the centenary of the end of the First World War, but in the aftermath of the nerve agent attack in Salisbury city centre became a timely reminder that the appeal for peace and reconciliation remains as powerful today as it was in 1918.

Working closely with members of the local community, multimedia artist Michael Pendry installed a flock of over 2,500 white origami doves that 'flew' the length of the cathedral nave. The doves were made, not by the artist himself, but by people in different communities. Before Salisbury this travelling exhibition had visited Jerusalem and Munich where many of the doves had been made by local people. The doves symbolised peace and, in the context of the cathedral, the Holy Spirit. In Salisbury a large community participation project was established alongside the exhibition, which saw shops, homes and schools making paper doves and displaying them in their windows as a simple but powerful symbol of the city's resilience. Evening events were staged with the great west doors wide open to draw visitors in. Pendry said, 'Although the doves are folded by different people in different countries, in their unity they stand for a fundamental human right – the right to peace and freedom.'

Most of Salisbury Cathedral's visual art exhibitions are funded not by the cathedral itself but through the generosity of external individual donors and grant giving bodies. Unfortunately, difficulties in sourcing funding can occasionally result in planned exhibitions not coming to fruition. Critical to the successful planning, organisation, and curating of each exhibition, large or small, is the role of the Visual Arts Advisor and Curator; this role is completely voluntary.

Celebrating 800 years of Spirit and Endeavour is a landmark and ambitious exhibition to celebrate the Cathedral's 800th anniversary in 2020. It is inspired by the influence, enterprise and effort of people who came together in the thirteenth century in the spirit of faith to achieve something extraordinary. Twenty iconic and important pieces of contemporary art by notable artists such as Henry Moore, Grayson Perry, Lynn Chadwick and Antony Gormley will be exhibited both inside and outside the cathedral. These works were especially chosen to illustrate the changes in thought and creativity over the past eight centuries and to explore the human condition in many different ways, seeking to understand what it is about human beings and faith that can inspire such extraordinary vision and creativity.

Fig 7: Tiles created by inmates of HM Prison Erlestoke for *Alternative Perspectives*. (*Jacquiline Creswell*)

Conclusion

Salisbury Cathedral is the only UK cathedral to have a dedicated arts programme and is renowned for its pioneering approach to displaying visual art. Particularly since 2008 the cathedral has promoted a visual arts programme and provided a spectacular backdrop to a series of wonderful, spiritually uplifting, and occasionally challenging installations and exhibitions. Art has the power to communicate beyond boundaries and between communities, transcending the limitations of language. It has the ability to reveal new ways of seeing, feeling and thinking, and to inspire visitors within a sacred place, offering new perspectives, challenging conventional orthodoxies and provoking dialogue and debate.

The art exhibitions and installations challenge us to reflect on ourselves and our legacy. The hope is that they help us in discussions about what it is that empowers people to harness their strengths, to find their voices and to echo the effort and achievement made by the extraordinary people who built a cathedral, and a city, of such distinction.

Notes

1   Salisbury Cathedral Archives (SCA), VA/2/18/1
2   SCA, VA/2/19/1
3   *Salisbury Cathedral News* Number 212, August 1997, 7, 13
4   SCA, VA/2/31/1
5   SCA, VA/2/31/1

Opposite: Fig 8: Michael Pendry, *Les Colombes*, 2018 (*Ash Mills*)

The Voices of Volunteers in the Cathedral Archive

Caroline Burrows

Many visitors to Salisbury Cathedral, particularly those from mainland Europe, are surprised to know that between 600 and 700 volunteers contribute to its welcoming and well cared-for character. (fig 1) We explain that this is in part due to the fact that cathedrals in Britain are not state-funded, which inevitably leads to reaching beyond the Cathedral staff to help run the building. This chapter sets out to describe the various volunteer roles and some of the people involved, by using transcripts from the Cathedral archive's Volunteer Voice oral history project.[1] It was also thought appropriate to delve back into the archive to find stories of people over the centuries freely giving their time and expertise to serve and support the Cathedral.

Although the archive contains many thousands of documents dating back to 1136, these rarely reflect the richness and variety of the lives of people in the Cathedral community, including the volunteers. The Volunteer Voice oral history project sought to redress the balance between official and social records and was run under the auspices of the Cathedral's archive as part of the National Lottery Heritage Fund Magna Carta project, and took place in 2015. To conduct the interviews, a new group of oral history volunteers were recruited to carry out the interviewing, transcribing and processing. Volunteers from over 27 different roles were interviewed to find out why they volunteered and to record for posterity the many different roles. The roles fall roughly into four definable categories: those involved specifically in the religious side of the Cathedral, those concerned directly with visitors and tourists, those who are seen and seldom heard, and those who work behind the scenes, seldom seen or heard by the general public.

Often the first group to arrive at the Cathedral each day is the holy dusters - seen, though seldom heard - and yet there are 43 of them. Equipped with a

Fig 1: One of the holy dusters at work in the choir (*Maureen Connolly*)

cloth duster and sometimes a feather-duster they silently dust the Choir and Presbytery furniture and, importantly, they put the books in order. They also dust the chapels. Wax polish is used twice a year, at Easter and Christmas; they do not use spray polish, as silicone can damage old wood, so if there are finger-marks on the pews, for instance, it is a case of elbow grease to remove them. In addition to holy dusters there are tomb dusters. Tomb dusters use paper rags, dusters and various brushes, depending on the material of the tomb. One of the difficulties with the tombs is that wax falls on them from the candles above: following the advice of a conservator they do not attempt to remove the wax, as this could damage the stone, they just report it.

The role of flower waterer may be unfamiliar, not only to the general public, but also to many volunteers. Tricia Durston waters the flower displays once a week - often aided by her husband. She is one of a team that shares the duties over the week. She says, 'the waterers have no hand in arranging the flowers week by week, but it feels good to know that we are honouring their beauty by cherishing them with regualar spraying and watering.' She describes her job as 'lonely', partly because she is in the Cathedral at 8.10am, but also as she works on her own. She also watered flowers for the Magna Flora flower festival in 2015, when she climbed up ladders and put handfuls of ice cubes on the surface of the displays so that the cubes acted as a slow-release dampener.

Flower arrangers form a large proportion of the volunteer force. Very much seen but seldom heard they love it when members of the public chat to them and ask what they are doing. A report in the archive from c1953 mentions the '... devoted help of those ladies, wives of the Canons and others, who week by week arrange the flowers in the vases in the Cathedral.' [2] It is not entirely clear whether being a wife was a prerequisite for this role! Today the arrangers are highly skilled and work under the guidance of Michael Bowyer, floral artist and Creative Director of Cathedral Flowers as well as Susan Branch (see an earlier chapter).

Many volunteers take up more than one role, for instance Jane Merian has been a floor guide, tower guide, chapter house guide, server, taperer and West Front guide. She started working in the Cathedral in 1993. In her interview she recalls the six weeks of training she received for floor guiding, takes us up a virtual tower tour and explains the jobs of taperer and server. Jane falls into the categories of interacting with the public and also being involved in the religious side of the Cathedral's activities. The longest-serving current volunteer, however, is Reverend 'Ben' Elliott. Ben has been volunteering for 52 years, first as a chaplain and then as a floor guide as well. When Ben started guiding in 1968 there were no lay guides during the week and the job was done by vergers and chaplains. He finally attended a guides training course in 2000, and on 5th January 2017 received a letter from Human Resources, saying, 'I'm pleased to confirm that we formally accept you into our team of volunteers'. Well, better late than never.

In the early 19th century floor tours were given not by volunteer guides but by the vergers, who charged a fee to supplement their salaries. This changed in 1866 when it was decided that 'The vergers must attend to the visiting public and provide information gratuity free. Visitors should have their names entered in the visitors' book and they should contribute not less than 6d to the Fabric Fund. For accompanied visits to the tower a further 6d should be charged. These rules and others concerning the vergers' duties to come into effect on 25th December 1866': as compensation the vergers' salaries were increased.[3]

Volunteers who come under the 'directly involved with tourists' category are clearly the floor and tower guides, the stewards, those working in the shop, the Sunday coffee volunteers and the education volunteers. The education volunteers have a very demanding task but also have fun. Many of them have been involved professionally in education and are therefore well suited to the job. In the interviews they talk about how much preparation goes into planning for school visits and workshops for the general public. A lot is done behind the scenes, preparing fabrics, paper, crayons and so forth. Rosemary Allen talks about how the education department was involved during the year of the Magna Carta celebrations in 2015 when children were shown how the original Magna Carta document was written and then had the opportunity to make an 'heirloom' using a quill, ink and a piece of pergamenta (artificial parchment): it was sealed with a mock King John seal and finished with a ribbon. The general public were also invited to similar events and Rosemary says, 'They couldn't believe when they came into the Cathedral that there were things that they could do' and see.

Jim Gillings recalls that, when he first started volunteering with the education department, they had their offices in Wren Hall on Choristers Green and the activities took place there. Then the offices moved to another building in The Close, The Gate House, which is not spacious enough to house the children as well, so the activities moved into the Cathedral itself. He had grave misgivings at the time, but later completely changed his mind, 'The benefit is that we are working in the Cathedral and the children are working in that space and when we get the eleven or twelve o'clock prayers we all stop and we listen ... I wouldn't actually now want to work outside of it.' Another comment of Jim's: 'this is a wonderful thing that we can be doing something completely daft and whacky ... [with] everybody around us and occasionally wandering through us to take pictures and so it is great that the Cathedral accept the children for what they are ...'

Volunteers working in the shop love the interaction with the public. As Andrew Whitney says, 'Everybody's in a good mood'. Andrew, like many, travels a good distance to the Cathedral. The shop team consists of between 15 and 20 people working in two or three hour shifts. Tony Male, another shop volunteer, relates how about 30 years ago he used to supply the shop with brass bells 'the best bell metal you can see.' Both Tony and Andrew say how privileged they feel to be able to work in the shop. The café, or refectory as it is called, was completely run by volunteers from parishes as far away as Lyme Regis in Dorset until 1997. Ruth Neame, currently a flower arranger, helped when she lived in Stapleford. She says, 'It was great fun, but then these hygiene checks and tests came in … so eventually it became a fully commercial business.'

One of the larger cohorts of volunteers is the floor guides. (Fig 2) Floor guides join a team that works for a whole morning or afternoon a week and each team seems to have its own identity. Peter Breeze, an ex-mariner, has been a floor guide since 2006. He points out that guiding is mentally quite tiring: 'I think it's because you're talking, but your mind is thinking about the next thing and you're also watching to make sure that everybody is there and you're answering questions.' Some guides specialise in guiding in the Chapter House where Magna Carta is displayed. Chris Basham is keen to explain Magna Carta's significance to visitors young and old, 'I tell kids who come along that it's a piece of dead sheep with some writing on it, and of course that's really all it is … it's

Fig 2: A small group of tourists with their guide by the font in 2019. The guide is pointing out the west window. (*Ash Mills*)

really up to guides like myself to bring it alive and to bring out its importance and to engage people's imagination because unless you do that … some people will just take nothing away they'll just walk past…'

As with the tower guides, floor guides never know who is going to be on their tour or who may approach them and request a tour. You have to make a mental assessment according to nationality, age and interests and adapt the tour to their interests. One of the first things many guides do is to find out whether there are any experts in the group. Caroline Burrows will ask at the start of the tour, when she is showing the group the materials used to build the Cathedral, whether any of them are builders, architects, masons, plumbers or carpenters. This always provokes a smile and usually a 'Don't worry, you can say what you like; no-one knows more than you!' and the group is immediately in a relaxed mood. There is, however, sometimes a carpenter, or perhaps a child studying design and technology, and she hands over the demonstration of the mortice and tenon joint to them. When children are on a tour, allowances have to be made for their often limited concentration. On tower tours this probably applies more to teenagers than to smaller children, who often are visiting such a huge place for the first time and are awed by the whole experience.

Arthur Bowden, one of the Cathedral's longest serving and oldest volunteers, gives tours in French. At the beginning of the tour Arthur gives French children a ten-minute lesson about the Cathedral, either in French or in English: 'and I make them repeat things.' Arthur goes to the trouble of learning a few words in a foreign language if he has advance notice of a particular group: he learnt ten things in Romanian to say to a Romanian group. Arthur, recalls how, as a sixth former at Bishop Wordsworths School he used to fire watch in the caathedral in 1943. Arthur and his friends slept in the North Porch and 'it was very amusing to do that because many of the young fellows that were there would be very active at night time in their sheets, running around imitating ghosts.' After the war Arthur became a teacher at the school. In the 1942 Friends of Salisbury Cathedral Report detail is given about how the Cathedral was equipped to fight fires, using volunteers, such as Arthur and his team, as firefighters.

The local authority also took over the supply of equipment to fight potential fires and themselves supplied 15 people each night to fire watch. (Fig 3) It seems that the cost of providing bedding and 'everything possible to make them comfortable' was covered to a large extent by donations from the Friends of Salisbury Cathedral.[4] Mention is also made of the use of the Chapter House as a shelter 'where people bombed out of their homes could be offered a resting-place.' Volunteers collected beds and bedding and other furniture for about 40 women and children to be housed temporarily.[5]

In the archive, nearly 300 years before the Second World War, we find another

Fig 3: A group of firewatchers on the cathedral parapet looking north (*Roy Bexon*)

reference to fire fighting. This was a fire at the Cathedral in 1672. A brewer's invoice for food and drink given to those volunteers who helped to put out the fire includes: '1 Humerkin of Strong Beere 12/9' and 'For Pipes and Bread Cheese 0.1.0'. The invoice concludes with the words: 'They had the drinke, and tapt it their selves, and drew it out, I looke not for a Penny Proffitt.'[6] Widow Lane of Salisbury carried pails of water to put out the fire and later fell ill. She was granted half a crown following a request for charity to the Dean because of 'a violent siknes'. A document in the archive tells us that 'she is not able to gett reliefe and is in want, therfor she doth humbly besech the reverent Deane to be pleased to extend some releife unto her that shee might be keept from perishinge and shee will be bound alwaies to praie for his worships prosperietie.'[7]

Volunteers give a variety of reasons for joining the Cathedral. High on the list is that they arrive in Salisbury, often following retirement, and look for a role that would suit them. Some worship at the Cathedral, feel they want to 'give something back' and then hear about the various volunteering roles and eventually sign up for one or two. Others follow suggestions from friends or are inspired from meeting existing volunteers; they simply want to 'do something useful'. There is also a social side to volunteering as most groups organise get togethers over a meal or tea, even trips to other cathedrals, and the free hot drink when on duty is a perk frequently mentioned in the Volunteer Voice interviews. Steve Hannath moved to Salisbury 'and I did a tower tour and it just blew me away and I thought well I need more of this so one thing led to another ...' Steve has been a tower guide since about 2007. He is keen on geology and says, 'I started to ask questions which nobody seemed to be able to answer so in the end I had to answer them myself and I've produced a small booklet that's for sale in the bookshop on the ... materials used to construct Salisbury Cathedral.'

Training for tower guiding was not always as thorough as it is today. When Caroline Burrows joined the tower guides in 1996 she was given four sheets of typed information and invited to do the tour three times with existing guides and then 'let loose'. Today's stringent health and safety regulations did not exist. Then, up to 20 people could go on the tour, with no restriction on children's ages or height. Today there is a strict limit of 12 with a certain ratio of adult to child and a minimum height of four feet. There were no rails on the spiral staircases, no fencing on the walkway in the roof and no steel barrier either on the walkway under the West Window or on the parapets at the base of the Spire. Now health and safety is very important; shoes are inspected – no high-heels or flip-flops as they could cause an accident. Caroline recalls a tour when two of the visitors were wearing flip-flops. Horrified that they would not be able to go on the tour, one of them said: 'How long have we got?' 'Five minutes', she replied. 'Right, we'll be back', they said and hot-footed it out of the Cathedral. Sure enough, they were back in time, panting heavily and clad in trainers. Fortunately, they were staying at Sarum College in The Close and did not have to go far.

Unlike today's organised tours it seems that in past centuries visitors were allowed to wander in the tower and roofs as they wished and even up the inside of the spire. At a meeting in August 1734 the Cathedral authorities decided that: 'No person or persons whatsoever except the workmen belonging to the said Church be from henceforth suffered to go upon the steeple any higher than the eight doors.'[8]

Stewards come under two categories: concert stewards and service stewards. Michael Joseph has been a service steward since about 2004. He wasn't trained for the job then and says, 'I learnt the hard way'. Now new stewards have a mentor who guides them. The job involves welcoming people and handing out service sheets. It also requires them to advise people of the evacuation procedure should there be an incident and 'just generally look after their well-being.' Some stewards are posted in the Choir and others in the Nave and the transepts and they work on a rota system. If they are posted in the Nave or transepts their responsibilities also involve keeping an eye on visitors to see that they do not disturb the service. Michael particularly likes meeting people from other parts of the country who have come to a service in Salisbury.

Mary Newman, another steward, says that on big occasions 'one of the most testing things is that people are not supposed to keep places for others … and so that requires a certain amount of tact' Mary joined as a steward in the 1990s. She points out that, not long before she joined, stewarding was very much a male preserve but that now 'it's pretty much half and half'. The original all-male Guild of Stewards was formed in 1966. However, mention is made of stewards in the 1950s book *Salisbury Cathedral: Its purpose, its staff, its finances.* At the end of a list of permanent staff at that time is added, 'In addition a number of voluntary workers help as Stewards, Collectors, etc.' Moira Dickson, also a concert steward, just loves the music which is so uplifting and she says how wonderful it is to attend the concerts while being useful at the same time.

One of the volunteer roles that definitely involves being neither seen nor heard is that of embroiderer, though the results of their work make a stunning visual impact in the building. Pamela Gueritz has been helping in the Cathedral since she first came to Salisbury back in the 1970s. When interviewed about her motivation to help she said, 'I thought how lovely to do some work which was likely to stay in the Cathedral probably for anything up to 200 years!' Henrietta Lear and Jane Weigall, both residents of the Close, were amongst the skilled needlewomen of Victorian Salisbury who produced beautiful altar frontals for the Cathedral.[9] Into the 20th century, the Salisbury Cathedral Embroiderers' Guild was formed in 1937 by Annie Morris, Florence Alcock and Mrs Daniell-Bainbridge; with other volunteers across the diocese they worked on the furnishings for the canons' stalls and choir stalls which was their first project. From the 1940s the group was led by Lady Jane Petherick, and continued making cushions and kneelers until they disbanded in about 1960. Re-formed some ten years later, a new group led by Lucy Judd, of which Pamela Gueritz was a member, began with the task of embroidering hassocks for the Trinity Chapel. One thing led to another and by 1982 the team was making new seat cushions for the Choir, then came cushions for the Chapter House and collection bags, and the list continues. Separately, Jane Lemon and the Sarum Group, formed in 1978, undertook high profile commissions of ecclesiastical embroidery, for Salisbury and other cathedrals in the UK and overseas. Their breath-taking altar frontals in regular use here include 'Energy' and 'Festal'.

Also seen and not heard are the archive and library volunteers. Helen Clarkson, who was previously librarian at Godolphin School, has been working in the library since help was needed with cataloguing. Helen and her colleague, Elaine Wood, another retired school librarian, started out by cataloguing books dating back to the mid-nineteenth century. 'We've got about 20 categories we have to fill in on the spreadsheet ... and you have to look at the book as well, to get a feeling of what it's about ... where you put it in the cataloguing system and then of course you get side-tracked because it's so interesting...' As a result of funding by the National Lottery Heritage Fund, Helen and Elaine have now moved on to working on the searchable digital catalogue which will allow anybody to access both the library and the archive online. When asked whether she feels lonely up in the library, Helen points out that they are not working on their own – 'a lot of the books have got letters and newspaper articles and bits and pieces in them, which link to maybe when the book was bought or who owned it, which is quite fascinating, so that's being catalogued separately.' Another library volunteer, recalls an old letter she found from an auction house in London, addressed to the Cathedral librarian, saying that they were bringing, 'a minibus of millionaires down ... and these millionaires would like to see the collection in the library.' The vision of a minibus full of millionaires struck a note of amusement.

In recent times further library volunteers have been recruited to work on a new project, also funded by the National Lottery Heritage Fund, to clean all 10,000 books. This project is called 'Beyond the Library Door' and a trained team of 16 are using mini vacuum-cleaners and fine brushes to clean the books. They also assess and record the condition of each book, tie it with tape if it is in a very poor condition, and measure it very precisely. The shelves, of course, have to be cleaned before the books are returned. As volunteers they do not feel guilty when a book is so fascinating that they just take five minutes off to look at it. There are also various projects involving the archive: translating medieval Latin

Fig 4: Cathedral volunteers photographed on 22 June 2016 shortly after the volunteer body was awarded the Queen's Award for Voluntary Service. (*Ash Mills*)

into English, cataloguing donated items, interviewing for the Volunteer Voice oral history collection and deciphering correspondence relating to the Father Willis organ.

Some of the more recently established volunteer roles are those of graffiti tour guide and works yard tour guide. The graffiti tour resulted from an on-going project to record and interpret the Cathedral's medieval graffiti. Most of the tour is conducted at floor level but a section of this journey into the Cathedral's past involves climbing around 70 steps via a spiral staircase to the triforium level. On the works yard tour visitors can see the masons and glaziers at work, visit the drawing office and discover that the techniques used to repair the Cathedral today are not significantly different from those used over the last 800 years of on-going repair and maintenance work.

In the seventeenth century, during the English Civil War, great efforts were made to prevent damage to the Cathedral helped by the fact that the Salisbury city authorities had assumed jurisdiction over the Cathedral and were themselves anxious to protect it. In addition, voluntary contributions were made and it is thought that members of the Hyde family secretly employed workmen to keep it in repair. Walter Pope tells the story of how, when asked who paid them, the workmen replied, 'They who employ us will pay us. Trouble not yourselves to inquire who they are ... they desire not to have their names known.'[10]

Public accolades are not anticipated, so when in 2016 the Cathedral volunteers were awarded the Queen's Award for Voluntary Services it came as a pleasant surprise. (Fig 4) This is the highest award such a group can receive in the UK and the equivalent of an individual MBE. It was created on the 2nd June 2002 to celebrate the Queen's Golden Jubilee.

Without exception, those who took part in the Volunteer Voice oral history project said how friendly they found the Cathedral staff as well as their fellow volunteers. Many talked about the pleasure they receive from meeting new people from all over the world. A final quote from Peter Breeze: 'I have never in all those years thought, "oh no, I don't want to go in today." I always enjoy going in because I enjoy meeting people...and I just think it's wonderful.'

Notes

1   All the Volunteer Voice interviews are catalogued in Salisbury Cathedral Archives under the reference VL/VV.

2   Smethurst, Arthur T, 1952, *Salisbury Cathedral. Its Purpose: Its Staff: Its Finances: What is it for; How is it Managed; What it Costs; How is it paid for; A Short Account for Interested Visitors*

3   Salisbury Cathedral Archives Chapter Minutes 1854-1877, CH/1/26

4   Friends of Salisbury Cathedral Annual Report 1942

5   Friends of Salisbury Cathedral Annual Report 1941

6   SCA, Receipts and Bills 1671-2, FA/1/5/15

7   SCA, Receipts and Bills 1671-2, FA/1/5/15

8   SCA, Chapter Act Book 1696-1742, CH/1/20

9   Howells Jane and Newman Ruth, reprinted 2019, *Women in Salisbury Cathedral Close*, 56, 59

10   Edwards, Kathleen, 1956, VCH, Wiltshire Vol 3, *Salisbury Cathedral*, reprinted 1986, 193

Index

(entries in bold are for illustrations)

Index

Index

Authors' Biographies

Rod Baillie–Grohman
Rod learned his masonry skills at Weymouth Technical College and Wells Cathedral. After leaving Salisbury he started his own small masonry and memorial business near Langport, on the Somerset Levels. Thirty years on he is still to be found working on or around village churches and vernacular buildings in the area.

Michael Bowyer
Michael Bowyer MBE has lived on the edge of the water meadows around Salisbury Cathedral for over forty years. He is a Friday afternoon guide in the Cathedral and for the past ten years has been Creative Director of Salisbury Cathedral Flowers with a team of over forty arrangers to assist him. He has been a designer for the Cathedral's highly successful flower festivals in 1990, 2008, 2011 and 2015. For over forty years Michael has been involved with *Musical Theatre Salisbury*, more recently he joined *Studio Theatre* and he also performs with *History at Large*. Michael's love of flowers has taken him far and wide. He is qualified with the National Association of Flower Arrangement Societies as a judge, demonstrator, teacher and speaker – all at National level. Later this year Michael becomes the Association's National President.

Susan Branch
Moving to Salisbury in 1987 with my husband, we joined Salisbury Cathedral and I became a member of the Flower Guild. In 2010, I took on the role of Administrator of the newly named Cathedral Flower Arrangers. In addition, in 2011, 2015 and 2020 I was Administrator for the Cathedral Flower Festivals.

Caroline Burrows
Caroline has lived locally for fifty years. After a variety of jobs, she graduated from Southampton in 1995 and then taught German, and English as a Foreign Language. She became a Cathedral volunteer in 1996, starting as a tower guide and then with the Education, Archive and Library groups.

Jacquiline Creswell
Jacquiline has been the Cathedral's Visual Arts Adviser since 2009 and has been instrumental in developing the Cathedral's pioneering Visual Arts policy. Raised in South Africa in a Jewish family, she has an arts background, having trained and practiced as a sculptor. Work in advertising, graphics and textile design broadened her already wide range of experience, and perhaps all have brought her to a point where she is most at home, making a marked

Biographies

contribution to the creative and cultural life of Salisbury Cathedral and its community. Jacquiline also curates for several other English Cathedrals including Ely and Chichester.

Richard Deane
Studied Chinese at Oxford and Leeds Universities, worked in the building trade and eventually trained as a stonemason at Salisbury Cathedral. In the mid-1990s he set up his own stonemasonry business and is now retired. He wrote the text of the primarily photographic book *Salisbury in Detail*, published by the Salisbury Civic Society in 2009.

Stephen Dunn
Stephen Dunn has been a guide at Salisbury Cathedral for 12 years and was formerly Head Guide. He stood down as Head Guide in 2016 to found and manage the Cathedral's Graffiti Survey Project – a three-year activity to record the significant examples of graffiti in the Cathedral as part of the 800th Anniversary.

June Effemey
Holding degrees in geography from the University of Southampton, and Archaeology from the University of Winchester, I gained a masters in Medieval Studies at Oxford, in 2017. Inspired by the University of Southampton's Old Sarum Landscape project, I am now researching the medieval history of Old Sarum and Salisbury for a PhD in History at Swansea University.

John Elliott
After many years as an accountant John took 'very' early retirement and studied for an MA in art and architectural history and a PhD in architectural history. He was then lucky enough to have a second career as a lecturer in art and architectural history at London and Reading Universities.

Linda Jones
Linda Jones has a PhD in English Literature, attained at Reading University where she taught part-time for eight years. She has been an Associate Lecturer with the Open University since 2004. Linda is also a tour guide at the Cathedral and has been involved in several projects at the Cathedral.

Jane Howells
Jane is editor of *Local History News* for the British Association of Local History. She wrote a new introduction to the 2013 reprint of Maud Davies' *Life in an English Village*. With Ruth Newman she transcribed and edited William Small's *Cherished Memories and Associations* (2011), and they are the authors of *Women in Salisbury Cathedral Close*, Sarum Studies 5, 2014.

Alastair Lack
Alastair Lack was appointed a consultant at Salisbury Hospital in 1974, retiring in 2003. He became a Cathedral guide in 2007, published a catalogue of Cathedral memorials and the *Salisbury Processional MS148* in 2012. He was elected a governor of Salisbury Hospital in 2011. His hobbies include golf, restoring old photographs, and writing books.

Emily Naish

Emily is the archivist at Salisbury Cathedral with additional responsibility for the Cathedral library: she has also worked with the archives of the British Medical Association, the School of Oriental and African Studies (University of London), and others. Emily has lived in Salisbury since 1998 and in recent years has joined the band of bell ringers at St Thomas' Church.

Pam Wall

Pam grew up in Yorkshire and despite long stints in the Midlands and Salisbury still considers herself a northerner. Nevertheless, she is very fond of Salisbury and since retiring a few years ago has, among other things, become a volunteer for the Cathedral Archives.

Alan Willis

Alan is a retired lawyer with a lifelong interest in the history of church music and architecture. He is a regular volunteer in various roles in Salisbury Cathedral. He enjoys making and restoring furniture, exploring and photographing old houses and churches, and walking, especially by the sea.